SOCIAL COMPETENCE
AND
MENTAL HANDICAP

To my family -

a small recompense for the many

evenings spent in writing this book

SOCIAL COMPETENCE

AND

MENTAL HANDICAP

An Introduction to Social Education

H. C. GUNZBURG
M.A., Ph.D., F.B.Ps.S.

Consultant Psychologist, Director of Psychological Services
at the hospitals for the mentally subnormal,
Birmingham Area, England

SECOND EDITION

The Williams & Wilkins Company
Baltimore

FIRST PUBLISHED 1968
SECOND EDITION 1973
Revised Reprint 1975
ISBN 0 7020 0459 6

©1973 BAILLIÈRE TINDALL
7 & 8 Henrietta Street, London WC2E 8QE

A division of Crowell Collier and Macmillan Publishers Ltd.

Published in the United States by
The Williams & Wilkins Company, Baltimore

Printed in Great Britain by
William Clowes & Sons Limited,
London, Colchester and Beccles

CONTENTS

PREFACE TO THE SECOND EDITION

In this new edition Chapter 5 has been altered to take note of the legislative changes made in 1971, and the teaching aids and methods in Chapter 7 have been up-dated. Appendix B has been considerably extended to clarify some points about the P-A-C system and to incorporate some new developments of importance. There has not been need at this stage to make other changes to the book, which was meant to provide a general introductory reading to the practical problems of social education for the mentally handicapped.

It is probably unavoidable that an introductory text over-simplifies the issues and a reader may be left with the impression that a systematic way of teaching, as suggested in this book, will provide most if not all answers to how to increase the mentally handicapped's social ability. However, 'social education' is not merely a technique for teaching more comprehensively a limited number of specific 'social skills', but must introduce the mentally handicapped to a mode of living where competence in social skills will make it simply easier to lead a more satisfactory life. Thus, 'social education' will have to concern itself also with those aspects[1] which have a subtle but very persistent influence in living practices, besides the design of a training programme, which is the particular subject of this book.

H.C.G.

July 1972

[1] The reader is referred to the author's new book *Mental Handicap and Physical Environment* (London, 1973) for a full treatment of these aspects.

Revised Reprint of the Second Edition

In this reprint of the Second Edition there have been adjustments to the first part of Chapter 5 and Appendix B. These adjustments are due to developments which have taken place recently, and I acknowledge with thanks the suggestions and information supplied by Mr. T. W. Pascoe, Dip Ed., Dip Spec. Ed. (Esn) for Chapter 5. Appendix B includes now, also, short descriptions of the Mongol P—A—C, the Personal Assessment Record and the Social Competence Index.

January, 1975

PREFACE TO THE FIRST EDITION

Society leaves a person to deal with life as best as he can as long as he requires no assistance from welfare agencies, keeps out of trouble with the authorities, supports himself financially, in fact conforms generally to a minimum standard of inoffensive behaviour. But a small proportion of people unable to fit in with those requirements have forced society to develop a multitude of rather expensive schemes for dealing with their problems: welfare agencies, institutions, hospitals, settlements, police courts, prisons, approved schools, borstals, etc., all of which attempt to protect the law-abiding and conforming majority on one side and to rehabilitate some of the misfits on the other side.

A number of these non-conforming people can best be described as socially inadequate or socially incompetent. Their offensive behaviour is not due to a deliberate breaking of society's rules, as in the case of the criminal and delinquent, or even to compulsive actions as in the case of the mentally ill, but simply to an inability to regulate behaviour sufficiently to conform to civilized life at a comparatively low level. In their case social incompetence seems to be linked with low mental ability and it is easy to show that generally, social competence decreases at the same rate as measured mental ability. Yet, there are many exceptions and there is nowadays strong evidence that the social competence of people with a mental handicap can be considerably higher than was assumed in the past.

The following pages will deal with some aspects of remedial action designed to ease the burden imposed on society by the mentally handicapped. It is essential to take more active steps to ameliorate the consequences of mental handicap and to adjust the mentally handicapped person sufficiently to society's requirements to make him less of a liability.

A new generation of researchers into mental handicap considers that remedial work in education and training must be based on a more complete and better understanding of the mental processes of the mentally handicapped than has been achieved so far. Methods of teaching will become more effective once we have learned to utilize the potential which has so far been inaccessible and the existence of which has not even been suspected.

The educationist, faced with the problem of preparing the mentally handicapped child to be more effective as an adult, cannot wait until research has advanced far enough to change methods and approaches as fundamentally as is probably needed. A practical way has to be found of organizing teaching effort—based on perhaps inadequate knowledge—to give the mentally handicapped child more skill and knowledge to prepare him effectively for the demands of society.

This book represents an attempt to make all those who have to deal with the problem aware of *the need for systematic observation in relation to stated aims,* and also of the need to define these aims concisely. Systematic observation is the first step towards systematic remedial action which is more likely to achieve 'success' because it aims at specific and concrete objectives which are modest, realistic and attainable. Efforts must be channelled towards 'first things first' and the teacher must be reassured that it is quite in order to press consistently towards the attainment of well defined skills, provided information is available that such attainment can be reasonably expected.

This book suggests a method for obtaining such important information and assessing one individual child against a background of relevant information. Drawing up a balance sheet of assets and deficiencies in an individual child may help the teacher to avoid frittering away well-meaning efforts on a pale imitation of 'normal, academic education' when in fact it needs all her energy to provide 'social education' which gives more adequate preparation for adult life.

This book is therefore directed to everyone who has a direct or indirect interest in the problems of mentally handicapped people. Whilst the teacher of the mentally handicapped will, it is hoped, consider seriously the practical implications of these proposals, everyone else in the field of mental health—medical, psychological, administrative, or welfare, etc.—should read these pages because

their awareness of the problems and their sympathetic and knowledgeable support for rehabilitation projects are essential if we are
to carry through a successful social education programme.

For the general reader who wants to orientate himself in the field
of mental handicap, which has moved so much into the open in recent
years, this book may provide an easy introduction to one aspect of
the work which is probably the most rewarding: the social salvaging
of people who were once considered incapable of living and working
in the open community.

Acknowledgments

Nearly all the evidence put forward in the following pages to
support the thesis of the need for social education has been
collected in the various hospital groups for which I act as Director
of Psychological Services. Acknowledgment is therefore made to
the Medical Superintendents for permission to use material obtained
in course of my work, and to the Hospital Management Committees
of the following hospital groups: Coleshill Hospital Management
Committee, Birmingham; Leacastle Hospital Management Committee,
Kidderminster; Monyhull Hospital Management Committee, Birmingham; St. Margaret Hospital Management Committee, Birmingham.

I am especially obliged for having been given access to the
surveys in the Junior Training Centres of Birmingham, which were
organized by Mr. B. Schiphorst. The data provided by three surveys
in Birmingham were essential for arriving at 'norms' for severely
handicapped children. I am grateful to Mr. Schiphorst for his
cooperation and assistance. Permission to use this material was
given by Sir Lionel Russell, Chief Education Officer, and Dr. E. L.
Millar, Medical Officer of Health.

Some material, summarized in the last section of the book, has
been collected when I was Psychological Consultant to the Board
of Management Hostel and Workshop in Slough of the National
Society for Mentally Handicapped Children. This gave an opportunity
to investigate particular aspects of social training and I am obliged
to the Society for its support and co-operation during that time.

I would also like to thank Professor A. D. B. Clarke and his wife,
as well as Methuen the publishers of 'Mental Deficiency, The
Changing Outlook' for permission to use the graph on 'Cognitive

Recovery from Deprivation'. Acknowledgments are also made for permission to quote and reproduce material from the following sources: Fig. 9 and Table XVIII, National Association for Mental Health and Miss A. Marshall; Figs. 46, 47, 48, 49, 51, 52, 58, S E F A (Publications) Ltd.; Fig. 50, Methuen Ltd.

The numerous quotations regarding the reading interests of the mentally handicapped were first published in a paper in the *Library Quarterly* and acknowledgment is made to the University of Chicago Press.

I wish to thank particularly Dr. E. A. Doll and the publishers of the Vineland Social Maturity Scale (Educational Test Bureau, American Guidance Service) for permission to reproduce graph material and figures from that important work. Those who are familiar with the Vineland Scale will see how much the P-A-C approach was inspired by that first attempt to measure social competence. A comparison of the aims of the two approaches reveals clearly that they are complementary and that it is desirable to use both assessment instruments because they give two different views of the same all important function—social behaviour.

INTRODUCTION

This book deals with children and young adults who require a
special kind of education—Social Education—on account of their
mental handicap. The children have such low intellectual ability
that they are considered unsuitable for education at school and are
not even admitted to the special school system for the educationally
subnormal pupil (E S N). Many of the adults are socially inadequate
and have to be educated and trained either in special training
centres, or in hospitals and hostels. The following discussion,
surveys and reports of research refer therefore to an intelligence
range of up to approximately I Q 55 when talking of children, but of
up to approximately I Q 85 when talking of young adults.

The thesis of this book is that society—once having made the
decision that the mentally handicapped should, so far as possible,
live outside the hospital and institution—must provide a type of
education and training which will make him competent to survive in
the community with relatively little support even if only for
comparatively short periods. The aim of this book is to examine the
practical implications of an educational scheme for the mentally
handicapped, not in terms of types of buildings, numbers of teachers,
qualifications of staff, etc., but by discussing the principles which
govern educational work aimed at the rehabilitation of the socially
inadequate.

The design of such a scheme must, of necessity, be based on the
personality, capabilities and attainments of the person who is to be
educated and trained, and will be determined by the aims which are
to be realized. The first two sections of this book deal, therefore,
with the mentally handicapped (section 1) and his attainments in
various fields of social knowledge and competence (section 2).
The following section 3 demonstrates that there is constant development in social competence even though this is delayed and extremely

1

slow compared with that of normal children. Maturing of motor skills, increased life experience, the effect of prolonged education and training and other factors may result in achieving at specific ages what may be termed landmarks in social competence. These will help the teacher to evaluate her work against the background of average achievements by the mentally handicapped.

Although our knowledge of the mentally handicapped person's achievements and development is inadequate and incomplete, the available data provide sufficient support for the thesis that the content of a rehabilitation programme should be *social education*, rather than academic education during the junior stage or mere work training during the senior stage. It should be guided by a careful assessment and evaluation technique as set out in section 4.

Once the framework which is at present available has been examined (section 5), the discussion turns to the contents of a social education programme (section 6). Without doubt there must be considerable education for the mentally handicapped child, but it must have a different content from that offered to the normal child. The deficiencies in social skills pointed out in section 2, as well as the fact that it is 'social inadequacy' rather than 'educational backwardness' which brings the mentally handicapped person to our attention, require a consistent and directed approach with emphasis on relevant education and training. Bearing in mind the slow learning speed and limited intelligence of the mentally handicapped and also the specific practical aims of social education, specialized teaching methods and teaching aids have to be developed which are tailor made for the mentally handicapped and not simply borrowed from the field of junior education (section 7). Finally (section 8), a summary of the evidence so far available regarding the social competence of moderately and severely subnormal people indicates that an appreciable number of them have succeeded in being relatively adequate socially and even useful without a concerted attack having been made on their social rehabilitation. It is suggested that the number of these people who could be socially more adequate could be increased were the present hit-and-miss approach to be replaced by a well-defined system aware of its aims and not reluctant to experiment with new methods of teaching.

The author found himself in the serious difficulty of not being able to call the person around whom the whole discussion hinges by a generally acceptable name. There are many reasons why the people whose education and training are discussed here are called mentally defective, mentally handicapped, mentally retarded, intellectually limited, or mentally subnormal, and the author considered that there was no particular need, in this context, to spend time justifying the merits of one description over another. Throughout the book therefore, all these terms have been used with reference to the same type of person even though of necessity one particular name has been chosen for the title.

Whilst there cannot be much misunderstanding as far as the general reference is concerned, many difficulties can arise in sub-classifications within this area. To avoid misunderstandings, the adjectives borderline, mild, moderate, severe, and profound have been used (following the practice suggested by the World Health Organisation) in conjunction with any of the descriptive terms mentioned above, i.e. a moderately retarded person is the same as a moderately subnormal person. This has been discussed in more detail in section 1 pages 25 to 28.

It is not possible in a book of this length, which deals after all with the practical points of rehabilitation, to cover every possible aspect of mental deficiency. Little mention has been made of the causes of mental handicap, of incidence and prevalence, nor even of some aspects of teaching, such as the role of play and music; psychotherapy and physical education have been omitted and various aspects, such as vocational training and workshop procedure, have barely been touched. The writer has little new to say on these particular aspects, but it is hoped that readers will pursue them none-the-less in the literature at present available. It seemed more important that the aspects that can best contribute to a definition of the aims, and an assessment of the present position should be given ample space, because it is precisely these aspects of our subject that provide the framework for further endeavours. Once these points are quite clear it becomes possible to select from existing knowledge, and adapt it anew to suit the needs of the individual child and the opportunities of each special situation.

This book must not be regarded as a textbook on mental subnormality nor even on one particular aspect of it. There are many excellent books of this kind which analyse in a critical and exhaustive manner the extensive literature which has grown up about this subject. The thesis of this book concerns one particular aspect—the social inadequacy of the mentally handicapped as seen from an educational-therapeutic point of view—and is thus, in a sense, *supplementary* reading once the topic of mental handicap has been explored in all its many ramifications. It is hoped that the approach adopted here will be considered as thoroughly practical because it deals with the first steps of 'what can be done about it ', rather than confining itself to presenting facts and figures illustrating the varying degrees of social inadequacy displayed by the mentally handicapped. When dealing with the practical implications of a social education programme one has to consider the immediate aims, the individual needs and the available educational provisions. This has been attempted in these pages, but it is fully recognized that the approach is, to some extent, one-sided and certainly not exhaustive. This has been intentional because it is felt that a one-sided and single-minded plan of action will provide a basis to work from and a direction to aim at. These are factors at present conspicuously absent from work in mental handicap, often because of the tendency to consider mental handicap as a 'disease' from which the patient is 'suffering'. In consequence, there have been anxiety and apprehension that an approach which does not pay attention to the sickroom aspects might impose too much stress on someone incapable of accepting it. As a result, little or nothing has been done other than to try to make the patient comfortable and happy.

It is the belief of the author that this over-anxious, over-careful and over-protective handling of the mentally handicapped child may do him a tremendous disservice and lead to a lower level of efficiency than need be. If the teacher is aware of the nature of the mentally handicapped child's limitations, and is also sure in her own mind of the particular goals that may reasonably be realized by employing specific teaching methods, much more can be achieved than hitherto without inducing nervous tensions in either pupil or teacher.

It is hoped that no prospective reader will be deterred from considering the proposals in this book by its multitude of graphs and figures. These diagrams are included as aids to the observation of the personality and make-up of a mentally handicapped individual in order to help him as a person and to make his education as relevant and effective as possible. The methods outlined have been developed primarily as an aid to teachers in providing the special education which the mentally handicapped needs, and will supply a practical background suitable for adaptation to the needs and conditions of different situations.

1

THE PERSON

Physical and Mental Handicap

The effects of a mental handicap can justifiably be compared with those of a physical handicap. In both cases a person's ability to develop the skill needed to adjust himself to the demands of a normal life in the community is limited to some extent. In the case of the physically handicapped person, patient training by those who make it their job to help him, the tolerance and helpfulness shown by ordinary people around him and, most important, his own determination not to give in despite his disability, all help to ameliorate his situation. A realistic assessment of what can be achieved and what cannot be attained contributes considerably to good adjustment to the situation and the ability to make the most of it.

In the case of the mentally handicapped, only the first two conditions for overcoming the disability are present. Devoted training by parents and special teachers is available and, nowadays, tolerance and practical assistance by the community. The third factor, however— the will to overcome the handicap—is apparently entirely missing owing to the nature of the handicap. Whereas overcoming the physical handicap represents a victory of mind over matter, when the mind itself is damaged or underdeveloped, the purposefulness, the will to strive against difficulties, the desire to reach specific and not easily attainable aims appear to be absent.

It will be noted that a statement on the *definite* absence of the will to overcome handicap has been purposely avoided: there may be a ray of hope for some. After all, the failure in the past to kindle the spark of interest and motivation which would assist the handicapped person to become a more adequate member of the community does not preclude the possibility of achieving this in the future.

A physical handicap can be sufficiently serious for the individual to require nursing and assistance; likewise, a profoundly mentally handicapped person may also need permanent nursing and care. On

6

the other hand, the disability may be comparatively minor and in many cases may prove disabling only if its existence is disregarded. This applies to both the physically and the mentally handicapped who will work reasonably well as long as the demands made upon them do not overtax their abilities. The same may also be said of 'normal' people, for there is a point at which we all crack and collapse under excessive strain. Having an initial handicap means simply that collapse will come sooner, and in apparently inexplicable circumstances, than in the case of the average person living a normal life. Whilst the profoundly handicapped person is obviously unable to live a normal life because he has virtually no ability to tackle even the simplest demands made by his surroundings, the less severely handicapped is in a different situation. He has some, even if rather modest, ability and can to some extent face up to the wishes and requirements of those around him as does everyone else. It is true, sooner or later the demands become too much for him: this may be early in life when he first meets competition from others at school; it may be later when he has to work for his living; later still when he no longer has the assistance of relatives who care for him. Nevertheless, there are some with similar handicaps who can successfully overcome all these obstacles and merge with the multitude of those who get through life with comparatively little assistance. Their modest social adequacy gives us justified hope that more can be done for those who require now so much support.

It is not always easy to decide where to draw the line between a handicap which incapacitates a person to the extent of needing permanent care, and a handicap which disables but does not incapacitate entirely. Nonetheless, with constant patience and first-class training even someone with a severe physical handicap can be helped to some degree of independence. The same applies to the mentally handicapped. It has, for example, been shown that people who have been regarded as severely mentally handicapped and are classified clinically as imbeciles, can work not only well enough in a sheltered workshop to satisfy employers, but can also lead useful lives outside the protection of an institution. The less pronounced the handicap the more likely is it that it can be overcome and be no more than what it says, a handicap, rather than a crippling, incapacitating and incurable condition of mind (see section 8).

This then is our task: to find ways and means to overcome the effects of a mental handicap and to adjust such a person to the demands of life. There are those who, like the profoundly physically handicapped, will not, in our present state of knowledge, benefit from any methods we may use; but there are many others who could be helped in their adjustment to life. In many cases this may mean some adjustment of their social circumstances, but not necessarily institutional or hospital care, and usually the aim will be to make them socially adequate within the open community.

The achievements of such rehabilitation work are neither very spectacular nor very glamorous. Trying to make people conform to life as it is rather than to encourage them to change it into something better appears to be an uninspiring task, yet there is fascination and value in bringing a human being, who would otherwise be condemned to almost vegetable existence, to a fuller use of his potential.

Mental Disorder

A mental *handicap* is not a mental illness; it is mostly an unfortunate state to which one is born, just as one might be born with a club foot or a hunched back. On the other hand a mental *disorder* or mental *disease* usually develops in someone who has previously achieved normal mental functioning. The various terms synonymous with mental defect—mental retardation, mental defect, mental subnormality—should not therefore be confused with the terms used to describe psychotic and neurotic disorders. Psychotic or neurotic patients have little in common with the mentally handicapped other than the adjective 'mental' and the fact that in England they are both classified under the same legal heading of 'mental disorder'. To refer to both types of people as mentally disordered is probably quite reasonable because, in both cases, their mental abilities are 'out of order'. However, in the psychotic person this is due to a disease process occurring *after* normal mental function has developed, whereas in the mentally handicapped, normal function of the mind has never been attained. In the latter case some event before or soon after birth has prevented normal mental development and a person of this type will probably always function below the average level of efficiency. On the other hand, the individual who has acquired a mental disease may be restored to normal functioning as a result of treatment or spontaneous remission of the disease.

It is unfortunate that the public generally does not realize that the different origins of mental disorders result in two entirely different types of problems for society. The disease of the mentally ill person is often discussed in hushed whispers because it seems to reflect badly on the family and on the patient himself. This unreasonable and emotional attitude is extended to the mentally handicapped person who should really be thought of as a natural occurrence as is a particularly ugly child or a very tall or very short person. It is only in recent years that parents of mentally handicapped children have come out into the open and talked freely about their problems and it is, therefore, only recently that the layman has begun to define a mentally handicapped person in terms other than those mentioned above.

This new attitude is characterized by stressing the importance of intelligence and suggesting that a mentally handicapped person is stupid or silly, that he cannot read or write and has a low intelligence quotient or low mental age. This concept, whilst not absolutely wrong, is very misleading because it over-simplifies the issues. What is worse it diverts attention from the relevant aspects and channelizes efforts to ameliorate the situation into directions which have led to only limited success in the past.

Intelligence and Social Competence

Let us look at the facts. Intelligence can be observed only indirectly in behaviour. Our impressions of the degree of intelligence of a particular person are drawn for example from observing his behaviour at school, which suggests the degree of academic intelligence, or his behaviour at work which suggests the degree of practical intelligence. Another more scientific but still indirect form of observation is based on testing in a formal test situation. Nevertheless, all these observations only enable us to assess a person's abilities with a higher degree of probability than if we had merely guessed. Even though the type of intelligence observed in the school performance or in an intelligence test influences quite substantially the level of functioning in 'real' life, there are other factors which perhaps have an even more decisive bearing on final achievement. The will to succeed, temperament and good or bad luck, for example, are among the factors which determine how far intelligence, as measured in laboratory situations by formal tests of intellectual functioning or as observed in the school situation, will become generally effective in later life.

The people we shall discuss in these pages have lower than average intelligence and they are also those who have attracted attention to themselves because socially, they function most inadequately. Those who are only mildly handicapped show an apparent inability to work properly or to apply themselves to work for any length of time and many of them commit small and silly delinquencies. A monotonous list of socially irritating mis-demeanours of decided nuisance value, but containing few items of major importance, can be drawn up as being characteristic of the social inadequacies of the mildly handicapped. Similar delinquencies and incompetencies can be perpetrated by people of normal in-telligence, and often the main difference between the petty delinquencies of people with normal and those with subnormal intelligence is simply the lack of skill in execution and covering up shown by the latter. The subnormal's approach to the socially nonconforming action is simple and direct, and because he is unable to foresee the consequences of his actions, his social incompetence is very marked and conspicuous. It might well be argued that the subnormal intelligence determines only the poor quality of various socially nonconforming actions but not their occurrence.

It is tempting to associate this low social competence with the low intellectual functioning high lighted by intelligence testing, and to assume a cause and effect relationship. It is usually argued that there is low intelligence and, in consequence, low social competence, but it is less often mentioned that there may be comparatively low social competence and, in consequence low intelligence test scores (Masland, Sarason and Gladwin, 1958; Kellmer Pringle, 1965). Another possibility could be that both low intelligence test scores and low social competence are the outcome of a third factor. This third factor could be described as a weakened ability and will to utilize the intellectual equipment and to apply it to social situations. It is interesting to reflect that the IQ is never thought of as an explanation of social inadequacy of a person with an intelligence test score of 130 or over. In his case the explana-tion of any incompetence is found in emotional maladjustment and neurosis. However, this argument is not applied once it is known that the socially inadequate has a 'subnormal' IQ.

Intellectual Functioning

Probably one of the thorniest problems in the whole field of
mental deficiency is the question to what extent social rehabilitation depends on intelligence as measured by intelligence tests.
The word intelligence itself has defied an agreed definition by
generations of psychologists. It has been said that trying to define
intelligence is like trying to define electricity. Everyone knows
what intelligence does, just as everyone knows what electricity
does; yet electricity has never been defined adequately, and
similarly intelligence has never been defined in such a way as to
satisfy everyone.

As far as the subnormal is concerned, probably the only demands
made upon his intelligence are that he should be able to adapt
himself to new uncomplicated situations, to foresee the consequences of his actions, to plan from day to day and be able to
profit by his own experiences. Experience suggests that he posses-
ses these abilities to only a very limited degree compared with the
average of the population, and to a certain extent formal testing of
his 'academic intelligence' supports this. However, testing cannot
indicate for certain whether the limited ability shown at the time
of testing will remain as limited in the future or in different
situations. Test scores, expressed in terms of IQ or MA, suggest
that, *at the time of testing*, the individual functions on a certain
level, and this can be compared with the average score of a given
population on the same test. They do not reflect a 'true' level of
ability, and no 'certain' prognosis can be made whether this level
will be permanently maintained. Any prognosis made is a matter of
a more or less skilful interpretation of the available evidence—
which is often insufficient and must certainly not be limited to test
results. Other factors have to be considered as well. The following
analogy may help to clarify the situation.

In Fig. 1 three vessels are shown in cross-section; they are of
different sizes and obviously have different capacities. The three
vessels symbolize the different intellectual capacities of persons
A, B and C. An individual inherits a certain capacity for intelligent
behaviour in the same way that he inherits his physique, the colour
of his eyes and hair, and various other characteristics. He can do
nothing to alter this genetic inheritance and he is therefore born
and will remain, either intelligent (person A) or not so intelligent
(person C). On the other hand his intellectual capacity may never

be fully utilized. Environmental circumstances, such as lack of schooling, emotional disturbances, lack of ambition and many other factors, may interfere and prevent him from fully utilizing his capacity. This is indicated in the diagram by the shaded content of vessel A, which shows clearly that the capacity is not fully utilized.

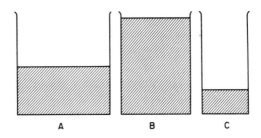

Fig. 1. The relationship between capacity (potential) and efficiency.

The second vessel, B, has a much smaller capacity than A, but it is fully utilized. In other words, good education, good opportunities and drive to achieve may have resulted in greater success than in case A, although B's capacity is much less. Vessel C is smaller than either of the others, and represents the intellectual capacity of the subnormal. The contents are also very limited compared with the available capacity, and even though this capacity is not as large as that of vessel B—a normal person—it may be adequate in an undemanding situation. However, case C under-functions similarly as case A. Nevertheless, A's functioning is still sufficient to cope with life quite satisfactorily, whilst the subnormal C, functions so much below the average level of requirement that he is socially inadequate. It is the task of social rehabilitation to help C to function more adequately by using his modest mental equipment fully.

Scores obtained by intelligence testing indicate the level of functioning at the time of testing; in other words, the contents indicated by the shaded portion on the diagram. We can only guess at the capacity of the vessel: we have to judge it but we cannot measure it. The better and more experienced the examiner and the more test results available on different aspects of someone's intelligence, the more reliable will be the judgment of his capacity.

Nevertheless, all that can be determined with any certainty is the degree of intelligence used at the time of testing for solving the problems of the test.

Probably no one is able to function all the time to his fullest capacity. The person symbolized by vessel A has much capacity but is under-functioning considerably. He will never achieve the distinction in life that is within his capacity if he continues to under-function. Compared with another normal person (B) who functions reasonably near his perhaps lower capacity, A will be far less effective. The subnormal symbolized by vessel C may also under-function and this may well be below the minimum level required for normal life.

It is unfortunate that we have at present no reliable means of assessing potential intellectual capacity and any speculation regarding possible higher intellectual capacity must therefore depend on the skill of the interpreter of the test. Sometimes there are indications in the test performance when, for example, an examinee is considerably better in some aspects than in others. Some examiners are inclined to regard these peaks of performance as indications of a higher potential which has not been utilized (Jastak, 1949, 1952). In other words, it is assumed that a person's performance on tests which score comparatively low is depressed and does not reflect his real ability. It can, of course, also be argued that the peaks of performance simply indicate special abilities in particular areas but not an all-round potential which has not been realized.

What is certain however is that since the test results indicate only functioning at the time of testing, assessment of capacity must take account of factors which are known to affect intellectual functioning, such as emotional disturbances and cultural background. This has been shown very clearly by a number of studies carried out by A. D. B. and A. M. Clarke and their associates (1954, 1958). They observed that a large number of mentally handicapped people made such gains in IQ points over a period after admission to hospital, that there was 'a considerable proportion of the certified feeble-minded advancing towards, or into, intellectual normality' (Clarke and Clarke, 1965). This phenomenon was explained when the researchers investigated the possibility that early adverse environmental circumstances might be connected with subsequent increases in IQ scores. Twelve criteria such as 'neglect',

'N.S.P.C.C. intervention' and 'cruelty' were formulated and
mentally handicapped people were separated into those from a
'very bad home' background and those from less adverse homes. It
was shown that the IQ point gains were consistently and considerably larger in the group with early adverse experiences than in
the other group. Clarke and Clarke concluded that such adverse
experiences tend to retard mental development for many years, but
that later the effects begin to fade and IQ increments begin to
occur.

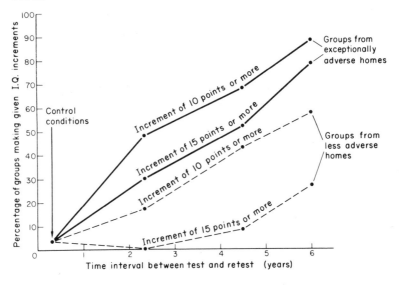

Fig. 2. Cognitive recovery from deprivation (from Clarke & Clarke, 1965).

These studies suggest that IQ scores may be much depressed at
a time of disturbing experiences and not always useful in predicting
final efficiency. Clarke and Clarke (1958) noted that at a later
stage relatively few patients from the group with very bad home
background were still in hospital. This underlined the better
prognosis of those from the worst social conditions.

The studies strongly suggest that increases in IQ points occur
in most moderately handicapped young people during a period of at
least 6 years after adolescence. The increases are most marked in
youngsters coming from very adverse conditions, but can be noted
in all cases. The apparently heightened intellectual efficiency is
probably due to entry into a non-adverse environment (such as

hospital) and removal from the often disturbing home environment, rather than to any positive stimulation such as training or education. It appears also that the increase in IQ points occurs in consequence of belated maturation. It is this personality development with its concomitant increased intellectual efficiency which could provide the fertile soil for educational and social training even in late adolescence (see pages 188 to 197).

Figure 2, from Clarke and Clarke (1965), summarizes the results of their investigations, and indicates very clearly the damaging effect of early adverse influences and the spontaneous remission in later years. This seems to be the more dramatic the worse the conditions were originally. There is nothing to indicate whether full utilization of the mental potential has taken place or whether the latest assessment of functioning is not still below the level which could have been reached had there been no adverse environmental influences. On the other hand it appears that environmental manipulation at a later stage can have most encouraging results.[1]

Social Competence

A descriptive and useful definition of 'social competence' is the following: 'Social competence is manifested by the extent to which an individual is able and willing to conform to the customs, habits and standards of behaviour prevailing in the society in which he lives; by the degree to which he is able to do so independently of direction and guidance; and by the extent to which he participates constructively in the affairs and conduct of his community' (Kellmer-Pringle, 1965). If social adjustment is to take place, it will be essential that the mentally handicapped learns to conform to the customs, habits and standards of the community in which he lives, which may be of limited nature as in a sheltered workshop or be the open community. This type of conformity must be the paramount aim of rehabilitation work even if it is in most cases only achieved in a mechanical-imitative manner. In many routine and

[1] The dependence of IQ scores on environmental factors is not confined to the field of retardation. Wall *et al.* (1962) point out that 'the norms on intelligence tests reflect the educative effects of good, bad and indifferent environments' and they refer to the 'general and significant trend with the improvement of general conditions since the last war for mean scores on intelligence tests of all types, and on tests of attainment to improve.'

everyday situations, the independence as required by above definition can be displayed by the mentally handicapped even though he
will require guidance and direction in unfamiliar situations.
Constructive participation which would need a comparatively high
degree of intelligence may well be absolutely beyond his ability.

Attaining a relatively low level of social competence in the sense
of being able to conform should be within the ability of most
severely and moderately handicapped people, even if proficiency
in many other aspects of social competence cannot be acquired.
Social conformity is not difficult to achieve. In many ways it is not
so much a matter of intelligence, as of experience, education,
social background and personality such as stability and persever-
ance. It is therefore an aspect which is far more accessible to
manipulation by straightforward teaching through imitation than the
acquisition of school-knowledge which depends much on a pupil's
verbal intelligence.

It is also an aspect which is far more accessible to assessment
provided it is simply regarded as a conglomeration of various social
skills and bits of social knowledge, which may reflect how
successfully somebody conforms to the social requirements of
his particular community. Attempts of measuring social competence
will have to rely on observing specific social skills but whether
these are relevant examples of conforming social behaviour is not
easily established. Whenever possible, direct observation will
establish competence under ordinary circumstances but very often
it is only practicable to establish 'knowledge' rather than 'application' and thus reference to 'social *competence*' may become a little
misleading. In fact, this term may be somewhat of a misnomer in
mental handicap because 'competence' suggests the independence
and constructive participation required by the definition quoted at
the beginning of this section. Nevertheless, the assessment of
social competence in the sense of assessing skills of conforming
provides a systematic technique of exploring the ingredients which
contribute towards social adjustment in the mentally handicapped
and is thus an essential procedure for directing and planning his
social education and training.

A comparison of relatively bright and relatively dull children in
the moderately retarded range, may lead to the disconcerting
observation that a dull child may be socially very much more
advanced than a bright child. In such a case, the difference in social

competence has to be explained other than by reference to intelligence. It may be due to bad schooling, to over-protection at home, or to severe physical handicap which interferes with the attainment of a reasonable level of social competence. The dull child may be older and may therefore have had more experience and opportunity to learn.

Comparison with children in the same age range and with similarly low intellectual ability, will help to draw attention to weaknesses in social ability which are not due to intellectual handicap. The question should be why children in the same age group, who have similar mental handicap, do not attain similar levels of social efficiency. Adequate reasons can be found in many cases, but a difference of three or four IQ points should never be regarded as an explanation for underfunctioning. Although social competence obviously depends to a certain extent on the level of intelligence, there are many skills and social accomplishments which are routine in nature and depend mostly on practice and experience, good teaching and training, and on maturity.

Assessment of social competence is not a substitute for assessment of intelligence, and both aspects have to be studied in order to obtain a full picture of functioning. The assessment of social functioning is concerned with whether social skills are known and practised. Many low-level social skills are acquired over the years by careful training, and thus the level of social ability is usually well above the level of mental functioning as established by an IQ test, particularly in older children.

Figure 3 shows the mental ages and social ages as scored on an intelligence test and a scale of social maturity by 31 mentally handicapped persons aged from 6 years 9 months to 33 years. The black columns indicate the levels scored on the intelligence test by each member of the group. The results are arranged from the lowest to the highest mental age; the shaded columns indicate the level of social achievement of the individuals on the Vineland test of social maturity. It will be seen that, in nearly all cases, the social competence ratings are above, sometimes well above, the levels of the mental ages. This suggests that most people were functioning on a higher level of social competence than one might have expected judging merely from their mental ages.

The diagram also shows that there is little relationship between social competence and mental level in the individuals tested. Where adjacent test results indicate similar mental levels, social competence may be far above mental level in some and very close to it in other cases. This seems to suggest that there is often no close relationship between mental ability and social competence, at least in the early stages of social development. Differences in social competence between people who obtain similar scores on tests of mental ability may well be due to prolonged experience, better training, more stimulation, etc. How much any one subnormal person can succeed in developing social skills cannot be predicted with any confidence at present. Intelligence will of course, in the long run, provide a

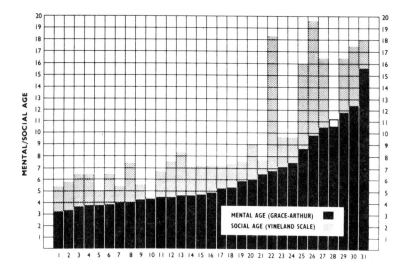

Fig. 3. Mental Age and Social Age (Gunzburg, 1964a).

ceiling to possible social achievement and no genuine subnormal will ever become thoroughly competent, but social attainments may be much higher than intelligence test scores would let us expect.

As far as social ability is concerned, it appears that education and training for adjustment to the open community can be planned without paying too much attention to the restrictions of the IQ score provided that there is minimal intellectual ability. This is probably somewhere around IQ 35.

Some factors seem to have a decisive bearing on the level of social competence obtained. Among them are the type of training, whether intensive and directed, whether academic or social; also, variety and length of relevant experience to which the subnormal was exposed. There is little doubt that the mentally retarded adult with many years of experience has a decided advantage over a normally intelligent child who has seen and experienced less than he.

Figure 4 shows the social attainments of a normal child and a subnormal adult, assessed on the P-A-C 1 of social development (see page 69). The shaded parts indicate skills which have been

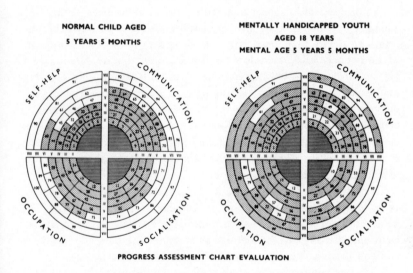

PROGRESS ASSESSMENT CHART EVALUATION

Fig. 4. Social attainments in a child and an adult of the same mental age (Gunzburg, 1964a).

mastered and the white spaces those not yet acquired. Skills, referred to by a code number, are arranged in the four areas: self-help, communication, socialisation and occupation. They are graded according to difficulty, with the easiest skills placed near the centre and the most difficult at the periphery of the circle.

The diagram on the left-hand side represents the social skills of a normal child of 5½ years of age. A very regular and normal development can be seen in the four aspects assessed, even though he is a little more advanced in one section than in another. On the right-hand side is the P-A-C 1 assessment of a subnormal man aged 18. On a test of intellectual ability he obtained the same test score as the child; he is therefore given a mental age of 5½. Nevertheless his social achievements are far advanced compared with those of the normal child. He has acquired many skills (shown near, or at the periphery of the diagram) which are obviously beyond the capacity of the younger child of normal intelligence, due to the fact that he has some 13 years more experience than the 5½-year-old. Therefore, if we were to consider only his mental age of 5½, his social ability would be considerably underestimated.

The diagram also shows that the social achievements of the mentally subnormal adult are very patchy. There are many achievements on a very high level but, compared with the P-A-C 1 diagram of the normal child, many low level skills are missing. Obviously his social development is very uneven and his attainments are very scattered. The social functioning of such a person would also be uneven, and at one moment he might give the impression of being more advanced than his mental age suggests, and at others of being extremely stupid. This inconsistency in functioning can often lead to difficulties in adjustment and to a misunderstanding of the true situation by relatives and employers.

To summarize, we may say that the measurement of intelligence is an important part of assessment, but that IQ and mental age scores are not so helpful as we would like them to be in the treatment and training of the mentally subnormal. The data may even mislead because the intellectual measurement is not always reliable and refers only to one aspect of the subnormal's functioning which is not as important as his general social behaviour.

It has been shown that the social functioning of the subnormal can be well above the level indicated by the test of mental ability. The discrepancy can be very large if good education and maturation have contributed to an advanced degree of social competence. However, the levels of social competence in various areas can also be very uneven as many skills which should have been learnt at an early stage may either not have been acquired or may have been forgotten for lack of practice. To compare a young, normal child with a mentally handicapped youth on the basis of M A or S A alone is misleading because the scores do not reflect adequately the different quality of their social behaviour.

The Personality of the Mentally Handicapped

No teaching or training can be in any way successful unless the pupil wants to be taught and trained. This is an essential aspect of all teaching. Most people have some interest in progress, some ambition, and a desire to develop and to achieve success in some sphere. These qualities appear to be inborn and may be responsible for the evolution of homo sapiens from the primitive apes. Without it the modern world would not exist. It is this force which makes people succeed; on the other hand, those with diminished motivation are often unable to make adequate use of their opportunities.

In many cases it seems that the real problem in the rehabilitation of the mentally defective is not his low intellectual ability or his mental handicap as such, but his greatly diminished drive to succeed. He has no ambition, seems to have no real desire to learn and, even more important, he will do little to overcome his difficulties and shortcomings.

It seems to be fairly typical of the subnormal who finds himself in hospitals or training centres that he displays a very marked degree of passive acceptance of the situation and of apparent lack of desire to try to change the situation. Many severely handicapped people vegetate in the wards of a hospital without concern about the future, and without attempting to improve their position. Though the more capable of them do not show this tendency to extreme, there is little doubt that even they do not deliberately strive towards a goal.

C. J. C. Earl (1961) stated that 'essential components of the inherently subnormal personality include weakness, poverty of the formative instincts, of the urge to develop, and later poverty of libido, an inability to strive toward a goal, to persist in effort or withstand frustration'. This weakness of drive is the basis of many puzzling and frustrating situations which occur in the course of rehabilitation work. Earl continues 'It is a more basic affair than simplicity or "low intelligence"; the inability to learn reflected in a low IQ, is often largely a function of weakness, both as failure of development of the highest psychoneural level, and of the inability to strive against the environment. Subnormal personalities suffer a double handicap; their simplicity renders ordinary school and scholastic situations more difficult for them than for the normal, while their weakness reduces their ability to strive against any difficulty. Yet weakness and simplicity vary independently of each other; many fairly low-grade patients are more capable of effort than some of the most intelligent patients. Indeed in high-grade cases there has to be considerable weakness—or gross emotional disorder—to justify special school or institutional treatment.'

Earl is careful to point out that not all failure to strive is necessarily due to weakness. It may be due to immaturity, emotional disturbance, personality inhibition or even to prolonged institutional residence. There is some dis-inclination to conform to the wishes of the community. The mentally handicapped may not want to do what he is expected to do. He is not interested in it; he has no desire to learn to read, to write or even to please us.

Such a mentally handicapped person without sufficient drive is the despair of his teachers and doctors. Intelligence testing has shown him to have the necessary ability to do comparatively well in a humble position in the community, yet he does nothing towards achieving this aim. He drifts, and the slightest mishap is sufficient to derail him and he stumbles back to the protective shelter of home and institution. In fact, the only drive which he displays may be a negative one, namely to preserve the status quo. In that respect, he may often show a remarkable skill—one that could be considered as a negative drive. Yet it is not mere opposition or negativism, and may be simply a result of fear, anxiety and apprehension, which make him feel insecure when venturing into the outside world. His social inadequacy is best described as a consequence of his 'weak ambition to overcome obstacles and to fight frustration'. Earl (1961) makes the pessimistic prognosis: 'the immature may become mature, the unstable may stabilize, the unintelligent be slowly trained, the schizoid, athletoid, neurotic may adjust; but the really weak are doomed.' This is probably true but it requires considerable clinical acumen to decide who is *really* weak.

Weakness of drive represents the basic problem for all those teaching and training the mentally subnormal for rehabilitation in the community with its many stress situations. No treatment or cure has yet been found to overcome this basic defect in a person who has no desire to help himself. All we can do is to place him in situations which are less demanding and less difficult—but he must be encouraged to try and to persist. In the face of too great difficulties he will collapse and become a problem to society.

It is possible that weakness of drive is a constitutional defect, but it may also be argued that the impact of such defect has become more pronounced as a result of the many frustrating and disappointing situations which confront the individual in the course of growing up. There may well be a very considerable overlay of fear and anxiety which results in even further weakening of the drive to overcome obstacles. If this is correct then remedial work must consist of strengthening the subnormal's confidence in his own abilities and giving him the assurance that, despite the complexities of life, he has the necessary equipment to tackle it on a simple level. If we succeed in restoring his loss of self-confidence by social education and training, we may be able to restore some drive and ability to tackle frustrating situations. The innate weakness and inferior mental equipment will however remain and will leave the mentally handicapped person still vulnerable even if he is less prone to collapse at the first sign of difficulty.

The interesting experiments of O'Connor and Hermelin (1963) suggest that much of the inability of even severely retarded people to carry out instructions or to learn, is due to shortcomings in communication between them and us. They do not grasp what is required because their knowledge of language has not developed sufficiently—largely due perhaps to our failure to teach vocabulary adequately. There is little doubt that the apparent incomprehensibility of the world around them will not assist the mentally handicapped to apply themselves with energy or to tackle constantly frustrating situations.

Claridge (1959, 1962) and Claridge and O'Connor (1957) suggested on the basis of their researches that the unequal rate of learning and application to work was related to personality differences rather than to intelligence levels. Basing their work on the clinical grouping of 'excitable' and 'apathetic' types of personality they showed that excitable and severely handicapped people tended to improve rather more than apathetic ones. On the other hand apathetic individuals tended to make further improvements, even when incentives were withdrawn, whilst the excitable people declined in their performance.

It may well be that far too little attention has been paid to the influence of personality factors on general efficiency, and that, in the attempt to explain failure, there has been overemphasis of the part played by general intelligence.

Definition of Mental Handicap

It is essential to define as clearly as possible the terms which will be used in this book. The terms and definitions will be those

put forward by the American Association on Mental Deficiency
(Heber, 1959) and used by the World Health Organization in the
eighth revision of the International Classification of Diseases. The
American definition states that mental handicap is a 'sub-average
general intellectual functioning which originates during the
developmental period and is associated with impairment in one or
more of the following: 1, maturation; 2, learning; and 3, social
adjustment'.

The implications of this careful definition are far-reaching.
Firstly the definition stresses 'sub-average general intellectual
functioning', and this implies the importance of an objective test
of general intelligence. Sub-average is a term used to refer to those
persons whose test scores consistently fall below a certain level
(standard deviation, see p. 208). Approximately one sixth of the
population fall within the definition, and their intellectual handicap
affects their school work and their ability to achieve economic
independence.

Though the employment of mental tests is considered to be
essential in evaluation, the American Association on Mental
Deficiency makes it clear that the test scores obtained should be
used in conjunction with other information.

The developmental period is considered to extend over approximately 16 years and it is thus possible to differentiate deficiency
originating during these years from that following damage during
adulthood. On the other hand the American definition does not
specifically differentiate mental retardation from other conditions
such as schizophrenia or organic brain damage. A child is therefore considered to be mentally retarded if he is functioning on a
sub-average intellectual level irrespective of the cause, and this
may mean that children whose only common characteristic is
sub-average intellectual functioning are cared for in a single
group. Differential diagnosis in childhood is often difficult and it
is probably better to describe behaviour in the agreed terms of IQ
rather than speculate in doubtful diagnosis.

Of particular importance is the fact that sub-average intellectual
functioning must be associated with and reflected in impairment in
one or more aspects of adaptive behaviour. The three aspects
mentioned, maturation, learning and social adjustment assume
different importance in different age groups.

In early childhood adaptive behaviour is assessed almost

completely in terms of sensory motor development: the acquiring
of the skills of infancy such as sitting, crawling, standing, walking,
talking and habit training. During the school years intellectual
ability becomes most important and any learning difficulties are
usually manifest during this period. In adulthood social adjustment
holds pride of place and indicates the degree to which the individual
is able to maintain himself independently in the community and in
gainful employment. It also shows his ability to meet and to conform to the personal and social responsibilities and standards set
by the community.

This is a very helpful approach to the problem of mental retardation because a child is in fact judged in his relationships to the
behaviour of others of his age group rather than in relation to
standards which are appropriate to adults.

Of particular importance in the American definition is the point
that diagnosis of mental retardation is made entirely on the basis
of behaviour at the time of assessment: a person is considered to
be mentally retarded as a result of poor performance on an intelligence test, and an observed lack of adaptive behaviour. No attempt
is made to predict future behaviour; it is acknowledged that a
person may be mentally retarded at one period of his life, but not
at a later stage. Such a person usually remains intellectually
inferior in terms of intelligence test scores, but the adequacy of his
adaptive behaviour enables him to be relatively independent within
the community. Research has shown that many who have been
considered to be mentally retarded during their school years have
succeeded in leading independent lives in adulthood (e.g. Charles,
1953). If social independence and gainful employment are regarded
as contra-indications of mental retardation, we must conclude
that the diagnosis of mental retardation in childhood does not
necessarily include a prognosis of retardation in adulthood.

Classification of Mental Handicap[1]

If one accepts the statistical convention of regarding all persons
as 'intellectually retarded' whose score on an intelligence test falls
below one standard deviation from the mean (see Appendix A) then
approximately one million people in Great Britain and one sixth of

[1] This section should be read in conjunction with the discussion of standard
deviation in Appendix A.

the population of the United States fall under this heading. It is thus desirable to provide a further classification into subgroups. The American Association suggests five groups according to measured intelligence levels. Although this is a convenient classification of intellectual functioning, it has no relationship with other systems based on medical or social criteria.

Intellectual functioning in relation to academic achievement can be assessed adequately by using the standard tests of intelligence, but it is far more difficult to measure adaptive behaviour which of course depends largely upon environment. In practice, therefore, emphasis is often laid on the results of intelligence tests, but this should not let us forget that deficiencies in both adaptive behaviour *and* measured intelligence should be demonstrated before the individual can rightly be considered to be mentally retarded.

A *borderline retarded* has an IQ between 70 to 84 on the Wechsler intelligence test (WAIS) or between 68 and 83 on a Stanford-Binet type of test. At pre-school age he would show only minimal sensory motor retardation and would probably be regarded as normal. Later, however, he will require special training in a school for educationally subnormal children and he will not be able to go on to a higher education. As an adult he will, with proper training and education, be socially and vocationally adequate, although under adverse social and economic situations he may need supervision and guidance.

The *mildly retarded* has an IQ between 55 and 69 on the Wechsler scale (WAIS) and between 52 and 67 on the Stanford-Binet scale. As a baby he shows a fair degree of motor development and can be managed with moderate supervision. He is perhaps slow to develop but he does learn to talk and to communicate. At school age he requires special education, but is capable of elementary attainments in reading and may, as an adult, be able to hold unskilled or semi-skilled jobs. He needs supervision and guidance in times of social or economic stress.

The *moderately retarded* scores between 40 and 54 on the WAIS test and between 36 and 51 on the Stanford-Binet test. As a baby he is generally unable to profit from training in self-help, develops only a few communication skills and shows poor motor development. When at school age he learns to talk and communicate and can be trained in self-help skills. He finds tremendous difficulty in learning academic skills and is unsuitable for education at school; he is therefore usually sent to special training centres or hospital schools.

As an adult he can contribute to his self-support in sheltered work-shops or sheltered work places in the community (see section 5). Although he is able to look after himself to some extent, he needs permanent guidance and supervision.

The *severely retarded* person scores between 25 and 39 on the WAIS test and between 29 and 35 on the Stanford-Binet test. He shows severe retardation in all respects from babyhood, and requires constant nursing care, although he can be trained to feed, wash and dress himself under supervision. During school age he still needs total care and does not really benefit from training for independence. Even as an adult his ability to look after himself is grossly deficient and he needs complete care and supervision, though he can also be trained to execute simple remunerative work in a sheltered workshop.

The *profoundly retarded* has an IQ below 25 on the WAIS test and below 20 on the Stanford-Binet test. Such people need complete nursing care throughout their lives and may be unable even to feed themselves or look after their toilet requirements. They are usually unable to walk or to do so only with help. At present we have no means of making them even relatively self-sufficient. They are cared for by their families and in special care units in the community and hospital (see section 5).

Once again it must be emphasised that a classification such as the foregoing does not provide a diagnosis, and therefore people with similar intellectual test scores and showing similar behaviour may function like this for completely different reasons.

In the following chapters terms are used with their specific meanings as outlined above. They refer, however, only to work behaviour and behaviour assessed in test situations and do not carry any etiological implication. For example, although it may be a reasonable generalization to say that people with IQ between 55 and 69 should be able to read, there may be individuals within the group in whom an inability to read may be due to a specific factor not connected with intelligence.

The association between intellectual level and social competence is not close enough to make it possible to predict the one after an examination of the other, and an individual may be found to be moderately retarded intellectually but only mildly retarded in social competence. The latter obviously requires intelligence when social demands are complex, but for the more primitive social skills, much

depends on education and training, experience and practice. Further-
more, intelligence tests have generally not been designed to assess
intelligent behaviour outside the school situation. Their original
purpose of assessing a child's school intelligence and predicting
his progress in the school situation has emphasized the academic
side of intelligent behaviour and has paid no attention to other
aspects of behaviour.

Etiology and 'Treatment'

The causes of mental defect have been investigated for over 100
years, and probably more time and energy have been spent on
exploring why some individuals are mentally defective than in
investigating their training and treatment. Despite their many varying viewpoints, investigators have generally ascribed the causes
of mental defect to either pathological or subcultural factors. This
essential dichotomy has been maintained even though the groups
may have been given different names and researchers have not
always agreed upon which aspects should be ascribed to pathological, and which to subcultural causes. It is, in fact, fairly easy
to classify mental deficiency theoretically, but in practice it is far
more difficult to determine the precise causes of the handicap in
individuals. Generally it is most frequently considered that the
condition is the result of an interaction of biological and socio-
cultural factors.

In the past, mental deficiency with IQs below 50 was ascribed
to trauma, toxic causes and infection, but recent research seems to
indicate that rare and often recessive genetic mechanisms may
cause severe subnormality as, for example, in phenylketonuria.

Mentally handicapped people with IQs between approximately 50
and 75 are very often the children of sub-average parents who survive only sub-marginally. The literature on this subject has usually
emphasized the unfavourable genetic mechanisms; but adverse social
factors may account for much of the intellectual inferiority, even
though genetic influences cannot entirely be excluded. Also there
must be mentally handicapped people who are intellectually subnormal because of genetic variation, just as there are people who
are above normal intelligence. Parents of normal intelligence who
provide their children with a normal upbringing may produce a sub-
average child just as they may produce a child of above average
intelligence.

At present we are able to ascribe only some 25 per cent of cases of mental subnormality to specific causes, which helps in the treatment of a few cases. Recently some spectacular successes have been achieved. In phenylketonuria (an inborn biochemical defect) for example medical treatment begun very soon after birth will usually prevent the development of mental defect. But much preventive action will probably be taken simply by improving the maternal and child health services, immunization against infectious diseases such as measles and rubella which lead to neurological sequelae, by better genetic counselling, family planning and by the establishment of registers of children at risk.

The large majority, generally the mildly and borderline handicapped people, show no particular genetic or biological abnormality and the influence of adverse socio-economic factors becomes very important. Many of these cases may have been affected by genetic and hereditary factors which are not always clearly identifiable, but there are also a great number of unfavourable environmental factors such as inadequate prenatal and postnatal care, poor nutrition, etc., which accentuate their condition. The majority of these people grow up in the poorer classes of society and the close relationship between comparative poverty and the prevalence of mild and borderline subnormality suggests that adverse social, economic and cultural factors have a major role to play in the prevalence of mental subnormality of this type.

Prevention of mental subnormality depends therefore not only on biochemical or medical treatment (i.e. avoiding obstetric hazards and those of rhesus factor incompatability) but also on tackling the socio-economic factors which are responsible for the spreading of mental retardation. President Kennedy's Panel on Mental Retardation (1962), stated that 'the conditions which spawn many other health and social problems, are, to a large extent, the same ones which generate the problem of mental retardation. To be successful in preventing mental retardation on a large scale, a broad attack on the fundamental adverse conditions will be necessary.'

If the prevalence of mental subnormality is, in fact, largely the outcome of conditions which are also responsible for the many other social problems society is faced with, then it is understandable that the prediction made by the President's Panel about preventing mental deficiency is not too optimistic. They expect that with present knowledge at least half, and perhaps more than half, of all mental subnormality cases could be avoided if society were to organize adequate preventive measures. If adverse social, economic and cultural factors can be corrected, then mental retardation could be prevented 'on a truly significant scale'. The provision of adequate learning opportunities and 'intellectual vitamins' will stop mental retardation which, once incurred, is essentially a permanent handicap.

These pages are not concerned with the prevention of subnormality but with the amelioration of the condition. If inadequate environmental circumstances have, in fact, contributed to or perhaps even caused social inadequacy, then it is reasonable to proceed on the assumption that what has been caused by environmental factors could, perhaps, be undone by environmental factors. This may, of course, not always be feasible, particularly since age plays a great part. Exposure to poor and adverse environmental factors in early childhood can, perhaps, never be entirely undone at a later stage. On the other hand, environmental improvement is our only chance at present to do something about a problem which is threatening to grow to unmanageable dimensions. To quote the President's Panel once again: 'mental retardation afflicts twice as many individuals as blindness, polio, cerebral palsy, and rheumatic heart disease, combined. Only four significant disabling conditions—mental illness, cardiac disease, arthritis and cancer—have a higher prevalence, but they tend to come late in life, while mental retardation comes early. Every year 126,000 babies born in the USA will be regarded as mentally retarded at some time in their lives.

One of the contributions which rehabilitation and training work can make is to provide, at a later stage of a child's life (but as early as possible), those learning opportunities or 'intellectual vitamins'—to use the Panel's telling phrase—of which the child has been deprived by adverse environmental conditions. The lack of opportunities, emotional disorders and many other factors 'appear somehow to stunt young people intellectually during their developmental period'. An attempt must be made to retrieve the situation, even at a late stage, and to salvage from the wreck as much as possible.

2

ASSESSMENT OF SOCIAL KNOWLEDGE

Three Basic Requirements

There is no industrial undertaking, no business enterprise, no educational institution which will not attempt to ascertain in some way first the 'potential market' or the needs of the consumer, and secondly the effectiveness of its organization and whether the methods and techniques employed produce the desired results. This applies to production, to marketing, to any form of industrial undertaking. This applies, of course, also to education in general and there is and must be a constant stocktaking of progress and achievement as well as revision and the introduction of new ideas.

As far as mental handicap is concerned, initial appraisal of relevant aspects which have a direct bearing on the social education of the mentally handicapped is completely absent and similarly no systematic attempt has been made to assess the efficacy of methods of teaching used and whether there is a need for adjusting outlook and approach in the light of experience properly evaluated. In fact, the general attitude appears to be that nothing much can be expected of people who are intellectually so limited. Thus no one can be blamed if there are few and inconspicuous results. It is indeed considered almost a miracle to find marked improvements and, if there are any, doubts are cast on the validity of the original diagnosis of mental handicap.

To an enthusiastic and conscientious teacher this situation could at times be demoralising, it is certainly frustrating and often discouraging. She cannot avoid asking herself the pertinent question whether her methods are effective and whether the results could be better. She is deprived of the constant stimulus of the many and often awkward questions asked by the normal child and there is no need for her to prepare herself (rather than preparing a lesson) for the inquisitive questioner. Nobody enquires into the reasons for persistent failures and no yardsticks or norms are available to judge progress, relative success and relative failure. It is quite possible that the demands made on the mentally handicapped are well below his capacity, but teachers are not encouraged to strive for higher attainments because it is assumed that the potential of a defective's social ability is as low as observed. This is a highly unsatisfactory situation.

It appears that three pieces of objective information at least should be available to the teacher confronted with the problem of developing the social competence of a child.

There must be first of all an accurate and detailed assessment of the social knowledge and competence of the mentally handicapped before teaching and training commences. This assessment should pinpoint missing or weak social skills and will thus provide initial guidance for teaching.

It will, secondly, be necessary for the teacher to know what level of attainments she should in fact expect from a mentally handicapped child. In normal child development it can be expected that the average child can carry out certain tasks but not others at specified ages. It is thus possible to compare the performance of an individual with the performance of other children and to assess whether he is relatively advanced or retarded in relation to the average performance of other children of his age. This is extremely helpful guidance, but unfortunately this information is useful only when applied to normal children. In their cases it can be said that a particular child is retarded, for example, in number work compared with the attainments of his age group. This should lead to remedial action because other information obtained (intelligence measurement) has established that the mental equipment is intact and, whatever the cause of retardation in number work, mental subnormality can be excluded.

Information of this character is of considerably less value in the case of the mentally handicapped. The observed retardation in his work will be associated with a low intelligence test score, and a direct cause and effect relationship will thus be assumed. *No information is available how advanced or retarded the mentally handicapped child is compared with other children of similar low intellectual standing.* This, however, is the piece of *essential* information for the teacher who has to judge whether Johnny could do better than he actually does. That Johnny is 'worse' than the normal child is, at this point, information of no consequence.

The third piece of objective evidence should be information

regarding a child's mental capacity. This refers of course to a valid intelligence measurement. The information of intellectual efficiency (at the time of testing) suggested by the IQ score, is important to provide a *classification label* which enables us to compare the social competence of children of one particular degree of mental handicap with others of approximately the same mental level. In other words, it would be misleading if one were to say to the teacher that the average mentally handicapped can do this but not that. It is more helpful for the teacher to know that Johnny, who has a measured IQ of 65 (and therefore belongs to the group of mildly retarded), does as well, worse or better than the average mildly retarded child of that age. It is solely for the purpose of being able to *compare* people that the IQ label is useful, it does not *explain* why people are effective or ineffective.

These then are the three pieces of objective information needed for an appraisal of the situation at the outset and for the regular re-appraisal of progress: knowledge regarding a mentally handicapped person's ability, knowledge of what he actually knows in social skills and knowledge of how much can be expected from people of his mental ability.

There is other knowledge which is important. It relates mainly to the reasons *why* people behave as they do; and medical, psychiatric and social histories are particularly helpful in this respect. A perusal of this evidence will help to explain much of the disfunctioning, or overfunctioning, but the objective appraisal of the individual and his social functioning must be made first.

The present section is mainly concerned with the description of selected aspects of social assessment and provides examples of surveys of social skills. A short discussion of some points relating to IQ and MA is included to emphasize the fact that no one should be misled by a seemingly accurate method of establishing mental functioning. Emphasis is also laid on the need to use even classification labels flexibly. However, the main part of the section, offering in a descriptive manner the results of some surveys of social skills, gives not only examples of the manner in which information can be obtained, but suggests the probable size of the problem which should be tackled.

The discussion of the third piece of important objective knowledge—what level of functioning can be reasonably expected from a mentally handicapped person in a certain age group who has obtained a particular score on an intelligence test—follows logically from the results of surveys of social skills. Having this knowledge available makes it easier to evaluate an individual's level of social functioning by paying due consideration to the intellectual handicap.

Assessment of Mental Ability

It has already been mentioned that mental handicap is characterised by subnormal intelligence, but this statement now requires a definition of the terms 'normal' and 'intelligence'. For practical purposes, it is generally agreed that subnormal intelligence is indicated by a low score on a properly standardised, and correctly administered, test of intelligence. Opinions differ quite considerably as to where to draw the dividing line between normality and subnormality and it is very difficult at times to talk of subnormal intelligence when the IQ score is near the range of normality. Nevertheless, an intelligence assessment is an essential part of the diagnosis of mental retardation.

It is, however, also important to realize that not everyone who attains a low IQ score is necessarily intellectually subnormal. A low IQ score may be due to different causes, and in some cases a low IQ may in fact mislead and even contribute to a wrong diagnosis.

It is unfortunately not widely enough realized that the score on an intelligence test provides only a label and not a diagnosis. In other words the result of an intelligence test will classify one person in relation to others; it will establish, with some accuracy whether he is above or below the average score on that particular test and also how far above or below the average his test result can be placed. From the classification point of view this is very helpful and the considerable importance attached to IQ and Mental Age indicates their usefulness. The IQ can be compared to a measurement of size and it is obviously helpful to know whether something is longer or shorter, bigger or smaller than the average. However, such a measurement can be unimportant and it can also be misleading. The late Dr. Earl used to say that if we were to classify on the basis of size alone we would find that a hunchback, a mongol, a man with both legs amputated, and a normal child would all fall into the same category (Earl 1961). This would obviously be nonsense. We must have some idea of the factors which go to make up the total. Accurate knowledge of one dimension only, without knowledge of other aspects, is practically useless.

This consideration applies also to the intelligence test where the score often attempts to express in one figure a number of different aspects of intelligent behaviour. There is one type of test which attempts to measure *one* single ability which is assumed to be representative of intellectual functioning. It is considered sufficient to measure one aspect of intellectual behaviour only, as for example planning and foresight, the ability to analyse and the ability to reason; typical tests of this type are the Porteus Maze test, Kohs' Block Design test and the Progressive Matrices test. In another type of test a number of different abilities is assessed by a battery of subtests; the well-known Wechsler Scale for Children (WISC) and for adults (WAIS) and the Terman-Merrill Test (Stanford-Binet), are the best known examples of this type. A person may do better in one subtest than in another, but the different scores obtained throughout the battery are averaged out to produce the final score or IQ. This type of test attempts to provide a fair and representative assessment of mental abilities, whilst the techniques which assess only one aspect of intellectual functioning can be deceptive. A person who happens not to be very good at the type of activity under test will have no chance to make up for his failure by success in another type of test. The 'single-shot' test is generally not, therefore, considered to be as valid as the 'multi-shot' technique, which gives a better total picture of a person's intellectual functioning.

Averaging out a person's score is obviously the only possible way to bring some order into the results of many different tests. Yet the average hides the many often very significant ups and downs in intellectual functioning. For example a score of 9 on one test and of 1 on the other test, averages 5, and a score of 6 on one test and 4 on the other, also averages 5. Yet in the first case, the excellent score in one test and the very poor score in the other, may be of considerable clinical significance. In the second case, both scores are round about the middle mark and suggest an even intellectual functioning.

The picture presented by a psychogram, showing the results of various subtests as a graph, can at times be very revealing. One may wonder whether the average score of, say, case A (Fig. 5) is a fair summary of that person's abilities. If such an uneven performance is contrasted with the even performance of case B, which obtains the same overall rating, it becomes understandable why many clinicians pay more attention to the 'quality' of the IQ than to its 'quantity' (Jastak, 1949, 1952).

It must be repeated again that the IQ or Mental Age is a means of classification only and not a diagnosis. And this is true whether the score is called mental age or developmental age or social age. It must also be remembered that the score may represent the average of several test results or, sometimes, the result of one test only.

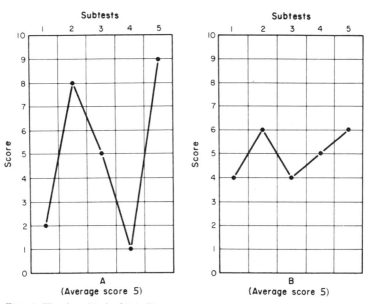

Fig. 5. The 'quality' of intelligence.

It can therefore be very misleading in both types of tests. Let us consider a hypothetical case—a woman, say 40 years of age with a good deal of life and sex experience, who has managed to raise a family and to earn a living, but is said to have a mental age of six. All that this means in fact is that she has obtained a particular score on a test claiming to measure a particular ability, and her score is similar to one expected from a normal child of six years. That this woman would obtain a similar 'low' score on another test measuring different abilities or even whether her test performance is closely related to her real life achievements, cannot always be predicted with certainty.

A more positive and more helpful approach to the problem of describing abilities and disabilities is represented by the so-called psychogram approach which does not attempt to sum up a large and diverse field in one single result. The psychogram is a visual presentation of the scores obtained through a battery of selected tests, each assessing a single skill or ability. The completed psychogram (Fig. 5) shows at once in which area a person does well and shows his strengths and weaknesses (see also Earl's Moron battery—Earl, 1961). Careful study of the psychogram may show that the low score in certain fields may be due to a variety of causes such as poor teaching, lack of experience, disinterest, etc., rather than to weak ability. It opens the door to remedial treatment by specialized education, training and treatment. This method pinpoints those areas which are in need of attention in a way that the single figure averaging high and low scores would fail to do.

To sum up: an intelligence test result classifies intellectual functioning of a particular person in relation to the normal population of the same age level and in relation to that particular test. In the case of the mentally handicapped person, the IQ indicates the size of the gap between his own, subnormal functioning and that of the average person (i.e. the average 40 IQ points difference between the 'normal' person and the moderately mentally retarded) and thus the mentally handicapped can be classified in relation to the general population.

The same consideration applies to tests intending to assess other aspects of functioning (e.g. Vineland social maturity scale for social competence). The result is always *a measure* relating to a standard of normality derived from an 'average' performance. Important as such measurement is in the assessment of both handicap and improvement, it nonetheless indicates efficiency at the time of testing rather than capacity. A reliable estimate of capacity must also take into account various other factors such as age, sex and educational background.

Surveys of 'Social Knowledge'

A comparison of social competence, or of social knowledge, of the mentally handicapped and that of his contemporaries with normal intelligence only re-affirms that the subnormal is less efficient and knowledgeable than the average. It does not show how developed are his social skills *in relation to his mental handicap*.

The result is, however, more valuable if a subnormal's social competence is compared with that of his peers. If the social performance or knowledge of a mentally handicapped person of known intellectual level is compared with that of others of the same intellectual level and the same chronological age, it is easy to establish how much better or worse he is in relation to the average level of others of the same age and intelligence. It is true that this 'average' does not necessarily represent the level of performance which a particular person of that group could achieve under optimum conditions and it may thus be an underestimate of possible efficiency. On the other hand a marked deviation below the norm of that group suggests an inadequacy in attaining a standard of social competence which is within the ability of the majority of those of similar age and intelligence.

It is probably not unreasonable to assume that the efficiency with which social skills are practised increases with age and experience. On the other hand, with increasing age, there may be less receptiveness of assimilating social experiences and learning from them. An investigation of the quantity and quality of social knowledge in the age group 16 to 25 might therefore provide information relating to the time when the mentally handicapped has already matured enough to benefit from social experience but is not set enough yet to be unaffected by it.

The following discussion presents a number of findings relating to social knowledge of mentally handicapped people in the age group 16 to 25. How widely applicable these figures are cannot be ascertained. They refer mostly to the young mentally handicapped whose social behaviour was difficult enough to warrant admission to a hospital for the mentally subnormal. It may well be that those who did not come to the notice of the authorities after they left school might have shown a higher degree of elementary social knowledge than was found in those admitted to hospital. But this is scarcely relevant when considering what should be done for those who have demonstrated by their behaviour that they are not able to live in the community without attracting undue attention.

The information used in the following surveys was obtained over the years by psychologists interviewing new admissions to the hospital and using the educational assessment form described elsewhere (Gunzburg, 1960), but now replaced by the P-A-C 2 form (see section 3). Some additional information was obtained by nurses interviewing new admissions on a prescribed interview form. Since this information was of a fairly concrete nature, it is felt that the percentage figures are reliable enough to indicate the extent of social knowledge in this type of population.

Information used for the following surveys relates mainly to the more capable groups of the mildly and borderline retarded. However, other information relating to the moderately retarded was incorporated when available, provided extraneous factors did not make the results unrepresentative.

Information obtained from the mentally handicapped himself is not always reliable or factual, and assessors may also differ amongst themselves as to whether to credit a particular social skill or not. In that respect results of assessments of social skills are far less reliable and valid than those obtained from intelligence and attainment tests. On the other hand, it is felt the numbers involved in the surveys assure that the trends are valid and that individual misjudgments do not affect the overall results.

However carefully interviews are executed, they can often establish no more than the *existence* of social knowledge; whether this knowledge is actually used when required is sometimes impossible to ascertain. On the other hand, *absence* of social knowledge suggests strongly that the person may not be able to function adequately in the field tested.

Surveys of this kind indicate the level of social knowledge reached by the majority of a given IQ group and the differences in social knowledge which might be attributed to different IQ levels. They also indicate the size of population which is below the 'average attainment level' of a given IQ group and is therefore particularly in need of attention, special education and training. There are many others who are well above the average of the IQ group and this suggests that our educational sights should not be set too low and that the present average levels of attainments should be regarded as transitional targets and not as final aims.

Reading

Traditionally, reading has been considered the most important skill to acquire before embarking on other school work. Although mechanical reading skill is by no means essential to the achievement of social competence, it is interesting to see the wide spread of reading ability at different IQ levels. Figure 6 shows the results of a survey of 457 young people admitted to hospital and tested on the Schonell test of mechanical reading. Since the survey covers admissions over twelve years, it can probably be regarded as representative of the subnormal with an intelligence quotient of at least 40, who is admitted to institutions.

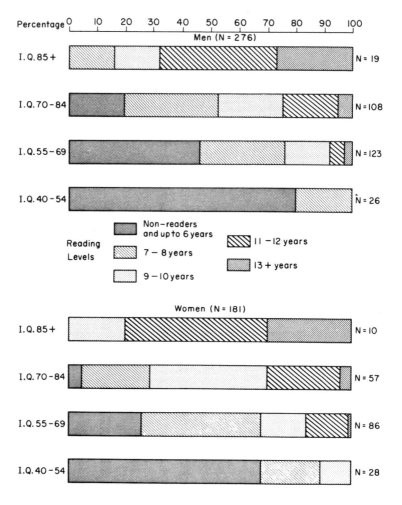

Fig. 6. Reading attainments of 457 young male and female admissions to hospital (CA 16–25).

There is obviously a relationship between intelligence level and reading skill as shown by the higher reading levels reached by the majority of each successive IQ group. Whilst the moderately retarded are generally unable to read more than a few words, more than half of the mildly retarded group (IQ 55 to 69) reach a reading level above 7 years. The borderline group reads at about the 9-year level and most of the dull normals are above the 11-year level.

These figures suggest attainment levels in mechanical reading skill which are comfortably within the abilities of the various IQ groups. These reading averages can be easily exceeded as shown by the fairly large proportion of people in each group who are better

TABLE I

Percentile ranking of mechanical reading ability (Schonell Word Recognition Test) based on a sample of 428 mentally retarded people (CA 16—25)

Percentile	Borderline retardation (IQ 70—84) N = 165	Mild retardation (IQ 55—69) N = 209	Moderate retardation (IQ 40—54) N = 54
100	15+	15+	11—0
90	12—4	11—2	8—4
80	11—6	9—8	7—4
70	10—8	8—10	6—2
60	9—11	8—4	5—2
50	9—3	7—9	—
40	8—8	7—1	—
30	8—1	6—2	—
20	7—4	5—5	—
10	6—2	—	—
0	—	—	—

than average readers. On the other hand, each group, except the dull normal group (IQ 85 +), contains a fairly large proportion of non-readers or semiliterate people who read well below expectancy. Whilst this is of little concern in the low IQ range, attention must be paid to non-achievers in the mildly and borderline retarded groups.

Table I sets out the percentile ranking of reading achievement for each group and offers an opportunity of establishing the degree of reading backwardness or superiority of individual young mentally handicapped people in relation to others of the same intellectual level and in the same age group.

The average achievement of each IQ group is represented by the 50th percentile. Young adults obtaining a Schonell mechanical reading age near the 50th percentile are average readers for their particular group, those falling below the 10th percentile are definitely retarded, and those falling above the 90th percentile are very superior for their IQ group. However, these placements do not indicate the level of reading skill which could be reached with good teaching and application.

The usefulness of Table I for comparing one person's reading level with the average performance of others with a similar intellectual handicap is, however, affected by the well-known observation that girls tend to be better readers than boys. Table II shows the distribution of reading ages of the same group as in Table I, but this time subdivided according to sex. Since the groups are now similar only the quartile distribution is shown. The 50th percentile again indicates the average, the 25th the upper limit of people with below average skill, the 75th percentile the lower limit of people with above average reading skill. It will be seen that, throughout the sample, the young women had acquired better reading proficiency than the men, and this fact should therefore be taken into account when studying Table I.

There is little doubt that there is much backwardness in the mechanical reading skills which cannot be explained in terms of intellectual retardation. O'Connor and Tizard (1956) remarked that the average mental age of the patients they tested was about 10 years (IQ approximately 70). However, the median mechanical reading age was only 8·6 years, a finding which is well supported by the distribution of means in the mild and borderline groups (Table 1).[1]

One analysis of subnormal adults (Gunzburg 1959) showed that, as far as hospital admissions were concerned, only one-third of the

---

[1] Deficiencies in mechanical reading skill are not confined to the unintelligent only. In 1947 the London Head Teachers Research Committee found that as many as 15·9% of pupils of average age 11½, failed to reach a reading age higher than 7½ years which, considering their age, meant that nearly 50% were backward readers. A Birmingham investigation of some 2500 children aged 14 in secondary modern schools, confirmed that some 50% fell in the backward grade and approximately 10% had reading ages below 8½ years.

Much depends, of course, on definitions and tests actually used. A far more recent investigation estimated only 3·6% of near or complete retarded young adults were able to read on a level appropriate to their mental capacity; another third was reading well below expectancy (2 years or more below MA), but one-third was superior in reading ability (2 years or more above MA). However, this does not take into consideration the fact that the intelligence score itself may have been lowered by the inability to read.

Despite the fact that comparatively large sections in the mild and borderline groups are backward in reading ability, there is probably, particularly among the women, as large a section which is well advanced in mechanical reading. Provided the right methods and the right approaches are used and there is some desire to learn, mechanical reading can be taught to most backward readers without too much difficulty.

TABLE II

Quartile distribution of reading scores according to sex, based on a sample of 428 mentally retarded people (CA 16—25)

Percentile	Borderline retardation M—108 F—57 Age in years		Mild retardation M—123 F—86 Age in years		Moderate retardation M—26 F—28 Age in years	
75th	9·9	11·2	8·9	9·7	6·4	7·5
50th	8·8	10·0	7·3	8·2	—5·0	—5·0
25th	7·3	8·7	5·5	6·9		

The other aspect of reading, comprehension of reading matter, is much neglected, largely because it is not often realized that it also presents special problems for education. The tacit assumption seems to be that comprehension will come of its own accord once the mechanics have been mastered. That this is quite wrong can be shown by comparing the mechanical reading age levels with the comprehension age levels obtained on one of the few specialized tests; but unfortunately there is little reliable information on this topic regarding the mentally handicapped.

Comprehension of reading matter is, of course, largely a question of intelligence—verbal intelligence to be more exact. One could

---

illiteracy in adults, and suggests that the number of pupils leaving school and of young adults who are nearly or completely illiterate are about 5%, whilst backwardness (reading age below 12 years) can be expected in 16% of the adult population. (All figures from 'Reading Ability', Ministry of Education, Pamphlet No. 18 (1950). London: H.M.S.O.)

assume with some justification that a child's capacity for comprehending what he reads is equal to his intellectual power, provided he has mastered the mechanics of reading and has grown up in a normal environment. Yet there is more to it than that. Many different skills are required to comprehend a paragraph of reading matter that is fluently read: an understanding of the vocabulary used is an obvious necessity, but so is the ability to concentrate, to remember and to associate, to grasp the general meaning of paragraph and at the same time to select certain important facts and details within it. These skills may be very unevenly developed in different readers, and everyone knows the fast but inaccurate reader who overlooks or even misreads many important details, and the slow, accurate reader who pays so much attention to the detail that he is unable to comprehend the general meaning.

The Gates basic reading tests were used in an investigation of the comprehension of reading matter by children in the age range 12 to 16, with IQs clustered round 70 (Gunzburg 1948a). Four specific skills required for a satisfactory understanding of reading matter are assessed in this type of test. Test A measures the skill to appreciate the general significance of a paragraph, and the group showed an average efficiency of 79 per cent in this aspect. Test B measures the skill to draw the correct conclusion from the reading matter, and here the group was on the average 71 per cent successful. When it came to assessing correct reactions to instructions in the reading matter (Test C), the group's average performance dropped to 53 per cent indicating inattention to detail, but even so they were able to grasp the details in their reading matter (Test D) sufficiently well to score the highest average performance of 82 per cent.

Many individuals, however, did not conform to this pattern and showed pronounced weaknesses in areas which were generally fairly well mastered by the group. Cecil A. a fourteen-year-old boy with IQ 71, achieved only 50 per cent on Test A, 28 per cent on Test B, but did well in Test C with 75 per cent and obtained top marks (100 per cent) on Test D. Joe P. aged 14, IQ 78, did well on Test A obtaining 84 per cent, succeeded near average on Test B (67 per cent), but showed extremely poor attention to detail both in Test C, 25 per cent and Test D, 44 per cent.

These two examples demonstrate how much the utilization of a mechanical reading skill depends not only on mental level, but also

on evenly developed comprehension skills. An educational programme which fails to pay attention to the problems of understanding
of reading, after the mechanical skills have been mastered, is
inadequate. It should concentrate on the various comprehension
reading techniques, not so much with the aim of heightening the
pupil's understanding (which is dependent on his mental level), but
in order to widen it. The problem is to assist the reader with
techniques which are quite within his mental grasp, but from which
he has failed to profit adequately.

It is unfortunate that so much attention has been focused on the
'barking at print' aspect of reading and little on teaching the
application of a skill so laboriously taught and acquired. High
mechanical-reading ages in school-leavers are a credit to the school
and to the reader—but this skill by itself may be useless if the
reader has not been taught how to make use of it.

Number Knowledge

An adequate ability to manipulate money sums is far more
important for social competence than a knowledge of mechanical
reading. There is simply no possibility of leading a relatively
independent life without some familiarity with the small financial
operations connected with shopping, paying bills, budgeting, etc.
Knowledge of the multiplication tables and the ability to do addition, subtraction, multiplication and division on paper is no
reliable indication of the ability to handle money in a shop. In
some cases the theoretical knowledge of paper-and-pencil sums may
be so divorced from the practical demands of working out a budget
on a weekly wage packet that a retarded adolescent is absolutely
helpless once he leaves school. Much of this unsatisfactory situation is due to teaching which relies on the mechanical execution
of exercises in number work without ensuring an adequate understanding of the operations involved.

Some idea of the lack of essential knowledge which is so
necessary to deal with day to day monetary problems is given in
Tables III to IX. They refer to 168 consecutive admissions to
hospital of 79 men and 89 women with a minimum age of 16 and
classified in the upper three IQ groups, whose knowledge of
elementary money operations was ascertained soon after arrival at
hospital.

Table III indicates that there is considerable uncertainty in the recognition of coins, and roughly one out of five mentally handicapped is not sure of the names of the coins; this is noticeable over a wide range of intelligence (IQ 40—84) and even the bordergroup showed some uncertainty.

A basic piece of monetary knowledge is the realization that the value of a sixpence can be obtained by different coins—one threepenny bit and three pennies, six pennies, or two threepenny bits.[1]

TABLE III
Recognition and naming of coins

	N	Complete recognition	Failure (partial or complete)
		(in percentages)	
Borderline	62	89	11
Mildly retarded	62	84	16
Moderately retarded	44	70	30
Totals	168	N = 138	N = 30

TABLE IV
Ability to give sixpence in three different ways

	N	Success	Failure
		(in percentages)	
Borderline	62	100	—
Mildly retarded	62	97	3
Moderately retarded	44	68	32
Totals	168	N = 152	N = 16

The mentally handicapped adult's ability in this respect was tested by handing over coins of various denominations and asking them to 'give sixpence' in three different ways. This problem presented no difficulty to the borderline group but some difficulty to the moderately retarded people (Table IV).

The same type of problem increases in difficulty when the amount is 2s. 6d. instead of 6d. Again three different combinations of coins from those presented were required to qualify for a pass (Table V).

[1] Knowledge of equivalents is an important element in money operations, but is also important when money is used as an incentive. Minor tragedies can be caused by paying out a one shilling piece or two sixpences instead of twelve penny pieces. Having learnt that twelve is more than one or two, it may take some time to understand that, as far as coins are concerned, this rule does not always apply.

How capable are mentally handicapped adults of adding small amounts presented in coins of different denominations such as they would find in their trouser pockets? Information on this aspect was obtained by asking the 168 adults to pick the named coins and to add them up using actual coins.

$$3d. \text{ and } 4d. = \qquad 7d.$$
$$7d. \text{ and } 9d. = 1s. \ 4d.$$
$$1s. \ 9d. \text{ and } 8d. = 2s. \ 5d.$$

There were 9 problems and in order to qualify for a pass seven answers had to be correct. Table VI indicates a fairly large degree of inability of working out small sums.

TABLE V
Ability to give 2s. 6d. in three different ways

	N	Success	Failure
		(in percentages)	
Borderline	62	97	3
Mildly retarded	62	84	16
Moderately retarded	44	52	48
Totals	168	N = 135	N = 33

TABLE VI
Ability to carry out simple additions with the help of coins

	N	Success	Failure
		(in percentages)	
Borderline	62	90	10
Mildly retarded	62	79	21
Moderately retarded	44	55	45
Totals	168	N = 129	N = 39

A fundamental stage in number development is the ability to realize what is more and what is less. This ability is often needed when estimating whether the money available is sufficient (or is more) or is not sufficient (less) than the price of the goods one wishes to buy. This is a situation which must be experienced almost daily by the mentally retarded living in the community. This ability was tested by showing the members of the group three price tags for 2s. 3d., 3s. 5d. and 4s. 8d. They were asked to select from the available coins those which they would hand over to buy the goods (the amounts and the coins had been selected to make it impossible to give the exact amount from the available coins). All three problems had to be answered correctly for a pass (Table VII).

Failure to answer these problems could also be due to an inability to read the price tags correctly. Whatever the reason for failure, the inability to handle such practical problems represents a sizeable handicap in the subnormal's social efficiency.

TABLE VII

Ability to realize which coins are required to pay for items costing 2s. 3d.,
3s. 5d. and 4s. 8d.

	N	Success (in percentages)	Failure
Borderline	62	85	15
Mildly retarded	63	73	27
Moderately retarded	44	39	61
Totals	168	N = 115	N = 53

Inadequate mastery of elementary money operations carried out by actually handling the money, obviously leads to pronounced difficulties when a budget has to be worked out. Tables VIII and IX show the achievements of 194 men and women in the age group 16 to 25 with a Wechsler full IQ between 55 to 84, who were assessed on admission to hospital using the educational assessment method described elsewhere (Gunzburg, 1960).

The Tables show the type of information which enquiry attempted to elicit and the proportions of mentally handicapped people whose responses were considered satisfactory and indicative of adequate knowledge, compared with those who failed to satisfy the assessors. The results of this investigation are borne out by Matthew's survey (1964) of 62 ex-special school pupils with a mean IQ 70.39 ± 10.2, which found that '74 per cent could do simple shopping sums involving calculations up to ten shillings; only 39 per cent, however, were able to do the calculations necessary for the purchase of larger items involving sums over £1.'

The ability to work out small amounts was assessed using the following three problems:

The 'bus fare problem': The fare from here to town is 8d. What is the cost of going there and back?

The 'luncheon problem': Lunch on Monday cost me 2s. 6d. On Tuesday I spent 2s. and bought a cup of tea for 3d. How much did I spend?

The 'change problem':   I bought a 9d. comb and gave the shopkeeper 2s. 6d. How much change should
he give me?

All three problems involved an understanding of simple arithmetical thinking on the 'shilling and penny' level and did not involve
pounds.

TABLE VIII
Ability to work out small money amounts relating to bus fares, lunches and change

Problem	IQ group	Satisfactory		Unsatisfactory	
		N	%	N	%
Bus fares	Borderline	54	73	20	27
	Mildly retarded	66	55	53	45
Lunches	Borderline	58	78	16	22
	Mildly retarded	68	57	51	43
Change	Borderline	46	62	28	38
	Mildly retarded	45	38	74	62

Total *N*: 193 = Borderline *N*: 74, Mildly retarded: 119.

As is to be expected, satisfactory performance decreases sharply
as soon as the financial transactions extend to pounds, even though
the sums involved are modest. This aspect was tested by asking
questions referring to cost of clothing and board.

The 'clothing problem': I have bought a shirt for £1 7s. 0d. and
a pullover at £1 13s. 0d. How much is
that together?

The 'board problem':   Lodgings cost £3 5s. 0d. and your wage
packet contains £6 0s. 0d. How much is
left after you have paid for your board?

The inefficiency with which simple financial transactions are
tackled, even by adults, in the borderline IQ group 70 to 84 is rather
alarming. There had been an ominous proportion of failure in this
group, in the simple 'shilling and pence' problems (Table VIII), but
the inclusion of pounds, which after all constitute a man's wages,
shows a high degree of inability which might have catastrophic
effects on the individual's social competence.

The ability to handle money is probably a prerequisite for social
survival in unsheltered situations. It is certainly far more relevant

to the business of living than the ability to read which has attracted
so much attention, and there is no justification for the inadequacy
highlighted by these findings. The percentage of success in each
intelligence group is high enough to indicate that this particular
skill is not beyond the ability of the mentally handicapped to
acquire. The only conclusion that can be drawn is, that there has

TABLE IX
*Ability to work out larger amounts of money relating to 'clothing' and
'board'*

Problem	IQ group	Satisfactory		Unsatisfactory	
		N	%	N	%
'Clothing	Borderline	46	61	29	39
Problem'	Mildly retarded	34	29	85	71
'Board	Borderline	35	47	40	53
Problem'	Mildly retarded	25	21	94	79

Total *N*: 194 = Borderline *N*: 75, Mildly retarded *N*: 119.

TABLE X
Ability to write one's signature in 'longhand'

	N	Longhand	Printing (in percentages)	NO writing
Borderline	62	87	13	—
Mildly retarded	62	61	37	2
Moderately retarded	44	36	45	19
Totals	168	*N* = 108	*N* = 51	*N* = 9

been inadequate teaching of number concepts and insufficient
practical experience which have lead to educational incompetence
in the most important aspect of school work which has a direct
bearing on social functioning.

Writing

Writing has been considered throughout the ages as a hallmark of
education, and it is one of the three essential tool subjects. However there are not many occasions when a mentally handicapped
person would really be embarrassed by an inability to communicate
by writing; he is a poor letter writer and would certainly not think
of making notes to help a failing memory. However there are times
when writing skill would be useful—filling in forms, applications
etc.—but since appropriate responses require a good reading
ability, an advanced level of vocabulary and, most of all, compre-

hension of the questions and the implication of the answers given, it is probably just as well that the mechanical skill of writing and spelling is generally well below his scholastic level.

Table X refers to the same persons whose number knowledge was assessed in Tables III to IX, and analyses their ability to sign their own names rather than to write it in block capitals. Inability to write the name in cursive writing is a handicap when a signature is required and, obviously, indicates a lack of mastery of longhand. The fact that well over one third of the sample in the mildly retarded range had not learned to write a signature reflects unfavourably upon their special school education.

The ability to apply knowledge of writing, whether longhand or printing, can be best assessed by asking the person to fill in an application form. This, of course, tests not only writing ability, but also the ability to comprehend simple questions which have to be read, and knowledge of a less familiar type of vocabulary (e.g. surname—employment).

One hundred and sixty-eight adult admissions to the hospital were asked to fill in the following application form:

APPLICATION FOR EMPLOYMENT

Name.............................. Christian Names...............................

Address ....

Age............... Date of Birth...........................(Single/Married/Widower)

Name and Address of Last Employer..

....

Reason for Leaving...

....

Date of Leaving...

Who should be notified in case of Illness or Accident?

        Name...

        Address...

Date...........................   Signature ....

Surprisingly, considering the number of different skills involved, the application forms are more competently handled than one would expect (Table XI). (It is true that, at times, diplomacy is conspicuously absent: one girl answered that the reason for leaving her last employment was: 'Because he kept moaning at me'!) Success at filling in an application form depends, obviously, on its complexity. Matthew (1964) tested a sample of 62 ex-special school pupils with a mean IQ 70·39 and found that only 48 per cent were able to complete the form satisfactorily. This figure is very similar to the 40 per cent found in this investigation for 62 mildly retarded, though the 62 borderline young people did considerably better with 77 per cent.

TABLE XI
Ability for filling in application form for employment

	N	Pass	Fail
		(in percentages)	
Borderline	62	77	23
Mildly retarded	62	40	60
Moderately retarded	44	10	90
Totals	168	$N = 77$	$N = 91$

Time

A neglected but very important subject for teaching is an adequate knowledge of the various mechanical skills related to time. This refers not only to the ability to tell the time from a clock face, but also to knowledge of days, weeks and months, and to an understanding of a time vocabulary comprising words such as punctual, fortnight, etc. Even so, ability in this aspect does not guarantee understanding or appreciation of the concepts involved, and the situation is paralleled by the subject of reading in which it is similarly necessary to make a distinction between mechanical reading ability and comprehension. The following tables and figures refer only to mechanical abilities in this field, mastery of which is a prerequisite for the practical application of these skills.

There is a close relationship between ability to tell the time and intelligence as can be seen from Table XII. The assessment of a sample of 73 subnormals suggests that most of them can tell the time even if not accurately. Nevertheless, 18 per cent of the sample either could not tell the time at all or could only tell the hours. The majority (44 per cent) had some difficulties and could tell time only approximately or only when the hands were in the main positions (half and quarter hours or at 5 minute intervals). A smaller proportion (38 per cent) was thoroughly competent and the majority of these people were in the higher IQ groups. (Correlation coefficient between intelligence and telling time is ·60 in above sample).

TABLE XII
Telling time
N = 73 (M and F)

	Moderately retarded	Mildly retarded	Borderline	Dull normal	N	%
Cannot tell time	2	1			3	
Can tell hours only	2	7	1	—	10	18
Can tell half hours and quarter hours but not minutes	1	2	1		4	
Can tell minutes in 5 intervals	3	11	14	—	28	44
Can tell time before and after	—	5	12	3	20	
Is thoroughly competent including telling time to the minute	—	—	6	2	8	38
N:	8	26	34	5	73	100

The ability to tell the time does not ensure an adequate knowledge of the various conventions which are important in the practical use of the skill. To a normal person its seems inconceivable that people should be able to tell the time but not know how many minutes there are in an hour, or how many hours in a day. Table XIII, based on a survey of 116 admissions of both sexes in the age group 16 to 25 indicates, however, a widespread lack of such detailed knowledge even in the borderline group.

What knowledge there is seems to depend to some extent on whether it has a direct relationship to the subnormal's own experiences; seconds and minutes are probably of little importance to him but hours are more meaningful. A similar observation can be made in Table XIV which summarizes familiarity with calendar times. The group was quite familiar (on both IQ levels) with the number of days in a week, but if a concept was not of immediate concern knowledge decreased markedly.

Most revealing is the quality of the incorrect answers given to simple questions relating to calendar times. Many of the answers are not just near misses but are so absurd as to indicate clearly that there is not the slightest awareness of the meaning of the terms. Among answers given to the question 'How many hours are there in a day?' were wild guesses such as 42, 50, 4, 3, 11; the

TABLE XIII
Knowledge of time elements
(N = 116, age group 16 to 25)

| Question | Borderline *N* = 58 | Correct | |
	Mildly retarded *N* = 58	*N*	%
How many seconds in a	Borderline	23	40
minute?	Mildly retarded	17	30
How many minutes in an	Borderline	35	60
hour?	Mildly retarded	19	33
How many hours in a	Borderline	43	74
day?	Mildly retarded	23	40

TABLE XIV
Knowledge of calendar times
(N = 116; age group 16 to 25)

| Question | IQ group | Correct answer | |
		N	%
How many days in a	Borderline	50	86
week?	Mildly retarded	44	75
How many days in a	Borderline	24	42
month?	Mildly retarded	10	18
How many months in a	Borderline	43	74
year?	Mildly retarded	23	40
How many seasons in a	Borderline	33	56
year?	Mildly retarded	15	26
In what month is Xmas?	Borderline	49	84
	Mildly retarded	38	65
On what day is Xmas?	Borderline	38	65
	Mildly retarded	28	48

question 'How many days are there in a month?' received answers ranging from 136 (from a borderline retardate) to 20. One would expect Christmas to be an event which would impress itself on the mind but nonetheless one borderline case placed it in September and others on such dates as the 7th or 14th of December.

Technical ability to tell the time or read a calendar is no guarantee that this ability can actually be utilized in practical situations as the following excerpts from educational reports indicate.

A young mildly subnormal man ' has a good capacity to read a clock but without proper comprehension of time concepts. For example, he did not know the number of minutes in an hour, and even after demonstration of how the clock face is divided he still insisted that there were only two minutes between any of the figure intervals on the clock face.'

A young borderline woman who had been able to read a clock for years and who knew the number of minutes in an hour, complained that a certain cosmetic preparation was useless. After questioning she was reminded that it said on the directions 'Don't guess the time; use a watch' and that she must leave the preparation on for 4 minutes but not more than 6 minutes. The next day she had a dermatitis, and investigation showed that she thought the 5-minute intervals on the clock face were 'about 2 minutes'.

Another mildly retarded young man who could tell the time insisted that '10 o'clock plus 1 hour is 20 minutes to 11; 10 o'clock plus 2 hours is 2 in the morning; 10 o'clock plus 5 hours is about next morning'.

A mildly retarded young man's educational report mentioned: 'Says there are 28 months in a year, yet he can read a calendar with speed and accuracy and rattle off the names of the months in parrot fashion. Although he can correctly identify the present month he cannot say how many months there will be to the end of the year'.

An examiner commented of a borderline youth: 'Says there are 240 days in a month and 8 months in a year yet he can read a calendar'.

These faulty notions must sometimes exercise a considerable and disturbing influence on the subnormal's behaviour because they interfere with the communication processes between him and his environment. If a common term such as 'fortnight' is misinterpreted as meaning 'four nights' or, less understandably, as one, three, four weeks, the misunderstandings arising from this can be very serious. A promise to a borderline subnormal that arrangements would be made for him to see his parents in a week's time was relatively meaningless to him because a week was 'hundreds and hundreds of hours away'.

There is often a complete inability to connect arithmetical knowledge with time concepts. One young mentally retarded woman who attended two types of educational classes with two teachers stated: 'Mr. L is on holiday next week and the week after. Mrs. S is also on holiday next week: that means I've not to go to classes for three weeks.'

Though the setting of an alarm clock is an easy skill to teach, difficulties are experienced in making the mentally handicapped realize that time allowances must be made for an effective use of the device. A mildly subnormal girl stated: 'I'll leave at 12 o'clock to be there for 10' and another one who worked as a domestic in a hospital was unable to work out the time on her alarm clock to allow half-an-hour to dress before going on duty.

Social Skills

Probably of more immediate and practical usefulness than a primitive mastery of the 3 R's is familiarity and experience with the many arrangements, institutions, services, etc., which are characteristic of modern life. Sooner or later the normal adult who is not in custodial shelter must use public transport, must obtain certain forms and information from the Post Office and elsewhere, consider the intricacies of deductions from his wage packet and consult a doctor. There are many other social skills required in everyday life which have become so habitual to a normal person that he is scarcely aware of the obstacle race they present to the subnormal.

The following Tables summarize the results of some 200 interviews with the mentally handicapped acting as their own informants. It is possible that this method overestimates actual knowledge and, of course, there is no guarantee that knowledge is actually applied. The questions are some of those contained in a Social Education and Assessment procedure (Gunzburg, 1960) and must be regarded as a sample of the many different social skills which are needed in an ordinary, uncomplicated, hum-drum life.

Handling of Finance

It is not surprising that few subnormals have an adequate idea of the purpose of the many deductions from their wage packet and the size of their weekly Income Tax, National Insurance etc., as shown on the pay-slip. Many a mentally handicapped has suspected his employer of embezzling part of his wages, and his distrust and apprehension of the world around him has not been lessened by finding that the wage packet regularly contained less than he had been led to expect.[1]

TABLE XV
Ability to handle financial situations

	IQ group	Adequate		Inadequate	
		N	%	N	%
Formulating a simple budget	Borderline	50	57	38	43
	Mildly retarded	52	40	77	60
Understanding the pay slip	Borderline	47	57	36	43
	Mildly retarded	33	26	92	74
Knowledge of prices:	Borderline	90	96	4	4
Small items	Mildly retarded	121	92	11	8
Personal clothing	Borderline	70	74	24	26
	Mildly retarded	84	64	48	36
Larger items (wireless, board and lodging)	Borderline	48	50	48	50
	Mildly retarded	56	42	76	58
Shopping	Borderline	73	86	12	14
(a) Small articles	Mildly retarded	116	91	12	9
(b) In special shops	Borderline	85	89	10	11
	Mildly retarded	106	81	25	19
Savings					
(a) Knowledge of one form of savings	Borderline	69	74	24	26
	Mildly retarded	79	60	51	40
(b) Knowledge of various forms of savings	Borderline	22	23	72	77
	Mildly retarded	16	12	114	88
Knowledge of H.P. and Credit System	Borderline	51	53	45	47
	Mildly retarded	64	50	66	50

Borderline   N = 83 to 94
Mildly retarded N = 125 to 132

Working out a weekly budget is made difficult by being unable to enumerate even the major items of weekly spending—board and lodging, fares, mid-day meals, spending money, etc. Knowledge of prices is usually very hazy and few subnormals are aware of the relative value of articles which they might have to purchase.

[1] Compare the story 'Trouble with Wages' in the series of social reading books 'Spotlight on Trouble', London: Methuen (p. 165 to p. 167).

Whilst they have little difficulty as long as items are small and within the purchasing power of their pocket money, their lack of experience begins to tell when buying larger items of personal clothing, and they are often quite at sea when asked how much board and lodging or a wireless would cost. These young adults' guesses were wild and suggested that financial transactions had been carried out by their parents, guardians or hospitals, even though many of them had been earning substantial wages. This is particularly obvious when enquiry is made as to what method is used for saving money. Irrespective of the intelligence level over 70 per cent of these young adults—many of whom had earned sizeable wage packets before their admission to the institution preferred or had been encouraged to hand over money to someone to keep for them. This was not due to ignorance of saving facilities since the majority knew of at least one form of official savings (although few of the group were able to name two forms of savings or realized that interests could be obtained).

Hire purchase contracts constitute a trap for the unwary and ignorant and only half of the borderline group had some idea of the implications of such arrangements. The situation in the financial field is summarized in Table XV.

Knowledge of Public Services

Enquiry into the degree of social knowledge available to the mildly and borderline retarded extended to assessing knowledge regarding Post Office procedure, transport facilities and medical arrangements. All young subnormals should have some sound working knowledge in these areas if they are to achieve any measure of personal independance.

Post Office Services

The Post Office acts nowadays as a clearing house for many public services and the dispensing of stamps and expediting of post is only one aspect of its duties. As writing is unlikely to be one of the strong points of the mentally handicapped not much sound knowledge can be expected. Though most of the group knew that postage is required for letters and that there are different rates for letters and parcels, there were often gross misconceptions of the time it would take a letter to get from one part of the town to another or one part of the country to another.

Generally speaking, the same rather high proportion of adults in the borderline group who had inadequate knowledge of elementary postage matters was also unaware of the variety of other services such as savings, postal orders, etc., obtained through the Post Office. The proportion is, of course, even higher in the mildly retarded group.

Transport Facilities

There are few in this group who have not made short, un-accompanied, journeys by public transport. However, the situation changes considerabely if the journey requires any change of transport: only just over half the mildly retarded claim that they have managed this, whilst the proportion is a little higher in the borderline group. Leaving the immediate neighbourhood and making the necessary enquiries leading to such a journey has been under-taken by only a comparatively small proportion. This probably reflects not only the lack of technical knowledge of how to proceed, but also a disinclination to give up the supportive familiar surroundings.

Medical Arrangements

The rather surprising and perhaps alarming finding was the professed ignorance of the group when asked what they would do about a small injury leading to loss of blood. The simple answer of bandaging or putting some plaster over it occurred to only just over half of the mildly retarded group, and the borderline group did not do much better. A similar helplessness is demonstrated by their ignorance of how to obtain a doctor's help, and many of the group had never heard of surgery hours and would not have known what to do in an emergency. The best many of them could do was the stock answer—go to hospital—but few of them actually knew where the hospital was.

Very few knew about medical procedure for the sick such as sick pay, sickness certificates and the like, and most of them had depended on the help of parents and guardians. Matthew (1964), dealing with 62 ex-special school pupils falling into the mildly and borderline retarded groups, found that only 48 per cent understood the sick note procedure which, whilst higher than the 37 per cent for the borderline and 22 per cent for the mildly retarded, shown by the present investigation, underlines the fact that not many of these young people understand a procedure which is very important for the working man.

The situation is summarized in Table XVI.

TABLE XVI
Ability to make use of public transport

	IQ group	Adequate		Inadequate	
		N	%	N	%
Post Office Services					
(a) Knowledge of current post-age for inland letters	Borderline	74	76	23	24
	Mildly retarded	109	83	23	17
(b) Awareness of different postal rates, etc.	Borderline	69	72	27	28
	Mildly retarded	79	61	51	39
(c) Knowledge of Post Office Services	Borderline	69	71	28	29
	Mildly retarded	72	60	47	40
Transport Facilities					
(a) Ability to travel short distances	Borderline	89	95	5	5
	Mildly retarded	105	80	27	20
(b) Use of transport involving change	Borderline	64	74	23	26
	Mildly retarded	78	60	51	40
(c) Ability to use transport for journeys outside immediate neighbourhood	Borderline	35	41	51	59
	Mildly retarded	32	25	94	75
Medical Arrangements					
(a) Knows how to deal with simple injury	Borderline	56	60	37	40
	Mildly retarded	69	53	61	47
(b) Knows how to obtain doctor's help	Borderline	54	57	40	43
	Mildly retarded	44	34	87	66
(c) Knowledge of sickness arrangements	Borderline	35	37	60	63
	Mildly retarded	28	22	102	78

Borderline   N = 83 to 94
Mildly retarded N = 125 to 132

Language Ability

Attention has repeatedly been drawn to the poor language abilities of mentally handicapped people (Spradlin, 1963). This refers not so much to pronunciation and ennunciation as to difficulties in comprehending what is said and in expressing one's self correctly and understandably. These weaknesses are, of course, associated with the subnormal's comparatively low intelligence level and with his poor socio-economic background which gives only inadequate and narrow language experience. Mastery of language is not a school subject and time spent in academic work at a special school is devoted to the 'tool' subjects of reading, writing and arithmetic, and not to the development of the use of language. This most important method of communication is left to take care of itself and the mentally handicapped must, like the normal, pick up an understanding of language and its proper use as best he can. Thus far too much reliance is placed on the sub-normal's ability to benefit by incidental learning.

The Sociologist Bernstein (1960, 1962) carefully investigated the speech patterns of the mentally subnormal and concluded that language deficit limits social growth. He points out that there are two kinds of language. 'Public language' is used by the uneducated and characterized by a lack of conjunctions and adequate sentence forms. 'Formal language' used by the more educated group, is on a much higher level which makes it possible to use language as a very flexible instrument of communication. Since the two sections of the population have to communicate with each other there will be difficulties if two different types of language are used. Examples of words in common use which were misunderstood and misinterpreted by the subnormal were given by Gunzburg (1962a). Some of the subnormal's so called foolish and incomprehensible actions could, in fact, be due to his attaching a personal, instead of the commonly accepted, meaning to a word or phrase, and acting accordingly. Gunzburg pointed out that the subnormal can often be regarded a stranger in his own country because he is unfamiliar with the language idioms, concepts and conventions of his home-land, in the same way that a tourist is in difficulty in a foreign country if he has only a smattering of its language (see section 6).

Earl (1961) referred to a 'subnormal language' and mentioned that 'the selective interests of their mind [the subnormal's] differ from the normal'. In consequence the 'outer generally agreed conventional meaning' will often be sacrificed to the subnormal's 'inner private and individual' meaning. There is also some evidence which suggests that intelligence as measured by an intelligence test is dependent on an adequate ability to use words. It has been said that the limitation of the subnormal's thinking as reflected in a low IQ are the result of his poor verbal development (O'Connor and Hermelin, 1963). It has also been shown that the verbal IQ tends to increase if children grow up in a stimulating environment (Tizard, 1962; Lyle, 1959, 1960; Kirk, 1958).

Considering how important language is for the rehabilitation of the subnormal in the community, it is disheartening to see how few attempts have been made to analyse the particular difficulties the defective experiences in his use and understanding of the spoken word (Sampson, 1962, 1966). The most frequent studies referring to this aspect of social functioning are investigations dealing with the knowledge and understanding of vocabulary (Mein and O'Connor, 1960, Mein, 1961). Most available tests are rather unsatisfactory for assessing how much the subnormal understands of the average everyday vocabulary, but even so some idea can be gained by studying these figures.

Table XVII shows the vocabulary ages and scores of 83 mentally retarded people aged 16 to 25 who had been admitted to hospital. In the test used (English Picture Vocabulary Test I) one picture illustrating the word pronounced by the examiner is selected from four alternatives. This method has a great advantage over other vocabulary tests which require the meaning of the words to be

TABLE XVII

Vocabulary ages and scores: 83 young mentally retarded people on the English Picture Vocabulary Test I (CA 16—25)

Percentile	Borderline retardation (N = 23)		Mild retardation (N = 31)		Moderate retardation (N = 27)	
	Score	Voc. age	Score	Voc. age	Score	Voc. age
100	36·5	10·5	33·5	9·9	34·5	10·0
90	33·4	9·9	31·2	9·1	29·8	8·10
80	32·6	9·6	29·5	8·10	28·7	8·8
70	31·9	9·4	28·9	8·8	27·8	8·5
60	30·8	9·1	28·4	8·5	26·6	8·1
50	30·0	8·10	27·3	8·1	24·7	7·9
40	29·1	8·8	26·3	8·0	22·9	7·5
30	25·5	8·0	25·6	7·11	21·9	7·3
20	24·7	7·9	22·7	7·5	19·7	7·0
10	18·8	6·10	19·9	7·0	18·3	6·9
0	−		−		−	

defined as this can be very difficult for the subnormal who may have a very clear idea of the usage of a word but is unable to give an acceptable definition of it. The English Picture Vocabulary Test, which is based on the well-known Peabody Picture Vocabulary Test standardised in the USA, avoids this particular difficulty by testing understanding of meaning without requiring a verbal definition.

The fiftieth percentile indicates the average vocabulary ages reached by each group. It will be seen that, on the average, a moderately retarded youth obtains a vocabulary age of only 7 years and 9 months; a mildly retarded youth scores slightly better (but scarcely significantly) with 8 years and 1 month; whilst the borderline retarded achieves a vocabulary age nearly comparable with that of a 9-year-old normal child. Since the borderline retarded obtained an IQ on the Wechsler Test of at least 70, which approximates to a mental age of about 10 years, it is easily seen that even the average borderline retarded person is under-functioning in verbal understanding. In fact his poor achievements in language are comparable with his poor reading abilities. O'Connor and Tizard (1956) reported a mean mechanical reading age in the borderline group of approximately 8-6 years and Table I (p. 41) showed an average reading level of 9-3 for that group.

Table XVII can be used to compare young mentally retarded people whose intelligence level is known, with the 83 young people in the group to estimate how much above or below the average achievement of that group their particular attainments can be placed. It must, however, be pointed out that there is no reason why the achievements should not be much higher than shown by the sample and it is most desirable that far more attention should be paid to the adequate development of vocabulary in the mentally retarded. It seems clear that the average mentally retarded—whatever his level of retardation above IQ 40—has no greater vocabulary knowledge than an 8- or 9-year-old child, and this must lead to considerable difficulties in his verbal communications with his fellow men.

Another very useful assessment of particular weaknesses in the use and understanding of language is the ITPA (Illinois Test of Psycholinguistic Abilities) test which has been developed in recent years in the USA by Kirk and McCarthy (1961, 1962). This consists of a number of subtests, each of which assesses a separate and distinct aspect of language ability. Figure 7 is based on ITPA results using 6 of the 9 available subtests of the battery (Gunzburg, 1964b). The graphs indicate the average attainments in various aspects of language behaviour of a group of 95 mentally retarded people. This sample consisted of three adult groups—moderately, mildly and borderline retarded young men aged 16 to 25, and a group of moderately retarded children aged 12 to 16.

Under the first column, visual decoding, are the results of a subtest which assesses the understanding of what is seen—a measure of how well the subjects interpret the visual clues offered by the world around them. The second column (auditory vocal association) assesses the ability to deduce relationships from what

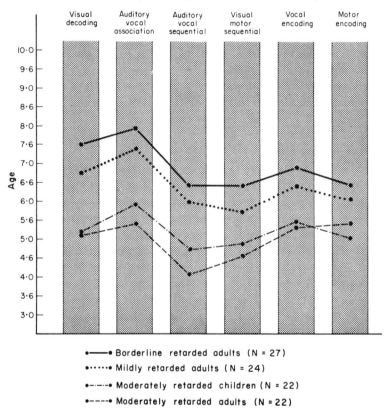

•——• Borderline retarded adults (N = 27)

•······• Mildly retarded adults (N = 24)

•—··—• Moderately retarded children (N = 22)

•————• Moderately retarded adults (N = 22)

Fig. 7. Communication abilities of mentally handicapped people.

is heard. The two following tests shown in Fig. 7 show the ability to recall immediately verbal and visual clues (auditory-vocal and visual motor sequential) and the last two columns indicate the person's ability to express himself either verbally (vocal encoding) or by gesture (motor encoding).

The test has been standardized on young children aged 4 to 8, and gives norms extending from 2½ to 9 years, but the average attainments of the four groups are comfortably within the 4 to 8 year range, even though approximately three quarters of the sample consisted of adults. The six tests are not easy even for adult subnormals with an average mental age of 10 (borderline retarded) and at times they achieve an average score comparable only with that of 6½-year-old children. It is intriguing to see that, generally speaking, the same type of language skill proves relatively difficult to an adult of comparatively low intelligence (moderately retarded) or comparatively high intelligence (borderline retarded), or a moderately retarded child. Intelligence level obviously has an effect on the average level of achievement, and higher average scores are obtained by the mentally handicapped of the higher IQ groups: however, one may speculate whether the slightly better achievement of the moderately retarded adults compared with the moderately retarded children might not be due to longer life experience and more opportunities for using communication skills.

Figure 7 suggests a definite pattern of poor communication abilities in the mentally retarded. Though the average mentally handicapped person has some understanding of a limited vocabulary (Table XVII) he has less ability to decipher the visual symbols which provide guidance and help in finding one's way about in life (visual decoding). Here he reaches only the average attainments of a normal child between 5 and 7½ years of age.

The mentally handicapped is relatively better in relating auditory impressions, but he is very handicapped by his poor memory for auditory and visual clues and, perhaps, by his inadequate techniques for recalling what he has seen and heard. Compared with his relatively better achievement in the understanding of the spoken word and of visual clues, the ability to express himself verbally or to use appropriate gestures is extremely impaired. Even the borderline retarded person is severely handicapped in this respect and is unable to use language adequately. This agrees well with clinical impressions. It is the difficulty of the mentally handicapped in making himself understood that very often interferes with his adjustment and gives the impression that he is much less able than he really is.

It should be stressed once again that among the various aspects of the education and training of the mentally handicapped, none has received so little attention as his communication abilities, yet they are vital to him if efforts to adjust him to the community are to have any lasting effect.

Concluding Remarks

The educational and social assessment of the mentally handicapped in the age group 16 to 25, many of whom are only mildly or borderline retarded, suggests a widespread lack of a certain type of social knowledge which is almost essential for adequate functioning. Though the evidence does not indicate the extent or the depth of social ignorance, it is suggestive enough to draw attention to a much neglected field of investigation and remedial action.

It must be remembered that practically all these people in the 16 to 25 age group have been educated in special schools. The borderline and mildly retarded in the sample had never been excluded from school and had received full-time school education to the age of 16. Yet nearly one third of that large group are ineffective readers with reading ages below 7, more than a quarter of the mildly retarded group find difficulty in handling simple coin problems, and approximately half of that group cannot deal with pounds, shillings and pence. Half of that group cannot fill in an application form, nearly half of them cannot tell the time correctly, or deal with many time concepts. They vary considerably in their understanding and knowledge of financial situations and public services, and are more often than not incapable of performing any other than routine social skills.

Distressing as these results are, considering that most of this elementary information is picked up by the average normal child at an early age, some of the evidence is encouraging. The Tables indicate clearly that intellectual limitation is responsible in a few instances only for the lack of elementary education and social knowledge. In most of the Tables a considerable number, usually the majority, possessed the correct knowledge. This suggests clearly that such elementary knowledge is within the capability of the various IQ groups, even though a large minority of persons fail to acquire it. It is reasonable to assume that knowledge which can be learned by the majority of an IQ group can also be acquired by the minority, and that the majority acquisition provides a standard towards which all work with the minority should be directed. There must be good reason (such as brain damage resulting in perceptual difficulties) for non-attainment of a simple standard achieved by the majority. A person falling considerably below the standard of his intellectual peers could justifiably be called a retarded retardate and this backwardness should not be regarded as being due to intellectual subnormality.

The comparative absence of social knowledge could contribute to increased feelings of insecurity and anxiety, which are conspicuous in the mentally handicapped personality. A person with an IQ of 55 or more has enough intelligence to realise that he is at a disadvantage, but not enough to do something about it. He knows that others of his age can read and write and work out their money transactions without difficulty. He is aware of the curious glances people give him when he has to confess that he cannot write his name or read an application form. He is often ingenious in devising camouflaging manouvres to conceal his educational shortcomings but most of the time he has to admit to these conspicuous gaps in his knowledge.

Once he has left school and faces a world less understanding and less prepared to make allowances, his conscious realisation of educational backwardness, and unconcious feelings of anxiety and insecurity engendered by his incompetence in day-to-day situations, combine to increase his feeling of personal inadequacy. This can easily snowball and one of the measures to be taken at this late stage could well be a direct attack on his educational shortcomings. With better skills he would benefit, not only by being more competent, but also by feeling less anxious, less insecure, and less apprehensive. Remedial educational measures relating to social competence could therefore be regarded as being of definite therapeutic importance and by their obvious relevance to the subnormal's conscious realization of his problems, may make him more accessible and readier to accept guidance in other fields of personality adjustment.

3

DEVELOPMENT OF SOCIAL COMPETENCE

Introduction

The preceding section dealt with various aspects of the three basic requirements for an adequate evaluation of the needs of the individual subnormal and of the success or failure of the educational approach used so far. Surveys show that there is an extensive lack of knowledge and social skills in adolescent retarded men and women, admitted to an institution, whose intellectual defects were often no more than mild. It is reasonable to expect even lower attainments in the knowledge of social skills in groups with lower levels of intelligence.

It has been suggested that the third requirement for adequate evaluation is a method whereby an individual's standing could be compared with the average attainments of a group of similar age and intelligence (e.g. Table I, p. 41 shows the percentile ranking of reading achievement in groups of specified intelligence levels, and Table XVII p. 62 refers to vocabulary ages).

This chapter will demonstrate the application of this method in a slightly different way—one which may be the only possible solution when reliable intelligence test results are not available. The surveys to be described deal with the social competence of mentally handicapped children under 16 years of age, who attended training centres in the community (see p. 104) and did not require hospital or institutional care. Even the most intelligent children were however not above the level of the moderately retarded: no mildly or borderline retarded children are included because these would have attended special schools for the educationally subnormal. The intellectual status of the group can thus be described with some accuracy, as far as the most able children are concerned but no IQ scores were available for the remainder. One can only say that the population consisted of moderately and severely retarded children with a proportion of profoundly retarded children.

Any generalizations based on a population of such diverse character will therefore be less useful than if well-defined groups with little variation in intellectual ability had been available. Nevertheless, it is felt that studies of so-called 'ineducable' or 'trainable' children—even if not 'stratified' by IQ levels, are of considerable value for general guidance. It should be remembered, however, that any 'norms' obtained will tend to be affected by the size of the group of profoundly retarded children in the training centres.

The P-A-C System of Ascertaining Levels of Social Development

The surveys already discussed have shown clearly that there are large variations in social knowledge within the fairly narrow limits of specific IQ groups. People with relatively high IQs tend to have better, and probably more effective, social knowledge than those with lower IQs. Nonetheless it is not possible to make a reasonably accurate prediction of social knowledge and competence even when the IQ rating is known.

Doll (1953) published a number of valuable studies dealing with the measurement of social competence. His Vineland Scale of Social Maturity is similar to an orthodox intelligence test because it establishes the ages at which certain social skills are first widely practised by the normal child. This technique is well known in paediatric practice where landmarks in maturation provide guidance to normal development in, for example, walking and talking. Doll extended this technique to cover social development well into early adulthood and established the ages at which 117 individual social skills were first mastered by the majority of normal children and young adults. The summing up of the individual performance in these various aspects of social competence is expressed as a social age (SA).

The SA of a healthy average child should be roughly the same as his chronological age (CA), just as his MA should be similar to his CA. An SA below the CA indicates retardation in social competence, an SA well above the CA, social precocity. The relationship of SA to CA can be expressed as a proportion in the form of a social quotient (SQ) in the same way as an IQ indicates the relationship of MA to CA. For example, an SQ of 100 indicates a close relationship between SA and CA, and an SQ of 50 shows that social competence is well below the level expected.

The Vineland Scale has proved extremely useful in directing attention to this most important aspect of functioning, and particularly in assessing systematically the early stages of social development. It is still used in the form in which it was first presented and no amendment or finer standardization has been added since it was published first.

Doll gives figures which indicate that the relationship between SA and CA, and between SA and MA, is high in normal people. But in subnormal populations correlation coefficients are often lower, and reflect the fact that institutionalization, diminished motivation, decreased opportunity and life experience affect social functioning to a large extent.

The comparatively low correlations between SA and CA in subnormal populations, as measured by the Vineland Test, important as they are for an understanding of the situation in general, do not help much in the practical work of social education and training. Whereas it is reasonable to expect a normal 10-year-old child to have mastered the scholastic and social skills practised by most members of the 10-year-age group, achievement levels for the mentally handicapped should not be based on those relating to a predominantly 'normal' population.

A widespread practice is to use the subnormal's mental age as an index of the level of attainments that are within his capacity. Thus a subnormal with an MA of 10 should be able to read, write and do number work on the level of a normal 10-year-old child, irrespective of his chronological age. This practice does provide some guidance, but it cannot be applied to social competence which can and should be well above the MA and depends on age and experience as well as intelligence (see Fig. 3, p. 18). It is clear that *an SA obtained on the Vineland Scale can indicate the level of attainment in relation to the normal population but nothing else.* The Vineland Scale will not permit to judge whether a mentally handicapped person is socially retarded *compared with other mentally retarded people,* because his social efficiency will always be below that of a normal person of his own age on account of his mental handicap.

This is an unsatisfactory situation. There is not enough knowledge available to advise with confidence whether a retardate should be encouraged to acquire more skills, and we may easily find that it is the individual pupil, and not his teachers, who decides how

far he can go. Since subnormals are usually lethargic and have no
ambitions, this situation will ensure considerable underachieve-
ment. The situation changes once teachers have the relevant facts
from which to assess the individual's position in relation to other
youngsters of the same age, and the same mental handicap. They
are then able to judge whether the child's performance agrees with
what might reasonably be expected of him.

Unfortunately, there are certain disadvantages common to all
measures based on averages; averaging very good, good, mediocre,
poor and very poor attainments could lead to the setting of a relatively low standard if the poor performers predominate. Using
too low a standard as the norm may easily result in the conclusion
that a pupil is up to the level which should be expected from
somebody of his age and handicap and the teachers may therefore
desist from encouraging further efforts. Instead of stimulating
development, she may in practice have put an artificial ceiling to
possible achievement. There is, of course, also the possibility that
a teacher, studying the attainments of the average mentally handicapped child, may urge a seemingly backward child to emulate the
performance of his age group. Yet a severe dual handicap may
make it impossible for him to reach the average attainment level
and he may suffer unnecessary hardship by being forced to attempt
things which are genuinely outside his reach.

But, as has already been stated, these are disadvantages common
to all norms based on averages, and it is the trained teacher's duty
to utilize information in the most appropriate way. The advantages
of having some guidance available are many and obvious. When a
teacher is faced with a pupil who falls below the average for his
age and handicap she must always ask herself whether the failure is
due to a particularly severe dual handicap, to a communication
defect, to lack of opportunities at home or at the school, to over-
protection, etc., or to some lack of training or a defect in teaching
method. There may be many reasons, but the important ones can
usually be found after study of the pupil, his circumstances and
his particular weaknesses. Having established a possible cause for
underfunctioning, remedial measures can be taken in many cases—a
talk to the parents, a change of the routine to provide new opportunities, a new approach to teaching particular aspects, and so on.

Having norms and standards available can thus ensure that the
attention of a conscientious teacher is directed towards many

relevant aspects of her pupil's life. Assessment is in the nature
of a regular stocktaking, which by being systematic and permitting
comparisons, is far superior to an intermittent gathering of
impressions into a collection of unrelated and sporadic pieces of
knowledge, compressed into a 'report'.

Establishing norms and standards of social efficiency is a three-
step process:
(1) Deciding what type of information should be incorporated in
an assessment procedure. This results in a list of social skills as
long or as short as the compiler wishes it to be.
(2) Applying this list to a large sample of mentally handicapped
people of different age groups to establish when particular social
skills have been generally mastered.
(3) Working out the average attainment levels of the various age
groups on the basis of the material previously obtained. This
establishes the norms and standards for each age group.

An assessment procedure of this kind does not attempt to measure
'social intelligence'. It is concerned simply to ascertain the
presence or absence of certain skills and items of social knowledge and practice in a particular child, and to relate his level of
achievement to the average attainment level in a well-defined
population. An assessment of social skills should pay particular
attention to factors which may interfere with the acquisition of
skills, because what is measured depends to a large extent on
opportunity and training rather than on innate ability. Thus the
norms may well be different in different populations: the mentally
handicapped child living in rural surroundings may have far more
opportunity to move about independently than has the handicapped
child in a traffic-congested town, and to adopt the rural norms for
the town child might set him an impossibly high standard; to
average the two performances would result in a meaningless norm
which would fail to give adequate guidance for either situation.

The Progress Assessment Chart of Social Development (P-A-C)
is essentially a check list of social skills. The skills were selected
partly because of the availability of research data and partly
because experience suggested that they referred to social knowledge which should be available to the child. Selection involved
much subjective judgment, and it might be thought that some skills
in the list could, perhaps with advantage, be replaced by other

more important ones. Teachers might be tempted, therefore, to draw up their own social assessment check-lists to include skills which had been omitted from the P-A-C.

The main disadvantage of such individually compiled lists is however the impossibility of putting these additional skills in a rank order of difficulty or maturation—a hierarchy which brings order into a medley of assorted social skills and permits comparisons and evaluation of the individual's achievement. In the long run a method which indicates the relative difficulty of each skill and is based on the results of research, outweighs the disadvantages of having to use a list which does not contain all skills.

The skills in the P-A-C 1 taken from available data, are placed in a sequence of development according to the age levels to which they had been assigned by researchers. There is in fact, less agreement among researchers in the ranking of skills than one might wish. Yet on the whole, the sequence of skills in each area of social achievement reflects well the gradual maturing of social competence.

The relationship between skills of different areas at similar stages of social development, and of skills in the order of maturation in a particular area, is shown in the P-A-C forms (Fig. 8) by concentric circles extending from the centre to the periphery. All skills (identified by numbers in the check list) which, in normal development, should appear at approximately the same time, are placed on the same level (referred to by letters) irrespective of the sector to which they relate, but skills learned early are nearer the centre than those learned later, which are situated nearer the edge. Stages in learning are referred to by letters although they correspond to chronological ages in normal development. This, it is hoped, discourages the tendency to reading off misleading mental ages from a chart the purpose of which is to *give a picture* of social function and dysfunction, rather than a figure suggesting a spurious placing on a scale.

The Primary Progress Assessment Chart (P-P-A-C) covers the period from birth to approximately two and a half years and is thus not only suitable for the normal infant but also for the severely and profoundly mentally handicapped. Progress Assessment Chart 1 (P-A-C 1) covers the span from about 2 to 8 years in normal development, and is the form most appropriate for work with the young mentally handicapped. Both forms are

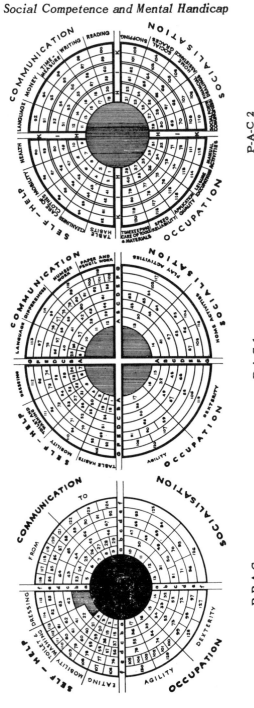

Fig. 8. P-A-C Diagrams.

based on research findings, but Progress Assessment Chart 2
(P-A-C 2) which relates to the more senior pupil, follows a
different procedure. Since there are no data available regarding
the sequence of acquisition of social skills necessary for the
young adult, it has not been possible to rank them in order of
their natural emergence. The alternative method of relating
skills to needs was adopted to obtain some grading according
to the social efficiency in three different situations. Thus the
comparatively simple skills necessary in a sheltered environment were placed nearest to the centre, and the more complex
skills required for working and living in an open community
with relatively little support, were placed further out in the
P-A-C 2 diagram (Fig. 8).[1]

The social skills are grouped under four section headings: Self-
Help, Communication, Socialization, and Occupation. Each contains
subsections referring to particular areas of social competence
(e.g. Self-Help is divided into Dressing, Washing, Table Habits,
Toilet and Mobility—see Fig. 58, p. 210). Published research does
not provide sufficient facts to list an equal number of social skills
for each developmental stage, but the total number of skills in
each subsection has been made constant to facilitate comparisons
(ten skills). Nevertheless, a straightforward comparison of the
number of skills acquired in various sections may be extremely
misleading because some skills may be comparatively easy to
acquire (i.e. using scissors) whereas others (i.e. learning the
Social Sight Vocabulary) require considerably more time and attention (see p. 157).

Assessment should be based on personal observation or reliable
information. No precise criteria for scoring the P-A-C had been
laid down in the past and most teachers were content with assessments based on their own standards. However, it is essential that
these standards should be well defined within the group or school
and *consistently* applied, both when comparing one child with
others and when studying successive stages in the development
of one individual. Unless the same yardstick is used throughout
each assessment period, the results will be suspect and hardly
worth the time spent in obtaining them.

[1] The grading of social skills adopted in the P-A-C 2 appears to be generally correct to judge
from the investigation carried out by Matthew (1964). Using the forerunner of the P-A-C 2—the
Social and Educational Assessment Record with some slight modifications—Matthew showed
statistically the internal consistency of the arrangement. Slight adjustments to the sequence of
P-A-C 2 skills were made following the research work by Jackson and Struthers (1974). These are
shown from the 10th edition onwards.

The situation is different when an attempt is made to compare a child's attainment level with that of others not personally known to the assessor (e.g. those taught in other schools, in researches or when applying the techniques of evaluation described in the following section). In these cases it is clearly essential to define as accurately as possible the level of performance to be used as a standard and for this purpose the scoring criteria of the P-A-C Manual must be used.

Once the P-A-C check list has been scored by assessing a child, it appears to contain only haphazardly distributed credits and failures. These are however organized into a suggestive pattern of failure and success by shading in the spaces of the Diagram (Fig. 4, p. 19). Spaces (referring by number to the skills on the check list) are heavily shaded on the Diagram if adequate mastery has been attained, and lightly if not. (Spaces for skills which cannot be assessed for one or another reason are left blank to avoid confusion.)[1] This procedure gives a telling visual impression of the strong and weak points of each child's knowledge and competence, and the results can be used to direct teaching efforts towards particular weaknesses. Information on social competence does not, however, predict intelligence level; social knowledge depends on many factors other than intelligence, and a mastery of many social skills suggests good training and opportunities for practice but not necessarily high intelligence.[2]

Marshall (1967) in her investigation of 165 children aged 14 and 15 in training centres presents correlation coefficients relating to the P-A-C 1 (Table XVIII). Using two vocabulary tests to assess the children's mental levels, she found the fairly low correlations of ·37 to ·42 between three subsections of the P-A-C 1 and the measures of mental ability. The highest correlations were between the communication sector of the P-A-C and the vocabulary tests ($r = ·60$, $r = ·61$), although this was to be expected considering that both assessments measured similar aspects. Correlation coefficients showing the relationship between the four subsections and the full P-A-C are comparatively high, and suggest internal consistency.

[1] In Fig. 4 the white spaces indicate inabilities and not skills which had not been assessed.

[2] Sellin (1967) showed that nearly all subtests of an assessment of social competence correlated at the 5 or 1% level with chronological age except certain subtests such as communication which correlated significantly with IQ.

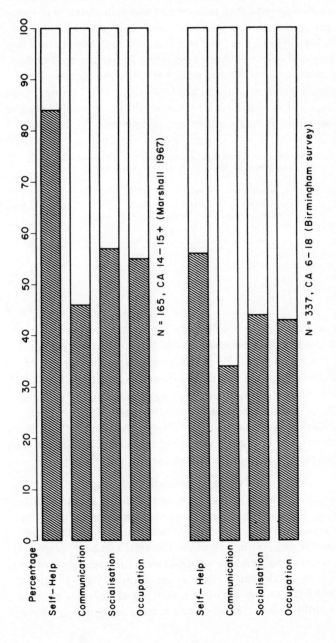

Fig. 9. Average social efficiency (from Marshall, 1967, and Birmingham Survey, 1965).

There is a general trend for self-help, occupation and socialization skills to be better developed than communication skills (Fig. 9). This strongly suggests that parents and teachers strive hard towards those aspects of social competence which make the child more self-sufficient. When he is able to dress and wash himself and to eat properly and occupy himself, the mentally handicapped child is a less constant liability and embarrassment and requires less supervision. Emphasis on these aspects of training, however, fails to encourage the development of those skills which would help the child to work and live with others and to overcome the barriers

TABLE XVIII

The relationship between language ability and social development as assessed by the P-A-C 1 (Marshall, 1967)

	Stanford Binet vocabulary	English Pict. Voc. Test	Full P-A-C 1	Self- help	Commun.	Soc.
Full P-A-C 1	·56	·57				
Self-help	·42	·43	·76			
Communication	·61	·60	·90	·56		
Socialization	·41	·41	·85	·64	·64	
Occupation	·37	·40	·86	·55	·65	·72

$N = 165.$

imposed by his handicap. Social education aims to make the mentally handicapped child reasonably able to take part in community life, but it appears that the very skills which would help him to communicate and to join in with others are neglected in his education. This situation is probably aggravated by the parents' inclination to protect the mentally handicapped child from scorn and misunderstanding and treat him always as a young child, and is not entirely due to a genuinely lower level of ability in the area of communication, or even socialization.

Norms and Standards

Mastery of individual skills, such as the ability to use a knife for buttering bread, depend partly on adequate training, partly on the development of muscular control. In a normal child the latter determines the earliest age at which the skill can be mastered, but it is his mother who provides the child with the encouragement and opportunity to develop his ability to use a knife. Doll (1953), investigating the emergence of this skill, found that the majority of normal children had learned to use a knife for buttering at the age of 7 and that by the age of 9 practically all children had mastered it. The subnormal child with an IQ under 50 takes considerably longer, and only about 6 out of 10 have acquired it by the age of 14 (Fig. 10).

Using a knife for such a routine performance seems not to require much intelligence, and the skill to do so should be acquired by a mentally handicapped child once the necessary motor control has been developed. Unfortunately, as every observer knows, the learning of this and similar skills by the mentally handicapped child takes considerably more time. It is instructive to compare the normal and the subnormal in this respect because it shows the difficulties of the latter in learning even simple, nearly mechanical, skills. Yet there is no evidence that such slow learning is unavoidable in the education of all mental defectives, and some speeding up of learning might take place if training and education were more purposeful, and more effective methods of teaching and training could be developed. This suggestion does not deny that it is unlikely that even simple social skills could ever be acquired as speedily and competently by mentally handicapped children as by normal children.

Figures 10 to 33 are based on surveys carried out in Birmingham. One of the purposes of the surveys was to study the development of competence in specific skills in clearly defined areas by assessing the proportion of skills mastered in successive age groups. Since Doll had used the same approach in his work (1953) it was possible to compare the rate of learning of specific social skills in normal and subnormal children. Figures 10 to 17 illustrate the extremely quick acquisition of some simple selected social skills by the normal child compared with the slow-learning mentally handicapped child.

Data relating to the Birmingham Survey of mentally handicapped children in the community are based on P-A-C 1 assessments carried out by teachers in training centres in Birmingham. Table XIX gives the age distribution of this survey and compares the composition of the sample with that used by Doll (1953). The Birmingham sample can be regarded as representative of those mentally handicapped children with IQ below 55, who have been excluded from the ordinary schools system as unsuitable for special education but not needing hospital care. (The children live at home and attend daily at a training centre.)

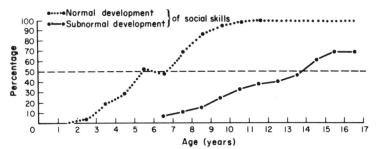

Fig 10   Ability to use table knife for "spreading" butter, jam, etc. (P-A-Cl, No5)

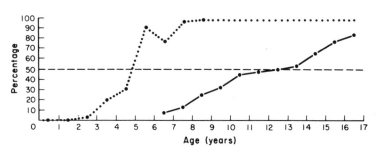

Fig 11   Ability to put on most ordinary articles of clothing (P-A-Cl, No74)

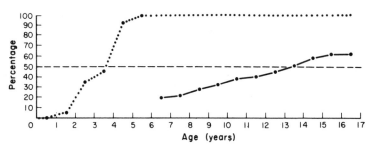

Fig 12   Ability to walk downstairs, one foot per step without supporting himself (P-A-Cl, No36)

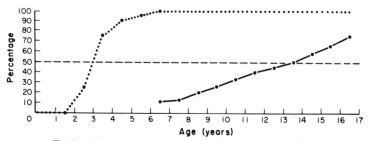

Fig 13   Ability to relate experiences in coherent way (P-A-Cl, No25)

by normal and mentally handicapped children.

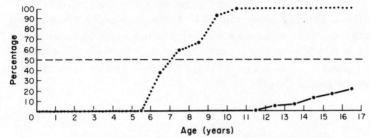

Fig 14   Ability to tell the time to quarter hour (P-A-C1, No98)

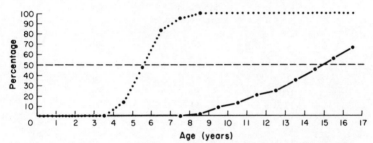

Fig 15   Ability to play simple table games, e.g. tiddly winks, dominoes, snakes and ladders etc. (P-A-C1, No84)

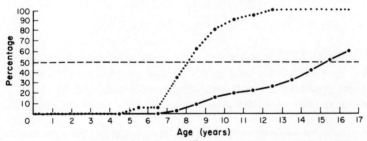

Fig 16   Ability to play co-operative team games and obey rules (P-A-C1, No117)

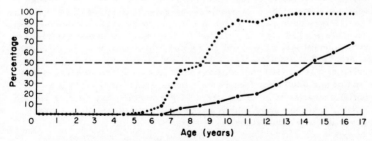

Fig 17   Ability to use tools, kitchen utensils, garden tools (P-A-C1, No107)

The data refer to the total child population attending training centres at Birmingham during 1965. Although, strictly speaking, all conclusions from these data refer only to the mentally handicapped child in this Birmingham community, there is no reason to suppose that a similarly handicapped child living in a similar environment would be very different.

TABLE XIX

Age distribution of P-A-C Survey, 1965, of mentally handicapped children and Doll's sample of normal children (1953)

	Mentally handicapped	Normal
C A	N	N
6	16	20
7	14	20
8	28	20
9	27	20
10	23	20
11	34	20
12	29	20
13	37	20
14	39	20
15	27	20
16	32	20
17	14	20
18	17	20
Total	**337**	**260**

Figures 18 to 29 indicate the percentage of successes on the P-A-C 1 check list for each group. As one would expect, increasing maturity is associated with increased competence, and the older age groups show therefore greater success than the younger ones.[1]

[1] Owing to the comparative smallness of the sample and the even smaller age groups resulting from this, the actual total scores showed, when plotted, a very rugged appearance. The score of one particular year might be 'high', but the score of the following year might be very low, though it 'should' have been 'up'. Nevertheless the general trend was very apparent and would have been seen clearly in all age groups if the sample had been larger. This would have compensated for the undue influence exercised by abnormal conditions, misunderstanding of instructions, inadequate assessment, etc. In the circumstances a statistical operation known as 'smoothing' was carried out, which results in evening out the excessive ups and downs due to the factors mentioned, whilst preserving the essential characteristics of the graph. A graph which has been 'smoothed' is, more or less, the graph which would have been obtained in a large sample under ideal conditions.

The subdivisions in each section of the P-A-C 1 contain 10 skills and the curves can be directly translated into percentages. For example, in Fig. 21, Self-Help, it can be seen that 60% of skills relating to dressing have been acquired by the group of mentally handicapped children, aged 13; in other words, the average 13-year-old mentally handicapped has acquired 6 out of 10 dressing skills.

It is obviously important to know how valid these findings are for the general population of mentally handicapped children. Does the 'average' mentally handicapped child go through the same stages of development at the same slow speed as the Birmingham child? No investigations that parallel this study have been carried out elsewhere as yet but, considering the representativeness of the sample, it is reasonable to assume that the graphs are a valid indication of what to expect. Some support for this assumption is found in data collected by Schiphorst (1968) which present the results of three successive P-A-C 1 surveys of the Birmingham training centres. Figures 30 to 33 (p. 88) indicate almost complete agreement among the three surveys, the children in Birmingham reaching approximately similar levels of competence at each chronological stage on three successive occasions.

The mentally handicapped child in hospital or institution may have special difficulties in acquiring social skills. He may be emotionally unstable, which necessitates his admission to hospital (see p. 104), he may be physically and mentally more handicapped than children at training centres and therefore requires special skilled attention; and he may have fewer opportunities to observe and practice social skills just because he is in an institution. It may well be that norms applicable to training centre children are not suitable for children in hospital.

Figures 34 to 37 (p. 89) show the rate of acquisition of social competence in a child population resident in hospital compared with a similar population at training centres. Though the children were comparable as far as their low intelligence levels were concerned the hospital children were often less competent socially than children living outside. Nevertheless it might well be possible to narrow the marked gap between the performance of the child in the community and that of an institutionalized child by providing more individual attention, increased opportunities, and more purposeful training.

It can be seen that neither the training centre nor the hospital

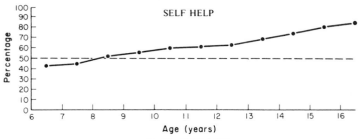

Fig 18   Table habits

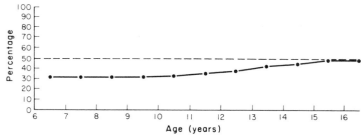

Fig 19   Mobility

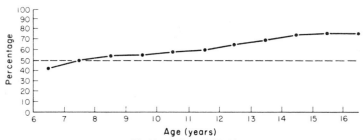

Fig 20   Toilet and Washing

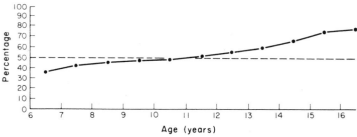

Fig 21   Dressing

successive age groups of mentally handicapped children.

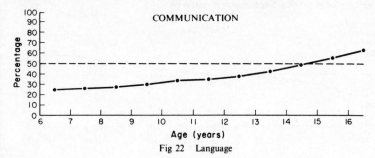

Fig 22   Language

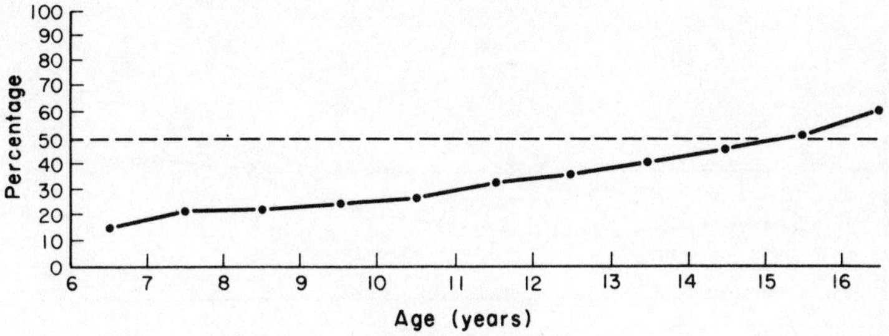

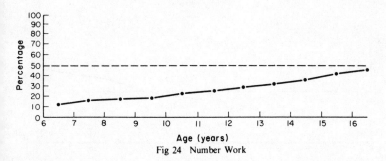

Fig 23   Differences

Fig 24   Number Work

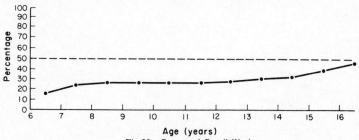

Fig 25   Paper and Pencil Work

Figs. 18 to 29—cont. The acquisition of social competence by successive age groups of mentally handicapped children.

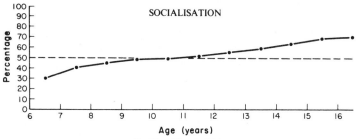

Fig 26   Play Activities

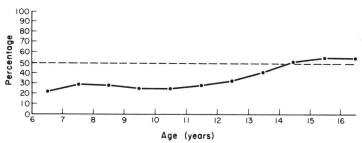

Fig 27   Home Activities

Fig 28   Dexterity

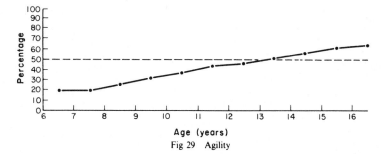

Fig 29   Agility

children normally succeed in reaching 100% competence in the
areas assessed; the most one can expect is that some 70 to 80%
of the self-help skills, and only 30 to 40% of the skills listed in
the other areas have been mastered by the age of 14 to 15. Considering that each age group contained profoundly retarded children
unable to respond to training, the situation can nevertheless not be
regarded as too discouraging.

The picture emerging from the data presented is unequivocal.
There is a proportion of severely mentally handicapped children
whose social competence develops slowly but steadily during the
11 years for which data have been collected. Generally children
of these age groups show 40 to 80% competence in the areas
assessed although some areas are markedly less well developed
(e.g. communication) than others (e.g. self-help).

The evidence of three successive surveys seems to suggest that
the various developmental stages are tied to age levels and are in
the nature of landmarks. This may be true in certain circumstances.
If a child is continually approached with the attitude that it is
cruel to demand too much of him because he is mentally handicapped, the result must be too low a demand on our side. If we
expect little we receive little in return. This attitude springs from
an uncertainty as to the capability of the mentally handicapped
child. Use of the mental age as a guide has added to our low
demands in those very aspects of social functioning which matter
most. Study of the graphs should help to by-pass the insidious
dangers of demanding too little most of the time and too much
occasionally. They provide guidance as to what should be regarded
as a reasonable level of attainment for most of the handicapped and
set the target towards which the educationist can strive with
confidence.

Once a clear recognition of these aims has taken place and the
teacher is more afraid of asking too little than too much, much more
deliberate and purposeful teaching could begin. The graphs, reflecting the mathematical average achievement levels of age groups,
should be regarded as indicating minimal targets for those age
groups. It may well be that striving towards more clearly defined
targets could result in 'success' consistently sooner than at the
ages suggested by the graphs. Since mastery of social skills is to
a large extent dependent upon the opportunity to learn, the graphs
should be considered as indicating achievements possible *under*

Figs. 30 to 33. Social development of mentally handicapped children as shown by three successive surveys on the P-A-C 1.

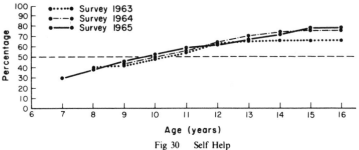

Fig 30   Self Help

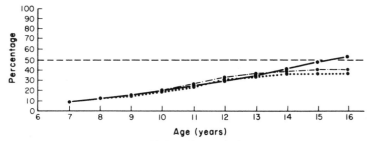

Fig 31   Communication

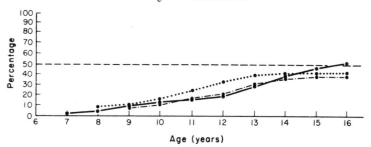

Fig 32   Socialisation

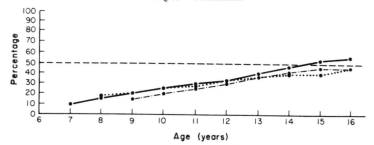

Fig 33   Occupation

Figs. 34 to 37. Social development of hospitalized mentally handicapped children compared with mentally handicapped children living in the community (from Schiphorst, 1968).

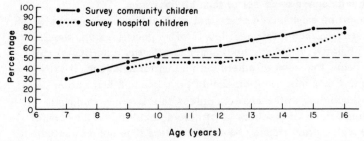

Fig 34   Self Help

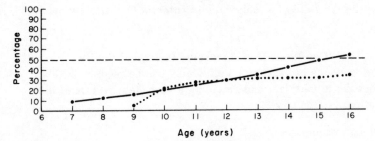

Fig 35   Communication

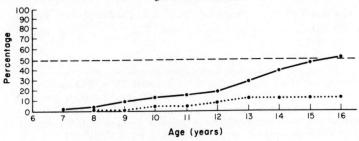

Fig 36   Socialisation

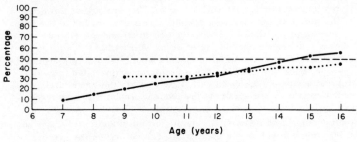

Fig 37   Occupation

existing conditions but not as reflecting an inability of the mentally handicapped to do better than he does now.

It must be emphasized again that such achievement graphs which represent average attainment levels of a specific group, should be used primarily to induce the teacher to ask why a particular child falls below the level of others with a similar handicap. It is essential that this question should be asked and that action be taken according to the answer. Unless this is done, the most well-meaning efforts of teachers and trainers could indeed be harmful since undue pressure may be applied where it is not warranted. Although this is a definite danger, it does not justify depriving the worker in the field of a tool which is potentially extremely valuable.[1]

Two Methods of Assessing Individual Pupils

Two methods of assessing individuals can be recommended as being easy to carry out and providing a very clear picture of the situation.

1. Group Comparisons

Figures 38 to 41 give four examples of a group of children in a hospital school whose attainments on P-A-C 1 were plotted against the norms obtained from training centres (Figs. 18 to 29, p. 86).[2]

---

[1] The graphs reflecting the growth of social competence in the Birmingham sample should be considered an underassessment rather than an overassessment of the capabilities of those under IQ 55. The sample had not been tested on an intelligence scale and the results refer therefore to a somewhat heterogeneous group from profound to moderate retardation. In a survey of 286 children attending the Training Centres in 1963, only 83 were found who had an intelligence test assessment, the others were so obviously defective that formal testing had been superfluous. The 83 children obtained an average IQ 42 which suggests that the remaining 203 children had an average IQ well below 42. The average social attainments of the group as a whole were therefore depressed owing to the great number of profoundly and severely retarded children and the attainment levels shown in the graph should therefore be well within the ability of the moderately retarded. The ideal procedure would be to obtain attainment levels for each age in each of the three groups (profound, severe, moderate) and compare each child with others within the same intellectual group. Until such data are available the present graphs will give some assistance.

[2] The procedure is as follows: Determine an individual child's age on his last birthday and select the appropriate age column in the graph referring to a specific P-A-C area, e.g. dressing. Check the number of skills acquired by the child in this specific area and make a mark on the

It can be seen from Figures 38 to 41 that a considerable
number of these hospital children scored well above the norms from
the training centres in certain aspects. However, plotting of each
child's performance permitted not only studying him in relation to
the group norm as provided by the training centre development
graphs, it compared him also with the achievements of other
children in the ward in which he lived and worked and with his
own performance in other areas.

An analysis of the relative positions of the various pupils in the
different aspects of assessment showed that many of them were
often better in certain areas than the average training centre child;
this was so particularly in dressing (Fig. 39), toilet and washing.
In other aspects there was not much difference between the two
groups, as can be seen when comparing the paper and pencil and
number work aspects of communication (Fig. 40, 41). Sometimes,
however, the performance of institution children was well below
that of training centre children, for example in table habits (Fig. 38).

It appears that children in hospital may be encouraged to help
themselves more than those in training centres. The latter may have
over-protective mothers who feel that they must help a good deal.
Those children master certain aspects of social behaviour less
effectively than children in an institution where comparatively less
help is available to them. This appears to be supported by the
observation that the institution children are poor in table habits
(Fig. 38). The large-scale feeding arrangements which must be
made in large wards permit little attention to individual training,
whereas the home probably provides more encouragement and
attention.

The foregoing is not necessarily valid generally, but a careful
analysis of achievements and deficiencies, using group comparisons, will direct attention to other, local problems which require
further investigation. It is also instructive to see that children

---

intersection between the number of skills read off from either side of the
figure and the age column. Identify marks either by initials or a reference
number. For example, in Figure 38 the child with the initial I 12 years
9 months old and has mastered only 3 skills. Compared with the graph of
the norm, she is well below the level of achievement of the 12 year-old
children in training centres who have, on the average, acquired 6 to 7 skills
in this aspect. Her performance in paper and pencil work is, however, above
the average attainments of her age group.

Figs. 38 to 41. The social competence of a group of hospital children compared with the Birmingham norms.

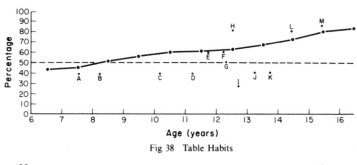

Fig 38   Table Habits

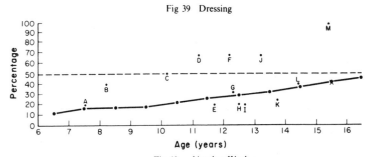

Fig 39   Dressing

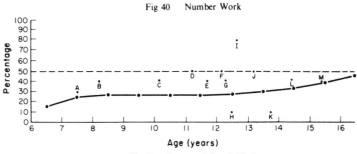

Fig 40   Number Work

Fig 41   Paper and Pencil Work

of one school class often tend to exceed the norm in one area and
not in others, which suggests that too much emphasis is placed
on an area due to a teacher's or nurse's particular interest, whilst
other areas are neglected.

Figures 38 to 41 show the relative positions of various individuals. Pupil M, for example, was consistently well above the level
of this group and of the norms provided by the training centres.
Attention was directed to him and subsequent assessment of his
intelligence indicated a WAIS IQ 71, which to some extent
explained why he deviated from the group norm. On the other hand
pupil I (WAIS IQ 46), whose scores were well below the norm in
most aspects, performed well above the norm of her group in paper
and pencil work; as a result more emphasis was laid on the neglected areas of her training.

The method outlined permits evaluation of the performance of (a)
a group and (b) of individuals in particular areas. It permits an easy
locating of 'stragglers' who need extra help.

2. Individual Evaluation

It is often desirable to compare the progress and performance of
an individual child, not only with the standards of his own age
group, but also with his own development through the years. For
example, it is helpful to know whether the slow progress observed
in a particular mentally handicapped child is nevertheless 'progress',
or whether it is slower than is usual in retarded children.

The diagrams of Fig. 42 correspond in layout to the diagram of
the P-A-C 1 (see Fig. 8, p. 74). Each subsection of the P-A-C 1 contains
ten skills and the diagrams of Fig. 42 (taken from the P-E-I folder—
Progress Evaluation Index) indicate by the cross-hatched parts the
average number of attainments of successive age groups in the
various subsections. The first diagram for example indicates that
the average 6-year-old has mastered four skills in self-help (table
habits) three in self-help (mobility) and so on. Another diagram
shows that the 10-year-old has acquired six skills in self-help
(table habits) and five in the area of self-help (dressing). The P-E-I,
relating to age 6 to 16 conveniently summarizes the facts which
were given in Figures 18 to 29 (see pages 84 to 86).

A child is compared with these norms by shading in the number of
attainments in each section and superimposing this block achievement over the cross-hatching of the relevant age group on the P-E-I.

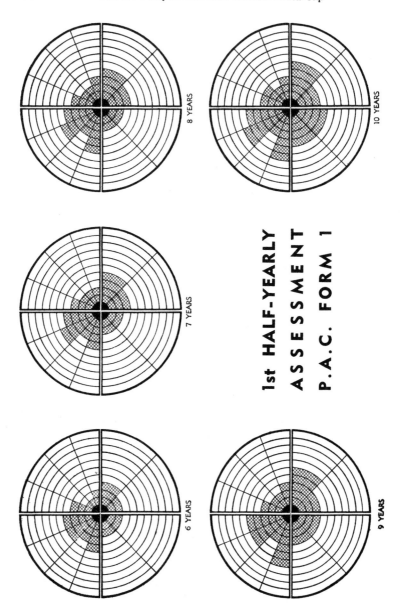

Fig. 42. Part of the Progress Evaluation Index (P-E-I).

The P-E-I folders contain the norms of the Birmingham Group and provide space for 20 P-A-C forms. The diagrams make it possible to summarize half-yearly assessments of the individual pupil and to compare him, at the same time, with his peers.

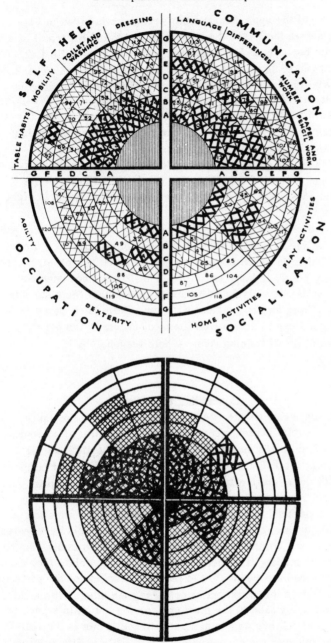

Fig. 43. P-A-C 1 and P-E-I of an individual child.

An example of the application of this technique is given in Figure 43 which shows the P-A-C 1 assessment and the P-E-I result of a 15-year-old boy. His P-A-C 1 showed proficiency in skills 1, 2, 18, 19, 34 and 93 in the subsection Table Habits. In consequence six spaces, starting from the centre, are shaded in the P-E-I diagram relating to the 15-year-old group. (The subsections of the P-E-I are arranged in the same order as on the P-A-C 1). However, two spaces on the P-E-I show still the cross-hatching indicating that children of that age-group have generally mastered 8 skills out of 10. The boy is very backward in toilet and washing compared with his age group and only 4 spaces can be filled in for skills 5, 21, 22 and 38, though the average attainment of that group is eight skills.

This youth must be considered as generally rather backward, and this may be due to over-protection at home for he fails to score in self-help skills in which assistance can be given by mother; he also scores very poorly in home activities. The boy has not been encouraged to assist actively at home because mother feels she has to do everything *for* him, and not *with* him. There is no gross physical handicap to account for the total failure in the agility section and lack of training must be held responsible.

Concluding Remarks

The assessments on the P-A-C and P-E-I indicate the quality and quantity of social achievements. Whereas the scatter of achievement on P-A-C 1 indicates qualitative features of the child's social performance, the P-E-I measures the level of achievement comparing it with the average attainment of his age group of similar intellectual functioning.

The two methods described can help to assess the situation of individual cases or of a whole group. It must, however, be repeated once again that, helpful as such procedure can be, it could also be extremely misleading if the assessor failed to appreciate that the results obtained are meant only to induce the asking of the pertinent question: Why is this child better or worse than others? It should not automatically lead to the teacher's forcing the child's pace in an attempt to achieve an average performance if this is not realistic. Dealing with the exceptional child of little ability requires much judgment and very careful evaluation of the individual factors which can be responsible for progress or backwardness. On the other hand, knowledge of what can be achieved by children with a similar mental disability could help to encourage training and education in aspects which might otherwise be neglected. Special provisions can be made to help children to acquire the experience and practice of which they have apparently been deprived.

It must be noted that the norms used in this survey are probably very low. They have been generally lowered by the inclusion of severely handicapped children in the Birmingham sample and do not indicate that a more advanced performance could not be achieved. In Figures 38 to 41 (see p. 92) for example, many of the hospitalized children are shown to have done better than the average child in the training centre, probably mainly because inadequate staffing necessitated the practising of skills with which the child would not have been entrusted at home by overprotective parents.

On no account should it be thought that norms are indicative of a *potential* for social competence. They simply reflect the average degree of social efficiency reached in particular areas by groups of mentally handicapped children at the time of assessment, and the ceiling level of possible achievement may be considerably higher.

4

THE LESSON: ACADEMIC OR SOCIAL EDUCATION?

We have seen that the mentally retarded person has handicaps which are partly of an intellectual nature, as reflected by low intelligence test results, and are partly defects in personality make-up which can be observed. The main features appear to be weakness of drive to overcome frustration, slowness of thinking, and immaturity. This unhappy combination of intellectual and personality deficiencies leads to many difficulties in the individual's adjustment to the demands of life and work. In many retarded people these handicaps are so profound that nothing much can be done to help them and the main task is one of nursing and general care, but in other cases certain adjustments can be achieved. There is some evidence to suggest that a minimum of social competence does not directly depend on intelligence as measured by an intelligence test, but on many other factors such as personality, experience, adequate training, and some desire in the child to learn and to understand.

The situation is so complex that it is impossible to say what is cause and what is effect in every case and in every area of social inadequacy. Observation shows that the mentally handicapped person often displays more ability to cope with a life situation than we would expect from someone of his intelligence. On the other hand a defective may give up a problem with the excuse 'I don't know', but persistent prodding frequently shows that the correct answer was known all the time yet he simply does not bother. Evidence has also been produced which suggests a continuous, though slow, learning process and acquisition of social knowledge in a good proportion of severely handicapped people. Compared with normal children their development is slow, laborious and incomplete but well-directed effort results often in a marked improvement (see p. 192).

The problems of education and training are very similar whether we are dealing with the young moderately retarded who has been to school but proves socially inadequate subsequently, or with the severely retarded whose pronounced intellectual handicap seems to make it impossible for him to learn, even mechanically.

It is the proven social inadequacy and not the mental handicap that attracts our constant attention. This inadequacy is associated with intellectual inferiority, although low intelligence is not automatically responsible for social incompetence. It has been estimated that at least one million people in Britain have an IQ below 70, but only approximately 150,000 are under hospital or local authority care. In the USA 5.4 million children and adults (3% of the population) are regarded as mentally retarded in varying degrees. About 400,000 are inadequate enough to require constant care or supervision and the remaining 5 million, though less retarded, present a considerable social problem. Discrepancies between the expected and the actual numbers of people who need supervision are to some extent due to the use of different definitions, but nevertheless they do point to the fact that social adequacy is possible *despite* intellectual deficiencies.

There is no evidence that the educational inadequacies discussed in chapter two are associated with the social incompetence which led to admission to hospitals after leaving school. Detailed records of the social knowledge of subnormals who have not come to the attention of the authorities are not available, and thus the question whether possession of social knowledge is associated with social success cannot be answered for the time being. However, it is reasonable to assume that the possession of relevant social skills will help the mentally handicapped both in the routine tasks of living and working in the community and in tackling new situations with confidence. It is also reasonable to assume that the subnormal, like the normal person, often underfunctions and does not always give of his best. Whereas a normal person can usually work and live sufficiently adequately on this basis, the mentally handicapped person's abilities are so inadequate to start with and his drive may be so low that he slides the more readily well below an acceptable level of social adequacy. The type of failure—social inadequacy— and the limitations of intelligence—shown by low IQ—call for education and training of a kind very different from that of the normal school. Many of the severely retarded are able to learn many, or most, of the comparatively simple social skills which would enable them to live and work effectively in an undemanding environment. The moderately and mildly retarded adult has sufficient intelligence to cope with the simple routine requirements of normal life situations, yet though he is well past the maturational stages of the young child, he has many deficiencies which are a constant source of embarrassment and frustration.

Lack of academic knowledge plays some part in the social inadequacy of the moderately retarded, but little in the social incompetence of the severely retarded. Some knowledge of school subjects would be helpful to the moderately and mildly handicapped although, if other factors are favourable— a stable personality, a supportive family, an understanding work situation— illiteracy is often scarcely more than an annoying handicap. If, on the other hand, those favourable factors are absent, the scholastic handicap can become the focal point of an increasing awareness of inadequacy. Feelings of educational inferiority can be very destructive and the treatment of personality troubles will thus be effectively supported by an educational programme which deals with the subnormal's academic backwardness. Illiteracy is often therefore only a problem insofar as the retarded himself is conscious of his failings. Some aspects of literacy are more important than others—reading is less important than ability to handle money, and it is more important to be able to add money than to multiply it. On the other hand, the individual might value higher the prestige of being able to read than ability to deal with his wage packet.

It becomes essential to clarify the relationship between academic and social education, particularly on account of the limited time available for teaching, the handicap of low intelligence and the social requirements of adult life.

In Figure 44A the inverted inner shaded cone indicates the growth of academic education given to a normal child. In the tip of the cone are the tool subjects, reading, writing and arithmetic, which are essential for the mastery of subjects to be studied later, and it can be seen that the whole of specialized and general knowledge rests on these comparatively modest skills. Education of the subnormal child could also start with the 3 R's, yet it is obvious that the acquisition of these skills does not lead to the more complex knowledge possessed by the normal child. We know that the subnormal will not acquire much geography, history or biology, and even if he were capable of learning these subjects this knowledge would be beyond his understanding.

Social education is represented by the outer cones in Figure 44. They surround the inner cones of academic education and it will be seen that social learning starts before academic education. Social education comprises the type of knowledge which usually need not be taught but is learnt informally during the early years of life. It has been said that the IQ indicates the ability to absorb incidental knowledge[1]. Thus a normal child with an average IQ will acquire such knowledge quite easily whilst the mentally handi-capped child has only a much impaired ability to gather such

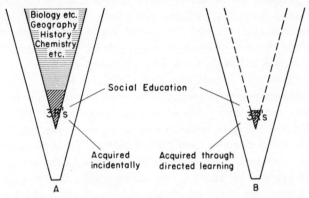

Fig. 44. The social and academic education of the normal (A) and sub-normal (B) child.

information. He therefore needs much more demonstration and explanation, and his attention must often be drawn to specific events and to the information to be deduced. Figure 44 compares the educational requirements of the normal and the subnormal child; A (normal child) shows the emphasis of teaching applied to academic education; B (mentally handicapped) indicates that much '3R work' may be unnecessary because the academic knowledge it is supposed to support will never be achieved, and social skills have to be taught which are of importance but need not specially be learnt by the normal child.

[1]Wall *et al.* (1962) maintain that an intelligence test does not measure largely *innate* capacity because it will always be contaminated by learning. The difference between an attainment test, such as a test of reading or arithmetic knowledge, and an intelligence test is, simply, that the first type of test samples learning 'which has been based on deliberate and systematic teaching', whilst the second type samples learning 'which has taken place in the wider, less structured environment of the home and community—as well as at the school.'

Considerations of this kind make it quite clear that the education of the mentally handicapped child, should be governed by other principles than those determining the formal education of the normal. Emphasis must be laid on those social skills which are necessary to achieve some relative competence in life. This requires not only that the general direction of the education of the mentally handicapped child should be clearly indicated as being 'different', but also that the targets to be achieved must be stated in as concrete and accurate terms as possible.

In many respects the definition of the targets is fairly simple. If the diagnosis of mental handicap is reliable, then the ceiling level of achievement is clearly indicated. There is no likelihood that a child with severe mental handicap will succeed in achieving a higher position in life than that of a semi-skilled worker and in fact most adults will do unskilled work. Only in the best cases could they be trained for a particular semi-skilled operation which is repetitive and requires little adjustment to new situations. In the social field too, not much flexibility or achievement can be expected from the mentally handicapped person. His social attainments will be modest, his interest in society will be limited and his functioning will be within a very narrow circle. The teacher therefore knows that she needs to aim only at very modest targets. Whilst this is of great assistance in planning the curriculum for the mentally handicapped, it must not be forgotten that his limited intellectual abilities slow down not only the rate of progress but affect also his power to apply many of the skills which he could learn in a mechanical manner. It is here that the challenge lies, and it is of little consequence to try to raise achievement levels for 'classroom use' when we can be quite certain that these skills cannot be effectively applied in day to day circumstances.

To sum-up, the education of the mentally handicapped child should be considered in terms different to those of the normal child. Because of his innate limitations, emphasis should be placed on those aspects which are of immediate use to him as an adult. Little purpose is served by using a syllabus designed for the young normal child. Since the purpose of education is to provide a reasonable all-round knowledge which will help in adult life, it is unreasonable to try to convey the same type of education to the subnormal with his considerable handicaps, as to the normal who will later take his full place in society. Education of the subnormal should therefore be directed from the beginning towards his limited role in later life and must disregard many aspects of the normal school curriculum, because they represent useless acquisitions and their learning takes up far too much time.

5

THE FRAMEWORK

Having considered the type of person we are attempting to help, his attainments, the methods for assessing and evaluating his achievements and having also come to some conclusion as to the form his education and training should take, it is now time to describe the training facilities in England.

Short Survey of the Existing Services for the Mentally Handicapped

Since 1971 all children of school age, including those who were formally known as ineducable or trainable children, have become the responsibility of the Education Authorities. This applies to all children whether living at home or in hospital. This was done through an amendment to the 1944 Education Act and it is now a statutory duty for local authorities to provide education for all children.

The statutory leaving age is 16, but many schools keep children within the educational system after that age. Depending on a place being available, and the head teacher feeling that a child will be able to benefit from staying on, special education is now available for children up to the age of 19 years.

After the child has left school, and if he still requires support he may, if living at home, attend daily a local authority training centre. Otherwise, he may be resident in an institution or hospital. There is, nowadays, a tendency to emphasize the desirability of keeping a mentally handicapped child in the family and in the community. Yet, sending a mentally handicappe child to a hospital or institution where special services are easily available, could be of more benefit to him than remaining at home. It would be wrong to say that hospital care should only be considered if everything else has failed, for in many cases it can be a positive advantage to the child if he is not brought up in an over-protected household and is given an early opportunity to develop some independence away from home. It will have to be decided in each individual case which type of attention will best serve his needs, and indeed whether the quality of attention available will be adequate.

Local Authority Services

(a) *Pre-School Provisions*

A comparatively recent development has been the provision by local authorities of special care units catering for profoundly retarded children, many of whom are physically handicapped and may be deaf, blind, spastic or epileptic. Many children are relatively immobile. Whilst there is obviously a danger that in these circumstances a 'caring' attitude will develop, which accepts these extremely disabling conditions, the educational purpose of these units is to stimulate the children and to help the children to learn to observe and thus to develop. Recent research work has demonstrated quite clearly that stimulation cannot begin too early, and that many of our difficulties in the management of the mentally handicapped are due to the fact that early stimulation has been completely neglected (see Gunzburg and Gunzburg, 1973).

The units also often accept children who are less retarded and would be suitable for the E.S.N. (S) school, but for the very disturbed behaviour which makes it impossible to mix them with other children. The existence of these units has made it possible for many parents to keep their profoundly disturbed retarded children at home (whereas in the past they had to go into residential care) and to initiate educational stimulation programmes on a far more individualized basis.

There is also an increasing number of pre-school units (either for the handicapped only, or for normal children) which admit handicapped children. Quite a few of these have been initiated by voluntary groups, but the local education authorities often make grants towards the running of them. Many local education authorities appoint peripatetic teachers to visit the homes of mentally handicapped children 'below statutory school age' in order to help the mother cater for the child's educational and other developmental needs, as well as to do a little counselling. In exceptional cases, these teachers will also attend to the needs of children of school age (see (d)).

(b) *Special Schools for the Severely Subnormal Child (E.S.N.(S))*

The former junior training centres for the severely mentally handicapped child have now become Special Schools and are part of the school system dealing with the educationally subnormal child. They are referred to as E.S.N.(S) schools to differentiate them from the E.S.N.(M) schools which deal with a mildly handicapped child, usually with an IQ above 55.

Many E.S.N.(S) schools, admit, nowadays, children below the statutory age of five years, and some of them admit children of about two years.

(c) *Adult Training Centres*

Around the age of 16 youngsters are transferred to training centres, known as adult training centres, industrial training centres or sheltered workshops. As explained above some of the older school children are kept at school even after the age of 16, and one can only hope that this tendency will in due course become a regular feature for the mentally handicapped child, who very often becomes receptive to more formal education only by that age.

Adult training centres also accept trainees with IQs above 50, many of whom have attended schools for educationally subnormal children (E.S.N.(M)) and thus the range of ability in the adult training centres is much wider than in the E.S.N.(S) schools.

Most of these centres are designed primarily to provide occupation and employment for those mentally handicapped people who, for one reason or another, cannot be trained to work in the open community. Many of them can, however, contribute, often quite substantially, to their upkeep. Industrial workshops are very often run in close liaison with industry, which provides work to be processed in the training centre and returned to the employer.

There is fortunately, realization breaking through that intensive industrial training *by itself* tends to put a ceiling on the mentally handicapped person's possible social achievements. Some progressive training centres have instituted training programmes which attach as much attention to social as to industrial training, and in a few notable cases, a very careful and documented training, programme has been developed which is designed to 'stretch' the trainee's abilities, rather than only to occupy him usefully (Morley and Appell, 1974).

(d) *Home Teaching*

Some mentally handicapped, both children and adults, are unable to attend any of the facilities described above, either because of geographical reasons or because they are so handicapped that they cannot be transported. For them, home teaching is the only possible solution as far as children are concerned, but this of course cannot provide the experience and stimulation afforded by a community of children under the supervision and guidance of a teacher. Similarly, handicapped adults are deprived of the companionship of others of the same mental level, and miss the opportunities of learning to live and work in a group.

Residential Facilities

The best education and training can be provided, in a majority of cases, by the combination of a good family setting and active school and training centre teaching. Yet there are often circumstances which make it advisable to consider the provisions made by the hospital which gives assistance on a residential basis. Profoundly handicapped children are typical nursing liabilities and may sometime become such a problem in the family that hospital care is advisable. In many other cases, the handicapped person's behaviour is so disturbed and fails entirely to respond to guidance, that neither the school nor training centre nor family supervision can adequately control it. In these cases, education and training away from home can often succeed in making the child or adult accessible and responsive and may result in his return to home and the community.

Most hospitals have residential E.S.N.(S) schools which provide the same educational assistance as E.S.N.(S) schools in the community. There are also a few comparable residential provisions for children which cater for a five day stay with weekends at home, but also if necessary a seven day stay.

On the whole the educational system has become very flexible, and many hospital schools have 'day pupils' and some hospitals send some of their residential children to E.S.N.(S) schools or other schools in the community.

As far as adults are concerned admission to hospital is generally as an 'informal patient' (voluntary) which makes it possible for the patient to leave whenever he wishes, even against the doctor's advice. Some mentally handicapped people who come before the Courts are sent to hospital on a Hospital or Restriction Order; they are detained there for their own protection and to safeguard society, but the patient and his nearest relatives have the right of appeal against the Order. Regular reviews of all cases under Hospital or Restriction Orders are made to ensure that no mentally handicapped person is detained longer than necessary.

The hospital provides for the adult mentally handicapped, training and education similar to that given at the local authority training centre. Some hospitals have social education units which continue the social education work of the E.S.N.(S) school, and they also provide for further education in evening classes (Bland, 1974). All hospitals have maintenance workshops which provide some vocational training for patients and occupation is available in special hospital workshops. The old fashioned weaving, brush-mat-and basket-making has generally disappeared and has been supplanted by industrial occupations identical with those found in the sheltered workshops run by the local authority.

It appears that the local authority generally provides services only during daytime, whilst the hospital provides a residential 24-hour service. However, many hospitals now arrange for day hospital treatment for patients returning home at night; and, on the other hand, local authorities have made hostel arrangements for young children at the residential E.S.N.(S) school which permit them to return home every weekend. Many hospitals also have short stay provisions for children and adults to help parents who have to go to hospital or who wish to go on a well-deserved holiday.

Group Homes and Hostels

Increasing emphasis is put on the provision of facilities for adult mentally handicapped people, which would permit them to live a fuller life in the community than residence in hospitals would permit. The realization that a good proportion of mentally handicapped adults at present residing in hospitals for the subnormal are there only for 'social' reasons (Leck *et al.* 1967; McKeown and Teruel, 1970) but do not require the nursing and medical care which one would expect to be needed in a hospital, has resulted in providing alternative accommodation in the community, managed on nonmedical lines.

Whilst it is recognized that many mentally handicapped adults are able to live an independent life in the community, and do not require constant support, there are many others who need help to different degrees (Browne *et al.* 1971). Mentally handicapped adults who require some form of humane 'hotel keeping' which insures that personal needs are properly met, are nowadays placed in hostels under the supervision of a warden or hostel parent. Many of the residents will go to regular work, but there are also quite a few hostels which cater for 'retired mentally handicapped people'.

The group home is a fairly new development and refers to a very small group of four to five mentally handicapped people who reside in a house in the community. There is no warden and the necessary help is given by friendly visits from social workers or other interested people when required. The group caters for its own needs, sharing in the shopping and budgeting problems, providing for their own entertainment and keeping the house in order. The members of the group go to work, have their holidays, and lead, generally speaking, as normal a life as most unmarried people in the community, who live by themselves or with friends (Gemmell, 1974).

Staffing

The training of teachers for mentally handicapped children is now the responsibility of the education authorities. The situation has changed dramatically compared with the very inadequate provisions available before 1971. There are now twenty colleges which provide a basic three year course for teachers of S.S.N. children, and a few of these provide facilities for a B.Ed. degree. The professional status of teachers of S.S.N. children is now comparable with that of the 'ordinary' teacher because they have either taken the basic three year course, or have fulfilled the requirements of five years service, after having taken the diploma which was formerly obtained via a one year or two year course.

The situation has not improved so dramatically in respect of the teachers of mentally handicapped adults. There is still no clear realization that the mentally handicapped adult requires social, rather than work training, for a few years after leaving school and thus professional training of the teacher of adults is not comparable with that of the teacher of mentally handicapped children. At the time of revising this chapter (November, 1974) the one year courses for the teachers of the mentally handicapped adult, which had been supervised by the Training Council for Teachers of the Mentally Handicapped, have been taken over by the Central Council for Education and Training and Social Work and further developments can be expected.

The Social Education and Training Centre, the Development Centre (General Principles)

Having outlined the provisions nowadays in existence the author proposes to give a short outline of a comprehensive approach to the task of providing Social Education and Training irrespective whether it is carried out at school or an adult training centre. As the term 'training centre' implies the task is training and not merely occupation. In fact, a training centre should provide directed education and training of a kind which cannot easily be given at home, because the parents do not have the requisite knowledge, skills or time. Its primary task is not to 'mind' the mentally handicapped child or to train the adult into a 'worker' but rather to stretch the mentally handicapped to the fullest of his ability during and after his school years. The term 'Social Education and Training Centre' or even better 'Development Centre' applies therefore, to any active social rehabilitation scheme of mentally handicapped people, whether child or adult, and simply indicates the emphasis which should be put on one particular aspect of education by developing latent abilities for social living.

The Social Education and Training Centre or Development Centre should cater in three stages for (a) young children, as is done in the pre-school provisions, and in the junior classes of the E.S.N.(S) school (b) senior children, (the older children in the E.S.N.(S) school and adolescent people in adult training centres), (c) for young adult people who are at present found in adult training centres and in hospital workshops. The centre should not deal with those mentally handicapped people who are profoundly retarded and in need to permanent protective care or who can work only in sheltered workshops.

In the following discussion of the Social Education and Training Centre, age ranges are mentioned to give some idea of the composition of the population in each stage. However, transfer from one stage to the other should be handled flexibly in accordance with the individual's maturity and application, and not be dependent on age.

(a) The Primary Development Centre

In view of the mentally handicapped child's very moderate abilities, the junior stage of his education should emphasize the learning of those skills and knowledge that will be of immediate use to him as an adult. In practical terms this means teaching habits and skills which make the mentally handicapped socially acceptable (self-help), assisting him in learning how to live with others (socialization), how to make himself useful (occupation) and lastly but not least important, developing as much as possible his ability to use and understand spoken language (communication).

Moderately and severely handicapped children are not only intellectually on a lower level than normal children of the same age, they are also emotionally very young, often physically under-developed, and they lag socially behind their contemporaries. Because they are emotionally young, they have the emotional needs of young children: they require love, emotional warmth, a feeling of security, and a feeling of achievement. Since they are intellectually in the preschool stage, formal educational work has to be postponed and reading, writing and arithmetic will very often not be learnt before the age of perhaps 14. Though they may be more advanced physically than intellectually and emotionally, compared with their contemporaries, they show gross disturbances in motor control, as seen in their inability to succeed in balancing exercises or simple ball games. Partly because of over protection at home and partly because of lack of encouragement, the mentally handicapped is also socially very often more inadequate than need be. Since severely handicapped children are emotionally and intellectually at a preschool stage, education and training should also be at that level, and play should be encouraged to stimulate a natural growth of the physical, social, practical and intellectual skills (Neale, 1966). In effect the nursery stage is extended to give the child ample opportunity of collecting important experiences. Play acting, singing, talking, taking turns and sharing with others, manipulation of objects and similar activities are important to the final aims of training. Play with sand and water, with sticks, blocks, dolls and other toys, provide an excellent foundation for acquiring fundamental concepts relating to number, length, size, space, which are essential for understanding the formal aspects of later more formal training.

Many severely handicapped children have to be stimulated and encouraged because they are physically handicapped or have auditory or perceptual difficulties. Their interests and needs have to be explored, otherwise they are unable to understand what is happening around them and feelings of insecurity may develop leading to a succession of failures. The child must be provided with opportunities for finding out, for learning by doing, and for experiencing and tackling new and unfamiliar situations. The aim should be to develop a curriculum which consists of activities which are undertaken because the children are interested in them and because they relate to their future life in their communities.

Despite the numerous activities and opportunities which should be provided for play and exploration in the general nursery atmosphere of the junior stage, the need for systematic teaching even at that stage should not be overlooked. These children have learning handicaps which are of quite a specific nature and they are unable to overcome them by themselves. They have, for example, very poor memories for comparatively meaningless stimuli — and indeed most stimuli of the everyday world are probably meaningless to them because they are unable to make them meaningful. They cannot easily and naturally assimilate verbal conventions and thus their spontaneous language development lags well behind. They are poor in their ability of incorporating stimuli in generalizations and associations and are thus handicapped in applying to new situations what they have learned in other contexts. Attention begins soon to wander because they cannot differentiate between relevant and irrelevant visual and auditory cues, and their visual and auditory world must be rather chaotic in the absence of firm landmarks. However, skills of this nature are essential at later stages when academic subjects (reading, writing and arithmetic) have to be learned and social skills have not only to be acquired but applied to many different situations.

The junior stage of the Development Centre should, therefore, set about to encourage those deficient primary skills without which the child will not be able to tackle the learning task at all. If he has not learned to perceive correctly essential features, to store information that can be recalled at will, to select from the store the relevant information and to reproduce that information adequately, all efforts directed to teaching 'school work' will be wasted because the basic skills necessary for learning are too under-developed to be of use. Exercises in the form of games and play activities will have to become a regular feature of the classroom syllabus at this stage to teach children 'how to learn' whilst leaving the actual contents of learning, (i.e. social and academic skills) mostly to later, more mature, stages. It cannot be emphasized too much that the subject-oriented school approach, consisting of a number of different courses of lessons such as number work, writing and reading, is quite unsuitable in the junior stage.

(b) The Secondary Development Centre

At one time it was thought that the mental mechanism had fully developed by about the sixteenth year and that any further improvement was due to experience and to the better application of acquired skills. Recent research, however, has shown that mental development continues well after the age of 16 and various schools of thought have suggested ages ranging from 16 to 20 and older. Thus, it is quite unjustifiable to deprive handicapped persons of opportunities of acquiring more useful knowledge and experience. The practice of offering only a limited workshop training after the age of 16 assumes also that mental, physical and emotional development proceed at the same rate and reach equal maturation at approximately the same time, and this of course is not necessarily true. In some cases physical development will be normal, but emotional development may be retarded even more than mental development. In consequence, transferring a youngster from a junior to an adult training centre at the age of 16 may be justifiable in terms of his physical development, but may be quite unreasonable considering his emotional development and should certainly not interfere with his further full social education.

At present the adult training centre is an adult environment—a work environment, and a trainee is expected to learn various work skills and to prepare himself for adult life, when he should be able to make a work contribution. The sudden change from junior-nursery environment to the adult workshop environment must often be an unexpected and terrifying experience. The demands of the workshop do not permit continuity of the educational approach practised at the junior stage and the adult training centre is not able to incorporate in the work situation the knowledge which the child has acquired in the preceding stage of schooling. In view of the fact that mental development does not come to a standstill at 16 and the subnormal has probably not acquired by then sufficient knowledge to use the skills he has been taught, transferring him to an 'one-sided' environment which is interested only in developing his manual skills will make it virtually impossible for him to obtain enough assistance in developing other essential aspects in personal and social functioning.

It has been argued that the social knowledge required by the young adult will be picked up in the workshop through the day-to-day routine. However, one of the most characteristic features of the mentally handicapped is his lack of curiosity, his weak or undirected drive and his inability to gather relevant information and to utilize it. The very experience which help a normal person to grow up because he is able to draw conclusions from what he sees, leave no impression on the mentally handicapped. It is misplaced optimism to assume that the mentally handicapped will be able to benefit by incidental experience in an adult environment in the same way as a maturing normal adolescent.

The transition stage between the junior-nursery and senior workshop stages will provide academic education, as far as necessary, but the emphasis will have to be placed on social education which requires the relatively more mature mind of the teenager. Formal training in industrial skills and habits can easily be postponed until the mentally handicapped pupil is older. Nevertheless, most of the materials, tools and machines used in the workshop, and the general approach to work can and should be introduced as an aid to learning. For example, screws, nuts, bolts etc., can by now replace the counters and beads of the junior stage as teaching material. Since these youngsters will soon have to move to an adult environment, familiarity with industrial materials will help to ease their adjustment. They should also be encouraged to use tools for repairs, for constructing and for hobbies.

Since the children are now more mature, many of the social skills required in life can be taught in practical situations, and running errands, taking messages, going shopping, using public transport, taking care of pets, shouldering minor domestic responsibilities should become part of the syllabus of this transition stage.[1]

It is noticeable that the mentally handicapped are generally better in the areas of self-help and occupation than in communication (Fig. 9, p. 77). The latter now requires particular attention and programmes should be developed to encourage the growth of communication skills rather than vocational skills which can be acquired later during the senior stage.

(c) The Secondary Development Centre (Upper Section)

The upper section of the Secondary Development Centre might seem to be identical with the adult training centre of the local authority and the workshops of the hospital. The classroom atmosphere of the transition stage has been exchanged for a workshop atmosphere, and social training which previously played such an important part, is now less prominent, though it is still important.

The adult training centre and the workshops of the hospital generally try to procure industrial subcontract work from the community, partly to familiarize the mentally handicapped with industrial processes and machinery and to train him for employment, and partly to keep him busy and content and to encourage a sense of responsibility and maturity. Compared with the Social Education and Training Centre the essential difference is one of *purpose.* In the Social Education and Training Centre, industrial contract work is used for training a variety of skills which could help towards social rehabilitation in the community. On the other hand in most adult training centres and workshops in hospitals, industrial work takes the place of old

---

[1] An account of the activities in the transition stage of the Social Education and Training Centre has been given by C. Moorman (1967).

fashioned occupational activities such as rug making, basket making and brush making, but is nevertheless not meant to be part of a comprehensive rehabilitation scheme. In these cases industrial work is an end in itself not a means to an end. It is essential to keep this distinction in mind when deciding the role of industrial work in the senior stage. There is little doubt that certain aspects of industrial contract work do not marry happily with the requirements of education and training in the senior stage, and are best left to the sheltered workshop where the considerations of a directed rehabilitation scheme do not apply.

The introduction of industrial processes into the senior stage has far-reaching effects, and has many advantages from the training point of view. The work is realistic and the trainee appreciates that this is the kind of work which would be demanded from him as a wage earner in ordinary conditions. In contract work quantities are usually large and help to maintain an atmosphere of 'busyness' and industry. The work requires the use of a variety of tools and sometimes simple machinery, and these help to make these tasks look more 'man-sized' and more attractive than many other occupations. Moreover, industrial jobs of this kind require little skill, yet the large quantities produced give the handicapped worker a feeling of satisfaction and achievement.

Much of this industrial work could provide learning opportunities for social rehabilitation. In practice, however, it is quite impossible to satisfy the demands made by subcontract work and still carry out a complete social rehabilitation programme, for few employers can afford to write off large wastage incurred in course of training, irregular deliveries or indifferent quality. In consequence, the adult centres must make use of techniques and arrangements which minimize the complaints and ensure the goodwill of firms and a continuity of work.

Jobs have been broken down into many very simple operations and the mentally retarded are trained to carry out one particular operation successfully; jigs have been designed to make it possible to execute satisfactorily and speedily some of the more complicated jobs in large quantities without much error. Nonetheless, the jig makes it impossible for a worker to learn by his mistakes, because a jig does not make mistakes. The more foolproof the jig, the less opportunity to learn, and so tasks which should be used to reinforce learning are executed mechanically and without thought. The presence of a jig deprives the learner of an important and realistic learning situation. If, let us say, a jig is built to enable a worker to cut off systematically and without error a 6 in. length of article, he will never have an opportunity to learn, by measuring, how long six inches are. As the senior stage is to provide opportunities for error and mistakes, and thereby for learning from mistakes, there must also be time to teach how to avoid the errors and mistakes, and learning opportunities must not be sacrificed to expediency. However, it should be pointed out that the use of jigs and assembly lines with jobs broken down into small manageable operations is fully justified in the sheltered workshop, (see p. 117).

Contract work is best left to the sheltered workshop and the senior stage should only accept industrial jobs which serve the purpose of training. For practical purposes it may be best for the sheltered workshop to arrange for all the industrial contract work and to make some of it available to the senior training centres. An agreement should be reached with the supplying firms for flexible delivery dates, and wastage and breakage should be paid for by the Social Education and Training Centre.

Much of the industrial work contracted out by firms and factories is of an assembly line character and is usually carried out by female labour. Though, obviously, some aspects of this work are very suitable for general work-training in the senior stage, it will have to be augmented by providing experience with other types of work. Local authorities can often arrange for other useful work such as repairing simple furniture, making concrete slabs, making seed boxes, etc. There is also a traditional, but lately rather neglected type of training in market gardening and farming. These types of work have tended to become overlooked in the enthusiasm for the more glamorous industrial work with its larger earning potential. Yet the efficiency required by industrial concerns can adversely affect the flexibility of a training scheme adjusted to the need of the mentally handicapped rather than to the needs of the employing industry.

The emphasis in the senior stage must be on learning on the job, utilizing, the industrial work itself which provides countless opportunities for measuring, weighing, counting, assessing and discriminating situations which are realistic and far removed from classroom practice. Specific weaknesses of the mentally handicapped such as lack of speed, application, workmanship, manual dexterity, timekeeping, attention to tools and material, could be improved in carefully worked out training schemes (Whelan, 1974). However, training on actual jobs in realistic working conditions is only part of the task and it is just as important to encourage the development of personal qualities, understanding of the social give-and-take, and ability to fit in with others. Work carried out during the transition stage must still be continued and trainees must, therefore, still practice the skills of how to cross streets, how to spend leisure time, etc. Schoolroom situations become life situations if trainees have to sign their names, enter their times of arrival and departure on time sheets, understand deductions from their wage packets and learn to relate their earnings to their shopping requirements.

It cannot be stressed too often that work training by itself is insufficient to make the mentally handicapped function adequately in society. He must be given many opportunities for learning, but no incidental learning will take place unless his attention is constantly drawn to the various important facts. This means that time must be available and teachers must be free to devote their energy to teaching and not to supervising a production line. Premature full-time work in a sheltered workshop may make the mentally handicapped socially more inefficient than need be unless the one-sided training of the workshop is supplemented by continuing training of the kind begun earlier in the transition stage of the Social Education and Training Centre.

The 'Finishing School' for the Mentally Handicapped

Towards the end of the senior stage, a decision will have to be made concerning the future of each trainee. A small proportion will be capable of living and working in the community. They will have been given careful training in essential skills, but, nevertheless, these skills must be practised daily and have to be applied to new situations to give confidence and experience. It may therefore be necessary to provide a 'finishing school' away from home for the mentally handicapped where their development can be further guided and encouraged. With some help, the young mentally handicapped adult, living temporarily in a new environment, is guided towards the experience of living in a community, of meeting other people and moving about in unfamiliar surroundings. Parents of mentally handicapped children are naturally overprotective and in consequence the children may continue to lack first hand experience of 'social know-how' unless some such 'finishing school' plan can be used to ease the transition from school to work in unsheltered surroundings. The results of such training are discussed on pages 186 to 195.

The Sheltered Workshop

The essential difference between the senior stage of the Social Education and Training or Development Centre and the sheltered workshop is that the senior stage *prepares* for work whilst the sheltered workshop *provides* work. Both Centre and workshop are, of course, 'sheltered' because they cater for those who are incapable at the time of taking their place in normal society. The Centre, however, provides a special education prior to settling in the open community, and the sheltered workshop a work setting specially geared to the needs of those who require a more less permanently protective environment.

The proportion of severely mentally handicapped adults who will never be capable of living in ordinary conditions, irrespective of the amount and quality of their education and training is difficult to estimate. It has been suggested that 10% to 20% of the severely handicapped population could work in sheltered employment outside sheltered workshops, and this proportion could well be larger if a determined effort were made to train people and to provide suitable work and living conditions in the community. Thus we should at present expect that at least 80% of the severely handicapped people will have to be found accommodation in sheltered workshops, either in the community or in hospital. These are people who have probably profited as much as they can from special education and training and must be taught the occupational skills which would help them to carry out satisfactorily some work operations.

The points raised in the discussion of the senior stage of the Social Education and Training Centre need no longer be considered since the purpose now is occupation and work. 'Occupational therapy' such as weaving or pottery can be introduced since the people in the sheltered workshop need not be prepared for outside industrial work. It may even be wise to encourage such schemes to provide alternative employment and occupation in case industrial supplies of work should become less plentiful for one or the other reason.

The jig and the assembly line, which permit a breakdown of work into many easily managed operations, will be the most characteristic feature of a busy sheltered workshop. In an efficiently run production shop ingenious arrangements can contribute greatly to increased output of work which might not have been expected from such a severely handicapped working population.

There is great need for the provision of this type of sheltered employment in conditions adjusted to very severe handicap. It is also very satisfying to the handicapped person himself, to his family and to those who are responsible for him, if he can contribute to his support by earning a financial reward rather than receiving pocket money. Some industrial work, e.g. assembling, dismantling, is ideal for this purpose and the financial return is most satisfactory. This must, however, not misdirect our attention from the fact that other forms of work can give the same satisfaction and keep the mentally handicapped happy and busy, and that it is not always necessary to insist on industrial work as being the only solution for occupying the severely mentally handicapped. (See discussion of 'occupational activity area' in Gunzburg and Gunzburg, 1973.)

Hostels

There is need for two entirely different types of hostel and as in the case of the adult training centre and sheltered w rkshop, it is necessary to ensure that the ultimate purpose is not sacrificed to administrative convenience. One type of hostel serves as a half-way house on the road to rehabilitation and is similar in purpose to the finishing school (p. 116). It is transitional in character and great care should be taken that hostel places are not occupied for too long by those who were thought to have a good chance of rehabilitation but who never made the grade. It is a stepping stone from the protected to the open community (Gunzburg, 1975).

The other type of hostel provides, essentially, a home for those mentally handicapped who cannot live independently in society but, nevertheless, do not require institutional or hospital care. Far too many hospital beds are occupied by subnormal adults who do not require medical or nursing care, although they need some supervision. Large hostels for them would be not only more economical, but could also be situated in the community and so have the advantage of being in close contact with normal society. Staffing need not be such a problem since all that is required is good home-making and housekeeping. Some of the residents would be in full-time, part-time or casual employment and thus be able to contribute to their support, but others would be pensioners in the full sense of the word although most would be capable of helping with the work of the hostel.

There is little doubt that a large (custodial) hostel would soon acquire the lethargic and unstimulating atmosphere so characteristic of the colony of old. This is probably unavoidable although it could be counteracted to some extent by having closer contact with the community than the colony ever had. If the hostels are not to have the same hampering effects on social development as the colonies had on young high-grade patients, it is essential that people with some potentiality for further development are tried out in a much smaller transition-rehabilitation hostel where staff can encourage social development.

The transition-rehabilitation hostel is intended to prepare for life in the community, and its atmosphere and furnishings should not be very different from those to be found in the homes of unskilled workers. By this means an unsettling contrast between the two atmospheres of the hostel and the subnormal's ultimate living conditions will be avoided and he will be adequately prepared for the realities of a modest and unassuming existence.

These considerations do not apply to the custodial hostels which are permanent homes and they should be made as comfortable and attractive as finances permit. Nevertheless, it should be borne in mind that the resi-

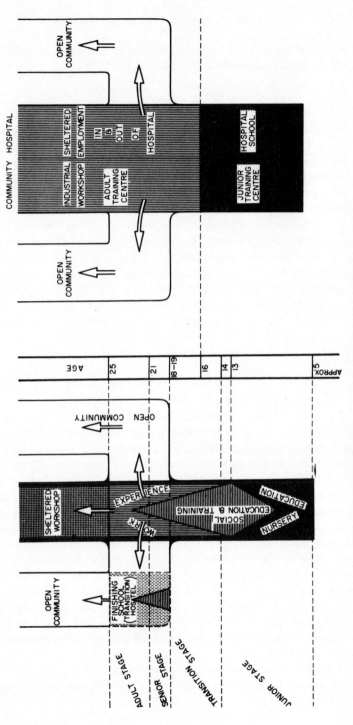

Fig. 45. The framework for a social education and training programme.

dents have simple minds and they are likely to feel at ease in small, homely and supportive surroundings (A. L. Gunzburg, 1974).

Staff

It will be clear that two types of staff are required. People working in the rehabilitative hostel should not be less well-trained than the teacher in the various education and training provisions through which the subnormal has passed before arriving at the hostel. The staff's role must be very active because it will be their task to help the subnormal to assimilate correctly the experience gathered during his working day and to encourage adjustment to the requirements of the community. The staff in the custodial hostel are not teachers in any sense of the word and what they have to give is of an entirely different nature. They should help to make the hostel into a permanent home for people who, although clumsy in their social affairs, do not require full-time skilled nursing or medical guidance. No specific training is given other than that needed to help the hostel residents cooperate effectively in the day-to-day running of their own home. This can generally be done quite successfully by a warm-hearted and kindly disposed married couple who show commonsense and an interest in those in their care.

Concluding Remarks

The scheme discussed in the preceding pages has been set out in diagrammatic form in Figure 45. Most of the components of the scheme are already in existence. However, their roles in the general framework of the education and training of the mentally handicapped have not always been very clearly defined and, as a result, there is confusion and uncertainty regarding the work they are supposed to carry out.

Whether provision for the care of the mentally handicapped is made by the hospitals or by the local authorities, the basic requirements are the same. The training scheme represented by the Social Education and Training Centre or Development Centre is shown on the left-hand side of the diagram, and at the right are listed the present provisions for the retarded. The system shown on the left-hand side starts with children of 5 years or less, and is essentially identical with the E.S.N.(S) school up to an approximate age of 14. Training should be on the lines of the nursery school and no formal education is given. There is free play and much opportunity for creative expression, play with sand, clay, paint and water, but also systematic 'learning how to learn'.

The following transition stage comprises the age range 13/14 to 18/19, or the senior group of the present E.S.N.(S) school, and the younger people of the adult training centre. Formal educational training should be directed towards social adjustment. The children should be encouraged to shoulder responsibility, to concentrate on realistic projects and should learn social skills such as shopping, handling money, using public transport, etc. Tools and materials should be introduced during this time but with the intention of using them for learning and finding out, rather than for teaching particular operations.

The senior stage shows a gradual dominance of work training on the job, but care is taken to use 'work' primarily as a learning situation and the development of production skills is subordinated to this aim. Much of the social training carried out during this time is in the nature of revision to ensure that skills which have been learnt in the transition stage are not forgotten but are consolidated.

In many cases it will be apparent by the age of 21 or as late as 24/25 whether a trainee is likely to require the protection of the sheltered workshop or whether he might be suitable for partial or full rehabilitation in the open community. Some of the trainees will therefore be transferred at this time to the sheltered workshop whilst others may be given a trial period in the open community. A further desirable development of social education and training is represented by the 'Finishing School'—shown in dotted lines—and it may well be that such training could increase the retarded pupils' chances for social survival quite considerably.

Mentally handicapped people who have gone through a training scheme as described, could live either at home or in hostels. Many of them can move freely from their place of residence to work and back again and can be entrusted to a certain extent with looking after their own leisure activities. They will always require a certain amount of support and guidance but adequate social education and training could succeed in reducing the extent of support required in individual cases. This is an important consideration and it justifies the great amount of care and attention which has to be spent in carrying out a training scheme which would result in giving the mentally handicapped a certain minimal degree of social competence.

6

THE CONTENTS OF A SOCIAL EDUCATION FIRST AID PROGRAMME

(A Stranger in His Own Country)[1]

Introduction

A mentally handicapped person, whether child or adult, is in somewhat the same position as a tourist in a foreign country. He may not know the language or the customs of the foreign country and may have difficulties with the coinage and the decimal system. Being handicapped by his inadequate understanding of the language and perhaps slightly flustered by the demands made on his arithmetical prowess, many a holiday-maker solves his shopping problem by simply dipping into his pocket and offering a handful of assorted coins to the shopkeeper, with the mute request to take his pick and to be honest about it. However, no intelligent person will maintain this mode of life for any length of time and there are, moreover, times when this no longer works—for example when tipping. The irritation he causes himself by his ignorance interferes with the smooth and even tenor of his holiday: at one time he overtips and feels that he has made a fool of himself in the eyes of the waiter, and the next time he undertips and quickly realizes from the waiter's disrespectful manner and audible asides that he is again at fault.

The mentally handicapped is in a very similar situation. He has to take much on trust, he has no standards of reference and thus he offers his handful to others and feels that they may have diddled him. When he tries to handle matters by himself he over-reacts to a situation—he overtips—and realizes he is considered a fool. And like most people, he prefers to be knave rather than fool—and he undertips, he under-reacts.

The mentally handicapped's typical instability, his explosive,

[1] The first part of this section is based on two papers published in 1962: *The School and Social Failure*, 26th Biennial Conference of the Association for Special Education; and, *Training for Employment*, Conference on Training and Employment of the Mentally Handicapped, National Society for Mentally Handicapped Children.

temperamental outbursts and impulsiveness, his drivelessness, un-caring attitude and his disinclination to tackle obstacles and difficulties represents the see-saw reactions of a man who is not too sure of himself; he is irritated, feels left out and inferior and is unable to regain his balance and a feeling of security. What has been a modest but probably sufficient mental capital to eke out a living with an employer who simply looks for a pair of hands, becomes inadequate simply because of his fear of using his ability and of meeting new people and situations. Even language, which should provide the link between the individual and the world around him has become a barrier because the common coinage of verbal expressions and terms is faulty or absent.

The difference between our handicapped adult and the tourist in a foreign country is, of course, that the tourist's stay is temporary and many of the mishaps he encounters can be laughed off as being of no consequence. He has some cash to pay for his mistakes and knows he will not repeat them because he will soon return to his own familiar surroundings. He also has some general knowledge which permits him to orientate himself on unfamiliar ground and, most of all, he has the intelligence necessary to adapt himself to novel, unaccustomed situations. The mentally handicapped lacks all these extra resources: *he is a stranger in his own country*, ignorant of its customs, imperfect in his command of its language, deficient in his understanding, suspicious of the intentions of others and bewildered by the demands of changing situations. It is the task of a social education and training scheme to provide some of that knowledge, some of the skills, some of the familiarity with every-day situations which will be necessary to make the mentally handicapped feel at home in his immediate surroundings—at least to some extent. He has much in common with the timid traveller but like him can gain assurance and enjoyment if he is helped to find out that the unknown is less frightening and threatening than he thought.

Once the mentally handicapped has realized that there are some guideposts, he may settle down and become receptive to the further support which a special environment can give him. A social education first-aid scheme is, therefore, a plan not only to prepare him for new situations but also to make him receptive for the further aid which he may require from time to time. Although it cannot give enough assistance to make him independent it can help to overcome many reactions of panic in new situations.

The aim of all teaching should be to prepare the mentally handicapped child to be a relatively efficient social human being when an adult; handicapped though he is, he should be able to carry on by himself on a modest level of efficiency. Academic skills (writing, reading and arithmetic) are taught only to the extent necessary to serve the aims of minimal social competence and training in the *social* needs of the adult are the primary consideration. Since we know that most of the academic education available is beyond the grasp of the mentally handicapped, emphasis must be put on those aspects which can help him directly to live and work in the community.

The minimal needs of the adult human being who lives and works with other people can be summarized under four headings:

1. *Self-help.* This includes all those skills and habits which make the mentally handicapped socially acceptable (dressing, eating, toilet habits etc.).
2. *Communication.* In this aspect are included all abilities relating to the use and understanding of the ordinary means of communication (language, reading, writing and arithmetical work).
3. *Socialization.* This comprises the skills necessary to live and work with others rather than in isolation.
4. *Occupation.* This includes that large area of skills which make a person useful and capable of contributing to his support, or enable him to occupy himself.

The social education first aid scheme is a programme which has whittled down to essentials the various skills in the four areas listed above. Only those skills are included which are directly useful to adult functioning (e.g. knowledge of money), or are basic to other more complex skills which will put the mentally handicapped more at ease in adult society, (e.g. recognition of words such as DANGER, LADIES and GENTLEMEN). These skills should be taught first and other academic skills should be added only after the first aid skills have been adequately mastered. In most cases not even these modest educational targets can be fully attained, but nevertheless partial achievement represents useful practical advance. The scheme must therefore be regarded as one that tries to develop systematically and intensively those skills, habits and knowledge which could help to achieve a minimum degree of social competence. It should not only stress elementary practical subjects but also contain a means of evaluating progress to check the efficiency of the teaching approach employed.

Such a scheme, even though it is limited and deals only with the bare essentials, does not suggest that all mentally handicapped people can and must achieve success in all areas and on all levels. Nor should it be assumed that relative social competence is out of the question if final targets are not achieved. But it is reasonable to assume that the mentally handicapped will find his adult life eased by some competence in most of these social skills.

I. Self-Help

Self-help skills are essential to the general social competence of the mentally handicapped child and, traditionally, most emphasis is put rightly on reasonable adequacy in this aspect of social behaviour. The real problem is very often not so much whether the child will learn what is required—most moderately handicapped children eventually acquire most of these skills—but firstly to decide *when* the child is ready to learn and, secondly, not to discontinue training too soon. Whilst the normal child's development gives an indication of the sequence of development of self-help skills, this knowledge does not help much in deciding when to encourage the acquisition of new skills in a mentally handicapped child. Sometimes attempts may be made to achieve skills before the muscular control is mature enough to cope with them. Sometimes stimulation and encouragement are postponed far too long out of mistaken consideration for the child's handicap. Parents tend to err towards over-protection, and the child's progress, slow as it is, may be halted temporarily or permanently because things are done *for* him instead of guiding him to do them for himself.

The mental handicap is real enough—but it is, after all, one that can be partially overcome like many other handicaps. The child is slow to learn, but learn he can provided he does not take advantage of the parents' concern and anxiety, letting them do what he could well do for himself. Mental handicap is very often not an inability to do something, but simply an inability to learn at the normal rate.

The most important subsections of the area Self-Help are concerned, during childhood, with good table habits, mobility, toileting, washing and dressing. These are the first self-help skills to be learnt, but afterwards further skills should be added relating to the use of clothes and to personal health.

Table Habits

The ability to eat properly without drawing undue attention is an important stage in social acceptability and except in the very severely handicapped, most children can be trained to use cutlery appropriately. Very often good table manners, washing hands before meals, use of table napkins, etc., are essential since people tend to be much harsher in their judgment when their enjoyment of food is spoilt by other people's uncouthness at table. The skills to be taught in this context are the ability to use cutlery, to serve oneself and to eat and drink without help.

Mobility

The ability to move about freely is comparatively easily learned by most of us and little attention is usually paid to the *quality* of movement, although in later life the clumsy and ungainly movements of the mentally handicapped tend to attract attention. Defects in muscular co-ordination are typical in mental handicap, yet attention to the ordinary activities such as walking could help considerably to remedy some of the more conspicuous weaknesses.

Generally, the aim should be to achieve good co-ordination in walking, good posture (no slouching), control over movement which makes it possible to deal with unexpected happenings, e.g. regaining balance after a slight push, stepping sideways, stopping suddenly etc. The ability to walk up and down stairs without having to hold on, without anxiety and with the even movement of the normal person, needs to be practised and is required everywhere.

Allowing the child to move out of the protection of the home is a step which many parents of normal children take only with great hesitation and anxiety, and it may become almost impossible for the conscientious parent of a mentally handicapped child to overcome his natural concern. In some cases the situation may be helped by geographical conditions, a low density of traffic and by most shops, friends and relations being within easy and comparatively safe reach. Very careful consideration must be given to the steps that can be taken to give the child experience and training in moving about in his neighbourhood—a skill which he will require later in his adult life unless he is to receive institutional care. At a later stage, the moderately and borderline retarded should be encouraged to acquire a good working knowledge of local transport facilities and some of the more mature severely retarded young adults can even be taught to use public transport on familiar journeys.

Toileting and Washing

The teaching and learning of toilet and washing skills probably provokes more anxiety and determined effort on the mother's part than any other. The minimal aim to be achieved in this area is the realization of the child that he needs to go *and* goes to the toilet. The next aim is to establish regular bladder and bowel control and to get the child accustomed to elimination at certain times. Similarly important is the ability to clean himself by using toilet paper, the management of his clothing and the washing of his hands before leaving the toilet.

There are many aspects to which attention should be paid: drying hands satisfactorily should also mean, as every mother knows, washing in such a way that the dirt is left in the water, not on the towel! Whilst the young child may be able to 'wash' his face in some just tolerable manner, the older child should learn how to wash and dry behind his ears and realize that the neck is customarily included in face-washing operations. Similarly, brushing his teeth and the adequate use of a toothbrush should be more stringently judged in older children than in the young child who has not yet acquired the manipulative ability necessary for the task. Generally speaking, the various skills in this section should, after proper training, be of a level and quality expected of a normal child of comparable age, provided an adequate degree of muscular control has been achieved. In this area more than any other, the mentally handicapped child who is not also physically handicapped should not lag far behind his normal contemporary.

Dressing

Learning to dress is a laborious and time consuming task. The difficulties are caused mainly by the need for controlled movements and by the fact that parents cannot always spend enough time on such a long drawn-out business. There is nearly always some pressure to get ready in time and, in consequence, the simplest solution is, of course, to dress the child rather than to assist him in dressing. This is a real problem and is probably best tackled by concentrating energies on one task after the other, rather than on the whole process at once. This means tackling first the simpler operations such as pulling off socks and putting on pants. By assisting the child to deal with only one task at a time while the parent performs the other operations, not too much time is spent on the whole procedure. Once the first task is learnt by repetition and encouraged by liberal praise, the next may be taught. Gradually, over a considerable span of time, one dressing and undressing operation after the other will be learned and included in the child's daily repertoire of skills. This gradual learning, step by step, is less confusing and more rewarding to the child and certainly less exasperating to the parent-teacher.

II. Communication

There is little doubt that mentally handicapped people are often accepted only with difficulty by the general public. Whilst the blind, the deaf and the physically handicapped person is a full member of the community, the mentally handicapped child and adult tend to be pushed aside and to stand aside.

Much of this unsatisfactory situation can be ascribed to the difficulties experienced in mutual communication. The mentally handicapped person does not understand 'normal' people and their demands. They, in turn, fail to understand readily the mentally handicapped person. If the ensuing rejection and isolation are to be avoided, it must be the primary task of social education to establish new links of communication between the mentally handicapped person and the community. This refers primarily to language and, to a lesser extent, to the communicative skills of reading, writing and ability to use number concepts.

Language

Language is probably the most important single acquisition which will ease the child's, and later the adult's, way through life. Yet it is often difficult to master since the mentally handicapped (and many 'normal' children) often prefer to retreat from this difficult task.

Three aspects have to be considered—comprehension, expression, articulation.

Comprehension of language precedes the ability to *use* language and speech and is probably the most important. Many of the difficulties experienced by the mentally handicapped adult in learning and applying what he has learned to new situations, stem from the original handicap of inadequate deciphering of the 'messages' of the spoken word from people around him. Not having an adequate understanding of what is said, the mentally handicapped person is obviously at a severe disadvantage in dealing with new situations and giving adequate responses. Though much of his incompetence may be due to the inherent mental defect, if enough time, energy and new thought are given to teaching with suitable techniques adequate understanding of language can usually be achieved.

The ability to use language—expression—also requires planned and consistent encouragement, particularly in the development of vocabulary.

The first stages of vocabulary development are concerned almost entirely with nouns and verbs. These are learned comparatively easily through constant repetition and because they are mostly of a practical nature so that the child can easily grasp their meaning and usefulness to him. However, an extensive vocabulary of nouns and verbs can be very deceptive and give the impression of a much better mastery of language than is actually available to the child.

The crucial test of language mastery is the ability to use and understand words dealing with relationships and therefore early emphasis should be put on the correct use of prepositions, comparatives, adjectives, etc. Exercises by themselves cannot by-pass the need for constant daily usage of a vocabulary of slowly increasing complexity which, together with planned speech practice, can help a good deal to prompt language development. It is a mistake to assume that natural growth of language will at a later stage make up for the absence of planned language teaching at an early stage. Language needs to be experienced and, since the mentally handicapped child's urge to learn and to seek out for himself is very limited, he has to be *taught* word meanings and word situations which the normal child discovers and uses naturally. The normal child requires little instruction other than correction in every-day use of language, even though he must be taught formally to read, write and do arithmetic. The mentally handicapped child should not be expected to pick up a knowledge of language and, for him, *every-day speech must become a subject of the curriculum* even though it is not taught in a formal way.[1]

---

[1] Much effort should be devoted to making the child sufficiently interested in what he sees and experiences to wish to communicate with others. The picture book entitled *Charlie Wants to Help* provides 'talking points' to induce language communication by showing pictures containing ridiculous, impossible or wholly incorrect features. These pictures should arouse curiosity and a desire to tell the teacher about the funny things. They also

Articulation, faulty as it may be, is of less importance than comprehension and expression. It may require the assistance of a trained expert but it may also gradually improve with the constant encouragement (but not nagging!) of the parent and teacher, who should be careful to pronounce words often, slowly and distinctly.

Development in comprehension, expression and articulation will be actively encouraged if the parent or teacher provide continuous stimulation and experience. Nevertheless development may be very slow, as in other aspects of the social education of the child, and may thus give the impression of having come to a standstill. But to accept this and to fail to encourage and guide the pupil to the next stage will result in the child's remaining at a language level which is below his real capacity. Since language is so vital to most activities this would adversely affect all aspects of his life.[1]

There is much evidence that the language skills of the mentally handicapped are below the level one would expect from a person of his age or even his mental level (see Fig. 7). This means that he is as retarded linguistically in relation to his mental ability as he is in the skills of reading, writing and arithmetic. If intelligence level, as assessed by an intelligence test, is indicative of the level of mental functioning at the time of testing (even though it does not indicate potential intellectual ability), then attainments which are well below measured mental level suggest that a pupil is backward in these respects.

The use of language by the mentally handicapped person—his verbal behaviour—shows certain characteristic features which differentiate him from a normal child of the same mental level. The mentally handicapped likes concrete words as opposed to the abstract ones used by the normal. The use of an object may

show foolish but possible situations resulting from lack of foresight, hastiness, inattention etc. Being everyday social situations they help to drive home some realization of the importance of the social graces and of the need to think before acting (Fig. 52, page 168).

[1] New research (Luria, 1963) draws attention to the mentally handicapped child's characteristic underdevelopment of speech which does not serve as a starting point for new associations and relationships, but rather as a means of repeating cliches. Since verbal discrimination and ability to generalize are fundamental to the development of thought processes, the mentally handicapped child's underdevelopment in this area affects his ability to think.

be *described* or demonstrated by the mentally defective in concrete terms but it is *explained* by abstract ones by the normal. Irrespective of mental age level, the mentally handicapped tends to use fewer abstract definitions than the normal child of the same mental age. It appears that the mentally handicapped does not develop his ability to use abstract terms to the same extent as the normal child, even though both may have apparently equivalent mental ability.

It has been shown in various experiments that people are able to learn better and remember more efficiently if they can accompany their actions by a descriptive commentary. However, the mentally handicapped child has not even learned to name objects adequately and is, therefore, handicapped from the start. Even though he may well understand the teacher's use of vocabulary he himself may find great difficulties in marshalling correct words from his 'store' of language in order to express himself. The task of language education is to help him to learn 'labelling', or verbalizing which in turn will help him to perform better in life and work. Abstract thought which at first appears to be missing in the mentally handicapped, may in fact turn out to be dependent upon labelling ability, and some research has now been done which suggests that the mentally handicapped person's difficulties are due not so much to his slow speed of learning, poor memory, or inability to relate one situation to another, but to his inability to understand what other people want of him (O'Connor and Hermelin, 1963).

For some reason which is not yet understood, severely handicapped children have acquired only a faulty understanding for speech. This may well be due to lack of attention and weak motivation, and once we have succeeded in making them attend and become sufficiently motivated there is hope that learning will take place. This learning is slow, but it has been shown that levels of attainment which were thought to be impossible in the past can finally be achieved. The fact that learning takes place only after a considerable delay in reacting to orders, explanations and demonstrations can be traced back to these difficulties in making out linguistic communications.

The mildly and borderline retarded, having mastered the more elementary skills of conversation and of translating into suitable actions any commands, warnings, exhortations etc. he receives, should be helped to gain an understanding of everyday vocabulary (i.e. time vocabulary, p. 52), the idiomatic use of language (the

'Spotlight on Trouble' reading books—see p. 165 emphasize this aspect), the different meaning of identical words, and the exact meaning of words (i.e. 'half' often being considered any kind of subdivision into two and not necessarily equal parts).

Later on, the adolescent mentally subnormal should be taught the more advanced skills required for conversation over the telephone and for the transmitting of messages.

The 3 R's in Mental Subnormality

It has already been pointed out that academic education for the mentally handicapped has to be reduced to a bare minimum. This is justified because competence in techniques which cannot be utilized by a person because of his innate mental handicap seems to be futile. Severely and moderately subnormal children with IQs between 35 and 50 can be taught reading, writing and arithmetic to a fairly advanced stage of technical skill. This is interesting but, in many ways, it is an academic and useless exercise because the child cannot make use of the skills in the same way as a normal child uses the skills to acquire knowledge and to entertain himself. In view of the considerable energy and time which has to be spent on teaching subjects which may be of little importance to the child, we must consider very carefully how far the 3 R's will, in fact, help a mentally handicapped child to be a socially competent adult, and whether this effort could be more usefully employed in teaching specific skills of living.

However, some pressure is exerted by parents. They may have little idea of the special skills which will make the child happy and competent in adult life, and, understandably, think of education in terms of the classroom knowledge which they themselves acquired in their youth. Parents may feel that their children, because of their mental handicap, are being unjustly deprived of an education which they have been brought up to believe is the birthright of every citizen: to omit the 3 R's from the curriculum appears to them to stigmatize their child unnecessarily.

It is important to overcome this attitude by enlisting the parents' support and making them understand that the aims of the education for the severely handicapped must be in some ways different from those of the normal child. This calls for a very close parent-teacher relationship and an appreciation of the fact that to each should be given according to his needs. This must be placed ahead of dessert ('To each according to his merit') and capacity ('To each according to his ability'), and an attempt must be made to 'bring the slow and the needy up to the levels of satisfaction enjoyed by the normal individual' (Neale and Campbell, 1963). Academic education, in the traditional sense, is merely the means to achieve this satisfaction for the normal child; for the mentally handicapped satisfaction will have to be obtained by some other form of education.

Lastly, but very important, is the attitude and the reaction of the pupil himself. Many, but by no means all of them, are aware of their shortcomings in academic work. They have become aware that reading, writing and arithmetic are valued by the people around them and that competence in these skills leads to approbation by their elders. The ability to read and write gives the mentally handicapped a feeling of achievement and increased self-confidence, and they derive considerable enjoyment from exercising these skills in a mechanical manner. This is an important consideration and it is desirable to create these feelings of confidence and achievement without trying to fill the child with useless and irrelevant knowledge.

Reading

Reading has always been of prime importance in education. Considerable efforts are made everywhere to overcome illiteracy and it is understandable that one of the foremost objects in the education of the mentally handicapped aims at overcoming his illiteracy. Yet a very careful analysis of the various skills required to exist on a minimum level of social competence suggests that there is very little need for reading. This is borne out by the many illiterates who survive happily and without undue discomfort or embarrassment in our society. There are some situations when illiteracy produces real difficulties but, by and large, there seems to be far less need to be able to read than to be able to deal with money.

In order to benefit from reading a satisfactory degree of mechanical skill is required, together with an adequate vocabulary and an understanding of the written word. The lower the IQ the less capable will the person be of understanding either speech or print, even if he can pronounce words correctly or, as has been said disrespectfully, 'barks at print'. Even a child with comparatively high IQ but living in a culturally impoverished environment will have difficulty in understanding a complex vocabulary though he may be capable of reading it. It is logical that the teaching of reading should be related to the use the person can make of it in later life. A moderately handicapped child whose IQ is well below 50 will have less need to read than a borderline child with IQ 70 or over. The teaching of reading will therefore be considered firstly with the needs of the moderately and severely handicapped child in mind and, secondly, in relation to the less retarded child.

Reading for the Moderately and Severely Handicapped

The severely and moderately handicapped person will not be able to acquire a reading ability sufficient to obtain information or entertainment for himself. Though he can be taught to read on the efficiency level of a 12- to 14-year-old child, the meanings of words on that level completely escape him.

It is therefore sufficient to teach him a Social Sight Vocabulary containing words he can see on notices, warnings, packages, etc. Most of these words such as EXIT, KEEP OUT, POISON, are a type of shorthand used by the community to give information and warnings in as short and cogent a form as possible. If a child learns to recognize these words in whatever style of print they appear, knows their meanings and is able to react appropriately, then a major purpose of literacy has been achieved.

A Social Sight Vocabulary should be taught by using the words as far as possible in their context. Generally the only suitable words which can be presented in the classroom are PULL, PUSH, ON and OFF which are used outside the school. It is useless to continue the practice observed in many classrooms for the mentally handicapped of putting little labels on the doors, walls, blackboard, window, desk and so on, each with the appropriate word on it.

A list of Social Sight Vocabulary words of general usefulness is given in Table XX and should be augmented by words which are of local significance and could help the child and adult to orientate himself in the community in which he lives and works.[1]

Words should be taught to groups or to individuals using flash cards (pp. 159 to 163), blackboard techniques, teaching machines

---

[1] There are some words in the list which may not seem absolutely necessary such as salt, sugar, and beans. However, these are words of increasing importance owing to the spread of self-service stores; not all products include explanatory pictures on the package and it is important that the subnormal who may be able to learn some shopping duties should be able to read the commoner words likely to be found on the label.

(p. 175) and special reading books. Words should be presented in different types and sizes and reaction to the message conveyed by the words should become as automatic as reaction to the red and green light signals at crossroads.

TABLE XX

A social sight vocabulary

Book

1	IN MEN EXIT	OUT WOMEN	PULL ENTRANCE KEEP OUT	PUSH ENTRY
2	GENTLEMEN OPEN HERE TOP ENGAGED	LADIES BOTTOM PRIVATE	NO SMOKING OPEN OTHER SIDE DANGER	
3	SALT CUSTARD SOUP POISON	SUGAR COFFEE BEANS SHAMPOO	LOW HOT BACK ON	HIGH COLD FRONT OFF
4	VACANT KEEP RIGHT CROSS NOW WET PAINT	CLOSED KEEP LEFT STOP PRESS	OPEN	

This list of 54 words provides the basic vocabulary of teaching reading in the four 'Social Sight Vocabulary Readers for the Illiterate' (CLUMSY CHARLIE) and the following series of 18 reading books to develop reading skill (OUT WITH TOM) (see section 7, p. 157 to p. 175).

Reading for the Less Handicapped Person

Most mentally handicapped persons who have reached some level of proficiency in reading do little better than a normal 8-year-old. This does not permit reading much above the level of juvenile fiction because most other reading matter contains vocabulary and content that are very alien and incomprehensible to the mentally handicapped (p. 169).

It will be a difficult and often disappointing task for the teacher to select from the available literature reading matter which is within the retardate's skill and understanding, yet is also interesting to him *and* will serve the aims of his education. This is often overlooked because it is difficult enough to find something technically suitable for adults of limited reading ability without complicating the issue by insisting that it should also be socially useful. However, if careful study is made of juvenile literature and of books specially prepared for backward readers in a younger age group, some suitable material should be found. Some courses of social reading books have been developed for this very purpose as discussed in detail on p. 165.

Generally speaking, the aim of reading at this level is to ensure that the skills and techniques already acquired are maintained and do not deteriorate through lack of practice. Only very few mentally handicapped adults will use their reading skill for more than acquiring casual information.

Writing

Writing is used very little by the mentally handicapped and although a moderately handicapped child can be taught to write a stereotyped letter, he is at once in difficulties if new information is to be conveyed. Inability to write is less embarrassing to the mentally handicapped than inability to read, for there are probably too few opportunities or too few incidents in his life when he needs to communicate to others in writing for him to be frustrated by his inability to do so. It might be argued that desire to communicate could increase once the skill of writing has been mastered, but this is very doubtful in view of his intellectual limitations.

For the moderately and severely retarded adult the only aspect of writing which is of definite social value is that of writing his signature (rather than printing his name). However, care must be exercised when teaching the very handicapped subnormal to sign his name, for without a real appreciation of the implications of his action, both the subnormal and his guardians could easily find themselves in some obvious difficulties.

For the mildly handicapped adult who has not learnt to write at school the aim can be higher but, nevertheless, a sense of proportion should be maintained. If the list of social deficiencies is long and time is short, writing should definitely not be a primary concern of the teacher. Those who are ready to learn to write should be taught to write their name and address and to fill in a simple form giving full names (Christian and surname), address, date of birth, age, occupation, marital status, address of last employer etc. The ability to do this legibly (even if not always with correct spelling) is of more social usefulness to the handicapped than an

ability to copy from a book page and even writing short essays.
The demands made by this form-filling age have often proved a
source of considerable embarrassment for the mildly and borderline
retarded, and it is as well to give some attention to this aspect
whenever time permits.

Number Work

The understanding of the meaning of number is more important than
learning to count well mechanically. It is easy to be deceived by a
child's ability to count rapidly and mechanically to 20 or more, but
unless there is systematic and intensive teaching aimed at an understanding of number relationships, this ability may be as useless as
the fluent reciting of words that may camouflage an inability to
understand what is read so fluently.

The steps which should be taken in achieving an understanding
of number are:

    (a) Number awareness
    (b) Number vocabulary
    (c) Number relationships.

(a) Number Awareness

The aim of this initial stage is simply to make the child aware
of the existence and wide usage of number terms. Some nursery
rhymes such as 'One, two, buckle my shoe', and counting games are
useful. Even better is the inclusion of as many number words as
possible in a running commentary with which members of the family
or teachers should accompany their actions; for example, when laying
the table—'we need four spoons, four knives and four forks, because
we are four persons, Daddy—one, Mummy—two, Jane—three and
John—four. Here we have only three plates, we need one more.
There are two big spoons for serving...' and so on. The vocabulary
should also include 'size' words: big, small, long, short, little,
tall, etc., and every opportunity should be used to draw attention to
the existence and meaning of these words.

(b) Number Vocabulary

It is essential that the child should realize that numbers enable
him to generalize as well as to be specific. If number words and
terms are used only in certain situations, the child may later have
difficulty in applying his knowledge to new situations. Counting
should use as many different objects as possible and not be limited

to one set of teaching devices. Practically everything can and should be used for number work: counters, beads, pencils, books, chairs, forks, children, windows, paper, etc.

There are many difficulties which interfere with the understanding of the *meaning* of number terms because the child relates the number vocabulary to objects in a special and concrete way. He is guided *not by what he knows, but by what he sees.* A typical instance is the fact that he is *misled by the appearance* of a number situation. Five coins lined up near together and compared with five coins laid far apart in a row may be considered to be fewer in number even though the child has counted both rows and has stated that both contain five coins. He gives the wrong answer because he sees that one row is longer than the other. The meaning of number words is not clearly recognized and the fundamental arithmetical idea of the *conservation of quantities* is not appreciated. There are many exercises which should be carried out to give the child an understanding of the idea of number (Isaacs, 1960; Lovell, 1961).

Difficulties of this type occur in normal children under the age of seven, and it will take many more years for a mentally handicapped child to grasp the fact that number is used in a general way rather than as an attribute of particular objects. Present evidence suggests that in a mentally handicapped child with an IQ of less than 50 number ability may not develop before the age of eleven at the earliest.

The work of Piaget (1952) is fundamental for developing a programme of systematic teaching of the first steps in number understanding.

(c) Number Relationships

The fact that numbers increase when units are added to them has next to be brought home to the child; understanding that 5 = 4 and 1, 6 = 5 and 1, is essential for further development. It is important to make the child understand that length, size and number can be greater or less and that size is not affected by other factors such as colour, newness or thickness. By practical experiment he can learn that one object is bigger than another and smaller than a third object which, in its turn, is smaller than the fourth, but bigger than the third. When the child can deal with such concepts without difficulty and with a growing understanding, he is ready to begin to learn the meaning of the symbols which are put down on paper.

The ultimate aims in the teaching of number concepts to the mentally handicapped child are modest. If he is able to manipulate small sums of money correctly, to recognize coins and relate them to the price of goods, to do small addition sums and to judge whether the price of an article is within his means—if all these aims can be realized, we have achieved more of substantial value than we would have done by teaching him to do 'sums' on paper without relating them to real life situations.

The teaching of number work has attracted much attention and many different systems have been developed, one of which is described on pp. 153 to 155.

III. Socialization

Next to 'communication' skills the area of 'socialization' is often very poorly developed. This means that those skills which would help the mentally handicapped to live and work *with* others and not merely *next* to others, are not available to him. He needs more help from others better endowed than himself, yet there are formidable difficulties interfering with his adjustment to the requirements of those people on whom he depends. Difficulties in communication have already been pointed out and they account for a good deal of the friction between the mentally handicapped and his community.

In addition, there are many other handicaps, some of which are due to the sheltered upbringing of the mentally handicapped child who has been overprotected by the parents. Of course this protective reaction is natural to parents, and to many people in the community who come into occasional contact with both the physically and the mentally handicapped. It is often necessary therefore to introduce the mentally handicapped child gradually to the social relationships outside his immediate environment and to teach him the social give-and-take which is necessary for successful socialization and will even be required in the protective shelter of institution or hospital.

The stages by which this development proceeds are fairly well marked. The childish play, at first completely independent of others, gradually merges into play *in the company* of other children and then becomes playing *with* other children. The child who, at first, is quite content to be served and looked after by the parents, later occasionally volunteers to help in the house; after that he may very often require only a minimum of encouragement to give regular routine help. His social activities should be extended to helping people outside his immediate surroundings and he should become familiar with the varying and sometimes conflicting demands of different people. A major difficulty in the work situation of the adult mentally handicapped is his lack of experience in adjusting to the demands of *many* different people rather than to only a few well-known ones. He finds it very confusing to work out for himself who comes highest in the hierarchy of work and social relationships, and it is a common excuse of mentally handicapped people that failure was due to 'too many bosses'.

During his childhood, environment tends to adjust to the mentally handicapped by making constant allowance for his shortcomings and the training centre and hospital school are designed around his handicap. However, when he is adult it becomes necessary for the mentally handicapped himself to adjust to the community and he must be prepared in good time for the less protective outside world where he has to conform to ordinary requirements.

The various activities which the growing child should be encouraged to participate in represent preparation for the responsibilities to be shouldered in adulthood. They familiarize him with *the need to give help and co-operation* to others. This must be encouraged even though it requires more heart searching, courage and persistence on the part of the parents and teachers than any other activity. Teaching these skills means taking the child out of his shelter and exposing him to a certain amount of unkindness and rejection from a society too busy or too unfamiliar with mental handicap to understand all its problems.

Some of the mentally handicapped child's difficulties in establishing and maintaining social relationships can be attributed to his slow learning development. Since the child is dependent on his immediate surroundings for much longer than the normal child, parental protection is often continued by sheer force of habit long after the time when it should gradually have been reduced from shelter to support. He is late in walking, late in thinking and without experience of independence and responsibility and so, because he mixes either with children similarly handicapped or with those very much younger than himself, he does not have the benefits of the stimulating and encouraging influence of his normal contemporaries. Unless a directed effort is made to overcome the consequences of this unfavourable set of circumstances, the child may remain on a much lower and less mature level of social competence than need be.

Play Activities

Play is a learning activity and has a most important and far-reaching influence on establishing healthy social relationships. It offers to the child an opportunity to experience the activities of other children who pay little attention to his personal likes and dislikes, and with whom he has to come to terms. Play gives an outstanding opportunity for teaching and guiding in most agreeable and acceptable ways and it provides, at the same time, opportunities for observing the child closely among other children.

A most important development in his social progress takes place when the child learns to take his 'turn' in adult-supervised games and to share with others at the request of grown-ups. He receives thereby his first lesson in the give and take of social intercourse. The little world where he is king with his parents attending to his demands crumbles under the impact of the other children who are as demanding and inconsiderate as he is himself. This situation will require adjustment from him, resulting in a grudging realization that others too have their feelings, their rights, their places, and that these may often take precedence over his own.

Home Activities

The first taste of co-operative work is provided by assisting in household duties and contributing a modest amount to the routine work at home. Mental handicap should not excuse a child from some regular duties and he should be trained to develop a measure of self-confidence and moderate independence, which in adult life will help to make him a more useful member of society.

Household duties should become more frequent and more complex as the child develops, and even though much of this is carried out as a kind of play, it can relieve the adult of small but time-consuming household chores. Among suitable tasks are helping to set and clear the table, sweeping up and dusting, feeding pets, watering plants and tidying up the room after play. It is important that these contributions should be asked for, should be appreciated when done well, and that disappointment should be expressed if the child does not do them properly and regularly. Breakages and incidental damage must be risked and written off as training expenses. Certainly the child must not become discouraged because he is too clumsy or takes too long. Boys should be trained to carry out domestic tasks alongside of the girls, and division of labour should not be determined by sex differences.

Mentally handicapped children should be made aware of how other unfamiliar people behave and that they also require consideration and the same social give and take as people whom they know. They should meet many people when sent on messages, shopping, etc., which will necessitate practice in being courteous and using the customary forms of greeting. This will help in widening the child's horizon and provide a gentle introduction to life outside the family.

The difficulties for the adolescent mentally handicapped increase considerably when he has to meet complete strangers who make no allowances for his shortcomings. In these circumstances, the mentally handicapped is hesitant and tongue-tied and eager to avoid the unknown. This leads to reluctance in using public transport to other than well-known destinations, unwillingness to venture away from his home area, shyness to visit other unfamiliar shops and self-service chain stores, and a general inability to make use of the many opportunities of finding out something new. Much patient encouragement is necessary at this stage because the mentally retarded adolescent is suffering not only from the deficiencies of his make-up, but at this and other periods of his life he experiences many of the normal adolescent's problems of growth and adjustment. Nonetheless, successful social interaction can be learned only in the community, and he must be encouraged to make trips from his training centre and hospital school if he is to overcome even some of his handicaps.

The teaching of social know-how is, in many ways, the most difficult 'subject' from an organizational point of view. It is obviously impossible to provide a detailed suitable syllabus which would take into consideration all the numerous social obstacles which might be encountered. Only the most conspicuous areas of ignorance can be tackled once they have been pinpointed by a diagnostic assessment of social knowledge, such as in the P-A-C 2 procedure. Those mentally handicapped people who could settle in the community should become proficient in the common daily politenesses of society and this may help to smooth their path with any impatient people they have to work with or under.

There is little doubt that living in a small protective and self-sufficient community such as the Colony of the past, or the hospital, or the training centre makes it impossible to offer learning opportunities which would acclimatize the mentally handicapped person to the demands outside those communities. However since it is our intention to rehabilitate as many subnormals as possible, training for living and working in the open community has to be arranged. Mock-ups of shops and cafes, staging of interviews, discussions and film shows provide rehearsals to later guided expeditions to shops, entertainments, cafeterias, self-service shops, banks or post offices and the use of public transport and so on. No social training scheme can be regarded as fully efficient which does not make arrangements for educational practical experience outside the school or training centre.

IV. Occupation

Work in various forms, be it remunerative or carried out as a hobby and leisure time occupation, fills most of the time of the adult. People tend to decline in efficiency unless they are able to occupy themselves adequately and, nowadays, work is considered of sufficient therapeutic value to be specially introduced in hospitals, old age homes etc. wherever there is some form of enforced leisure.

In view of this it is understandable that training for occupation in general should have taken a predominant place in the training of the mentally handicapped child. Recent research has shown that even the severely handicapped adult is capable of work on a far more skilled level than has been assumed in the past, though he takes longer to learn than a normal person. It will be easier for him in later life if he has been made familiar in childhood with the basic elements of work and has acquired good control of his muscle movements.

Motor skills involved in occupational training are, of course, learned when pursuing such targets as walking or manipulating a knife and fork or pencils or coins, when playing and helping with household chores. But this incidental learning of motor skills should be supported by a direct attention to improving muscle control. Physical exercises, dancing, certain crafts and play are all important in acquiring a degree of physical competence which could contribute considerably towards greater occupational adequacy in later life.

Junior Stage
Practising Fine Finger Movements

Playing with cubes and building structures, threading and sorting will help considerably to improve the use of finger muscles and to gain dexterity, besides serving the main purpose of finding out about things and doing something with them. The large blocks are useful for clumsy fingers, but sizes should gradually be decreased to allow the development of finer finger movements. Care should be taken that blocks are not too smooth, leading to frequent frustrating collapses of structures.

The skills of purposeful handling of objects, fitting together, taking advantage of clues offered by size, shape, colour, etc., mature by stages. It is important to realize that this type of apparatus should be graded according to stages of development in order to guide the child's understanding for the principles of sorting, classifying, ordering etc. Woodward (1962), who investigated the application of Piaget's theory to the training of the mentally handicapped, points out that 'the child's manipulative interest and the method he uses are pointers to the functions he is developing. If young children, or at any rate emotionally stable ones, keep on at the same activity, it is likely that they are learning something from it . . . if the child uses a particular material in an inappropriate way, then that material is too advanced for functions which he is developing; if he tackles it in a trial and error manner, then it is useful in encouraging the appearance of developing functions; if he tackles it by the most efficient method (e.g. being guided by size and form in the nesting and form board problems) then the function has already developed and the material has little development value for him'. She continues by suggesting a scheme of using various teaching aids in accordance with the developmental stages as described by Piaget. In the first stage, hollow containers and small objects such as bricks, spinning objects and water and vessels for pouring are needed. This is followed by a stage when bricks are neatly and closely fitted into a box. The next stage is concerned with nesting problems, simple picture puzzles which help to develop perceptual motor co-ordination in relation to size and form. When the ability to use size and form has developed, more complex formboard material is appropriate.

Utilizing Fine Finger Movements

Once a child has overcome his clumsiness and is able to apply his motor skills constructively, he becomes more settled in his play. He enjoys using his skill and it is important to give him as much practice as possible. No elaborate apparatus is needed, and with a little imagination many household gadgets can be collected which fascinate the child and hold his attention, provide a learning situation and give an opportunity for practising the finger and hand movements of turning, twisting, pulling and pressing (small bottles with corks and screw-tops, matchboxes, envelopes and pieces of hardboard to go into them, padlock and key, are a few suitable objects).

Exercising Muscle Control

Unless a child is very much handicapped physically, efforts should be made to make him participate in activities which require the use of the whole body and not only hands and fingers. The larger type of toy car, carts, trolleys and trucks which can be loaded up and be pushed and pulled about are very useful. Very soon the child should be given an opportunity of digging, hoeing and raking in the garden and helping with various jobs requiring physical effort. Many mentally handicapped children have particular deficiencies in walking, running and balancing, and these tend to become more conspicuous the older they are. Physical exercises should be planned to deal with these shortcomings, aiming at muscular co-ordination rather than muscular development.

The typical slouching or shuffling of the mentally handicapped should be tackled by the teacher and parent as energetically as is permissible considering any genuine physical handicaps. Even if the child no longer trips over his own feet, there are often pronounced deficiencies in muscular co-ordination shown in the difficulty in stopping suddenly, turning rapidly, or stepping backwards and sidewards without stumbling. Striding along and swinging the arms is, for many of these children, nearly impossible but much can be achieved by persistent training. Considering that the mentally handicapped adult has only his labour to sell when entering the competitive field of employment in the community, it is important to develop his physique and stamina. The mentally handicapped is generally inferior in muscular performance, co-ordination, equilibrium, speed and staying power and special efforts should be made to develop these skills.

The correct use of kitchen or garden tools is an important step towards achieving vocational adequacy later on. No longer are the various gadgets used indiscriminately for play, but they are now employed purposefully in the manner for which they have been designed. Hammer, saw, screwdriver, pincers, should be applied to mending and constructing jobs, needles and cotton to sewing and

mending. The older child should be encouraged to use these tools
and utensils and should be made aware of the dangers to himself
and to others if the implements are used carelessly. Accidents may
happen, but they are less frequent and less dangerous than over-
careful parents usually believe. A child who has attained this level
of competence is pretty near the stage when more advanced training
can begin on vocational tools and machines. It is well worth while
to make the child familiar with the correct use of dangerous implements before this stage has been reached.

Senior Stage

By the time the primary stages have been mastered and the
necessary muscle control has been attained, severely subnormal
children are very often in their late teens and are transferred to an
adult work environment. Progress should be judged by a pupil's
ability to handle tools and materials reasonably well, not by the
finished product which only too often show the instructors' dominant
contribution.

Much of the arts and crafts side of the occupational work should
now be supplanted by activities such as simple repair work which
requires some adaptability and provides an opportunity to use
different tools and materials. Girls can be taught mending and a
reasonable proficiency in this will make a girl welcome in any home.
Both men and women should be taught to cook simple meals such as
toast, scrambled egg, welsh-rarebit, grilled tomatoes and tea. It is
far less important to be able to make fancy cakes and pastries than
to be able to organize the timing, sequence, preparation and arrangement of unpretentious meals. Getting breakfast or tea ready at the
right time without any help requires organization and knowledge,
and should be taught systematically as the main target of instruction
and other meals dealt with only for a change and to maintain interest.
The basic skills of boiling, frying, grilling and mixing should also
be taught.

The general principles governing the utilisation of
industrial education and training have already been discussed
(p. 114). Besides learning how to handle tools and small machinery,
many other important skills should be acquired. No attempt should
be made to teach trades or to develop manual skills to a high level
of craftsmanship. It has been shown only too often that the
tremendous time and energy which has to be put into teaching the
mentally handicapped a good mastery of specialized skills is

wasted because in outside employment he is unable to compete with a normal person's speed, adaptability and workmanship. However, many mentally retarded people can compete in unskilled labouring, and training should therefore be directed towards acquiring acceptable work habits and work efficiency, rather than skill in particular operations. Trainees should be made aware of the need to keep up sufficient speed to produce a reasonable quantity of work without affecting the quality of workmanship. It is necessary to teach the mentally handicapped to attend to his materials and tools, to general tidiness and to his work. Many training establishments have simulated real factory conditions by introducing clocking-in and clocking-out systems and using incentive bonuses. These are important aspects of work training but they are only effective if somebody takes his time to explain the relationships between the amount and quality of work on one side and financial reward on the other side. It is by no means certain that mentally handicapped people always understand that the harder they work the more money they are able to earn and, therefore, the more things they are able to buy. It is also by no means certain that the mentally handicapped trainee understands that coming late to work usually means less pay and therefore less buying power. These simple relationships, taken for granted by most of us, must be pointed out frequently and in detail, if they are to be fully understood by the handicapped worker.

Concluding Remarks

There is much need for planning the syllabus of a training scheme from the junior stage through the transition and on to the senior stage as one consistent whole. At present there is too much haphazard and half-hearted playing at school and industrial work. On the one hand, an ineffective attempt is made to emulate the school of the normal child, thereby wasting both teacher's and children's time on inessential learning; on the other hand, an all too successful method is developed to produce factory robots whose industrial efficiency is reflected in rising production curves and increased wage packets. Whilst the junior stage often limits itself to minding and occupying the children, the adult workshop, by over-emphasizing one aspect to the detriment of others, may succeed in making the mentally handicapped an efficient worker, but fails to assist him as a social human being. It is only by adjusting our teaching to the needs of the mentally handicapped and making room for important knowledge by throwing overboard educational ballast which does not further social competence, that it will be possible to help many of these people to live and work with less support than they require at present.

TEACHING AIDS AND TEACHING METHODS

Introduction

The preceding sections have tried to define, in some detail, the immediate aims of social education and have shown that the mentally handicapped person's knowledge and application of elementary social techniques and social 'know-how' is very limited. It has also been demonstrated that many mentally handicapped persons have an adequate degree of social knowledge which suggests that where there are deficiencies they are not entirely due to intellectual limitations. Inadequate training and insufficient experience may contribute a great deal to the social inadequacy of the mentally handicapped. It has also been suggested that more effective social training could be given if one examined carefully and in detail why a particular mentally handicapped child has not acquired certain skills when most others of his age and with his degree of mental handicap had managed to acquire them. It has been suggested that rehabilitation work in mental handicap has failed to advance significantly because, in the past, the aims were considered to be training for a custodial existence and more recently, training for sheltered industrial work.

Unfortunately little is known of how best to teach social knowledge which must take its place as an essential aspect of educational work. It may be that the methods used so far would be more effective if the targets were clearly seen and evaluations were regularly made; but it could also be that other methods are required which take into consideration the particular personality shortcomings of the mentally handicapped. This will have to be a matter of careful investigation and constant experimenting in the same way as the education of the normal child is constantly investigated, queried and adjusted under the influence of new ideas and re-evaluations of existing practices. The various methods in education and training of a mentally handicapped child will have to be judged by the effect they have on the happiness and social efficiency of the mentally handicapped adult. It is certainly too early to do this now or to advocate definite approaches which have not been tested adequately.

The present section is therefore concerned with less definite suggestions than the preceding sections. It will illustrate the need for new approaches by giving three examples of assisting in learning specific skills. The emphasis is on *assisting* because it will depend entirely on the teacher how the tools are used—the tools by themselves are only as good as the teacher who handles them.

Communication is the most under-developed area in social competence compared with the other three aspects of social functioning assessed by the P-A-C (see Fig. 9). It is also in that area that content is nearest to, and often identical with, the work carried out in schools for the normal child. Whilst the training centre and hospital school have had to develop their own approaches to the work required for the development of self-help, socialization and occupation, in the field of communication they lean most heavily on the methods of the normal school. This may not necessarily be good practice and it is desirable to consider carefully the special requirements of aids designed to teach communication skills to the mentally handicapped child.

A. Teaching Aids for the Mentally Handicapped

The term teaching aid covers a wide range of apparatus from the reading book or picture to highly elaborate teaching machines. As is to be expected, most teaching aids have been developed for work with normal children and relatively few aids are specially designed for the mentally subnormal. It is therefore usual to use aids designed for normal children in work with older but educationally very retarded children. This can lead to certain difficulties and these will be discussed in the following paragraphs.

Teaching aids have been designed to help the teacher to achieve better and quicker results by helping the child to understand and learn more readily than is the case if only explanations and blackboard diagrams are used. We have already argued that techniques leading to social usefulness are those of most importance to the mentally handicapped person. Teaching aids can not therefore be borrowed indiscriminately from those designed for junior or nursery school children, simply because they facilitate the learning of something, and it is necessary to judge rigorously whether a particular teaching aid is one that will further our special educational requirements.

Important factors are that the mentally handicapped have a very slow speed of learning and the steps which lead from one piece of information to another should be both small and repetitive. If a teaching aid does not allow for such small and repetitive steps, it is unsuitable for the mentally handicapped child. Unfortunately, most teaching aids are designed for the normal school child who, even if backward, can easily bridge the gap between successive steps of learning. Some of the teaching aids nowadays available are self-correcting in which the pupil's answer is mechanically checked and which indicates, usually by a 'non-fit' mechanical arrangement that a particular 'answer' is wrong. Although a normal child will probably attempt a more systematic approach to the task after he has made a wrong answer and will learn by his mistakes the mentally handicapped child will not be inclined to re-think his problem. On the contrary, the possibility of arriving at a correct solution by trial and error, e.g. sorting mechanically until pieces fit, encourages the mentally handicapped child to go on haphazardly rather than apply his shaky knowledge to the problem on hand. Self-correcting apparatuses are therefore wholly unsuitable in this situation and should be avoided.

It is also important to use teaching aids in such a way that they follow the previously defined programme of learning step by step. This can be illustrated by reference to a teaching programme of arithmetical concepts.

Number Work

The understanding required for applying mathematical skills to new situations has been compared by Locking (1966) to a closed telescope. In this state it contains all the component parts which make the instrument serviceable—the parts are telescoped rather like the components of the arithmetical skill of computing—two- or three-place additions have to be considered as essential stages which *precede but are contained in the final result*. Unless all the initial stages are fully understood, the more complex skills of later stages cannot be applied.

In order to give the child a serviceable understanding of number, it is necessary to follow a course of teaching which is based on the stages through which number knowledge develops. It will also be necessary to subdivide these stages into very small easy steps, thereby avoiding jumps which cannot be bridged by the intellectually limited child.

Locking's programme (1966) consists of five stages.

Fig. 46. CLUMSY CHARLIE FLASHCARDS

First Stage

The aim is to enable the pupil to answer such questions as:

(a) How many are there?
(b) Give me the same number of chairs as there are dolls.
(c) Give me five (or eight or ten) dolls.

The pupil is taught to determine the numerical quality of two sets, e.g. two blocks and two dolls. He uses the 'one to one' correspondence and can, therefore, determine how many there are in any given group. (Ability to count does not imply that the child necessarily appreciates that six is more than five or less than seven, but simply that he is able to establish the correct total by careful counting.)

The main aim of teaching must be to give a thorough understanding of the fact that number remains constant whatever the position of the component parts (e.g. three pencils are still three pencils whether together in a box or spread out; four cubes on top of each other, making a tower, are the same number as four cubes in a row or a heap; three big books are the same number as three little books).

The target at this stage is the pupil's ability to answer questions such as: Which is more, three things or five things? Tell me a number which is less than seven, and so on.

Second Stage

The second stage deals generally with the ability to appreciate the meaning of the terms: more or less as applied to length, size and number.

The general point to be understood is that number increases or decreases like objects arranged according to length and size, and that this applies to everything that can be counted. This can be demonstrated in different situations using sticks, dolls and beads of different lengths and size and requesting the child to arrange these objects in proper order.

Third Stage

The aim at this stage is to enable the pupil to answer questions such as: How much more is five than two? What is seven and three?

A pupil at this stage can *predict* the outcome of a counting operation, e.g. if he has three objects in front of him and is to be given another three objects, he can predict that there will be six objects, whereas a pupil at stage 1 will have to count the objects, mostly by touching them.

Fourth Stage
The work at this stage should result in an understanding of the multiplication tables. The pupil should now realize how the adding up of equal amounts results in certain numbers which can be predicted by the use of multiplication tables.

Fifth Stage
This stage represents the most advanced mathematical knowledge a mentally handicapped child might acquire and includes a knowledge and understanding of the carrying process.

These five steps are very large ones which have to be subdivided. Very few subnormal children will be able to attain the higher stages, and all will take a long time over the learning of each.

Time

It is almost impossible to teach such an elusive, abstract concept as time, and the mentally handicapped person will seldom become 'time conscious' in the sense of using time cues flexibly for arranging his activities. On the other hand it may be possible to make him *aware* of time to show him the connection between certain times and certain events, and to teach him how to tell the time. Unfortunately it is doubtful whether ability to tell the time will have any regulatory effect on his actions—the knowledge that it is now 4.30 p.m. will not induce him to hurry up so as to have a job finished by 5.00 p.m.

As well as teaching the mentally handicapped child to tell the time from a clock-face, attempts should be made to give him an understanding of 'one hour before' and 'one hour after'.

The aim will be to help the pupil to *become aware of time* rather than to help him to tell the time. It is desirable that he should realize that time does not relate only to his sphere of experience: *his* tea-time is at 4 o'clock and *his* bedtime at 9 o'clock, but time is also everyone's time irrespective of where he happens to be, so that if the time is 5 o'clock here in the classroom, it is also 5 o'clock in the next town.

It is extremely difficult to give an understanding of concepts such as the co-existence of events in time (e.g. whilst Mr. Smith is having his breakfast at 6 a.m., Mrs. Jones next door has just arisen to go to the bathroom, young John is still asleep but workers at the bus depot have been at work for some time), and a grasp of the succession of events in time which requires an understanding for 'after' and 'before'.

Terms commonly used by the normal adult may present linguistic obstacles to the mildly or borderline retarded, and should be used with care. Words in this category are: frequent, regular, punctual, every other, fortnight, etc. They are obviously part of the language programme to be learned, but special care must be taken that the meanings of these terms are made quite clear to the mentally handicapped by using them accurately and constantly in everyday life.

More advanced and capable trainees should be assessed for their knowledge of numerical relationships in different contexts, e.g. half, quarters; length, weight, time, money, goods. They can be taught to use the footrule, and common measures required at work and at home should be practised very frequently since they help to form a basis of communication at work and in domestic situations.

B. A Social Reading Course

As in every other aspect of social education and training, the teaching of reading should be governed by the special needs of the mentally handicapped and by his intellectual limitations.

Comprehension of the written word will always be extremely limited and there is little effective time in which to teach reading (because of the much later age at which the handicapped child is ready to learn with understanding). Reading instruction must therefore be of a special kind, and should concentrate on those aspects which are of immediate use: what is learnt should be useful at once, and is not merely a stepping stone to a higher level of efficiency at a later date which will mostly not be attained anyway. Thus, for example, to learn at first to recognize the word DANGER and to act appropriately to it, is a more useful piece of knowledge to the mentally handicapped than the ability to read a phrase such as 'Here is the ball'.

Teaching should begin with learning the social sight vocabulary (Table XX, p. 137) which ensures that the laboriously acquired technique of word recognition serves an immediate purpose. Since teaching of reading should commence probably comparatively late (perhaps not before the child is twelve or thirteen years of age) this social knowledge is relatively advanced, and words of the social sight vocabulary have now more meaning and interest for him than

DANGER

meant that he must be careful or he might be hurt. Where there is a notice saying

NO SMOKING

and another saying

DANGER

you should be careful because smoking might easily cause a fire. If Charlie had looked at these notices and read them carefully he would have known at once why the notice said

NO SMOKING

The room was a storeroom with lots of papers and books everywhere. The notice

NO SMOKING

had been put up because paper catches fire very easily and this might happen if people smoke. The notice saying

DANGER

was to warn people of this.

Charlie should have seen all these notices. There were notices saying

NO SMOKING

and

DANGER

on each wall. He knew quite well that people must not smoke when there is a notice saying

NO SMOKING

5

NO SMOKING

DANGER

"Look what it says here! Can't you read?" the man shouted.

7

Fig. 47. Sample pages of the CLUMSY CHARLIE Reading Books (Book 2: Clumsy Charlie at Work).

they would have for a much younger normal child who is about to start learning to read.

It would be ideal if reading instruction could be continued after this stage in such a way that every further stage had immediate social usefulness. This is not always possible, but the course of social reading outlined in the following paragraphs has the advantage that *some useful* reading knowledge will have been acquired at every stage even if reading instruction has to be terminated prematurely. This course is suitable for mentally handicapped people irrespective of age provided they are not less than about twelve years old, and not profoundly retarded. Everyone is started off on the social sight vocabulary, but further steps— based on the social sight vocabulary—are only taken if time permits and mental capacity is adequate for an understanding of more advanced reading matter.

The Social Sight Vocabulary

The words of the vocabulary (see Table XX, p.137) can be taught in various ways. They can be learned by moderately retarded people using a teaching machine (p. 178) or in the traditional way with the teacher using blackboard and flash card techniques.

The Clumsy Charlie FLASH CARDS, and the four CLUMSY CHARLIE books have been designed to make learning of the words enjoyable and meaningful, for there is little point in reciting mechanically words which have been learned by rote unless the specific meaning of each one is understood.

The FLASH CARDS show the words of the Social Sight Vocabulary on one side and a 'cue-picture' on the other side. The 'hero' of the series is a young man known as Clumsy Charlie, and the illustrations depict the meaning of the words in a humorous way. (Fig. 46). The cards can be used for different games but ordinarily the printed word is exposed to an individual or group and if necessary lagging memory is helped by turning the card over to show the cue picture.

[1] Most teaching devices are self-explanatory so that no further assistance from the teacher is required; examples are the self-correcting teaching aids as used in number work (p. 153) and the flashcards on which each word is illustrated by a well-known object or symbol with which the word is associated. This approach leads to relatively few mistakes because few faulty associations are formed, but it also encourages stereotyped concepts, inadequate stimulation and an inability to generalize. Most teaching aids available give the idea of 3 by showing three *identical* dolls, 4 by

to escape the blow. She was very angry and her eyes were furious. She swung her umbrella and hit Charlie hard on his behind. At the same time she shouted at the top of her voice, "Hey, my lad, can't you read what it says here?" Charlie turned his head and looked up at the notice above the door. There in big letters it said:

WOMEN

Over the other door was a notice which said:

MEN

Oh dear, he had done it again. These were all notices which he could read but he had not even looked for them.

Charlie stood up. The lady glared at him once more and then walked away muttering to herself. Charlie only heard one word—clumsy.

Of course, she was right. "Clumsy Charlie" once again. Why didn't he read those notices? Clumsy Charlie indeed.

It wasn't only notices saying

MEN
and
PULL
and
WOMEN
and
PUSH

which Charlie did not bother to read. There were other words such as the words

14

Charlie turned his head and looked at the notice above the door.

15

Fig. 48. Sample pages of the CLUMSY CHARLIE Reading Books (Book 1: Clumsy Charlie and those Doors.

It is obvious that the acquisition of a sight vocabulary, consisting of many isolated words, does not represent a proper reading skill. Reading a book may be a real incentive both to the child and to the parents, and this extra motivation to acquire a useful skill should not be disregarded even though book reading proper is beyond the understanding of many mentally handicapped children and adults.

The books of the CLUMSY CHARLIE series have been designed to assist in this particular aspect. The four books of the series (Clumsy Charlie and Those Doors, Clumsy Charlie at Work, Clumsy Charlie at Home, Clumsy Charlie at Large) contain the words of the social sight vocabulary printed in different styles and sizes and constantly repeated throughout the text (Figs. 47 and 48). The teacher reads out the text stopping at the words of the social sight vocabulary which are then read by the pupil. This provides good practice in recognizing the words of the social sight vocabulary in different types of printing and puts them into their appropriate context.

The books illustrate the adventures of Charlie, who is known as 'Clumsy Charlie'. He never looks out for the words in the real 'life situations', although he has learnt to read them. In consequence, he finds himself constantly in trouble because he fails to pay attention to the notices on doors, labels, boxes and tins. Each story illustrates Clumsy Charlie's misadventures as a result

showing four *identical* houses, 5 by showing five *identical* cars and so on. By encouraging the child to count only identical objects he can easily fail to grasp the idea that counting refers to things and that things can be counted irrespective of their similar or different appearance. Counting is a generalizing process which enables us to form collections of objects based on properties other than appearance, e.g. use (pieces of furniture), composition (made of glass), etc., and this must be taught. Similarly, words of the social sight vocabulary seen and taught only in one context, acquire only a particular meaning and do not, therefore, help in grasping the general meaning of the word. Although a normal child learns the general meaning of a word simply by responding to the general usage, we cannot be sure of such a natural development in the severely retarded. The words 'IN' and 'OUT' are usually taught in connection with doors and are related to ENTRANCE and EXIT. IN and OUT refer however to movement in relation to a static object which may be a door (as in the Clumsy Charlie series), or a drainpipe (as in the Flashcards). IN and OUT are general words relating not only to doors but to many other actions and contexts, and so it is necessary that aids employed to teach vocabulary should stimulate the development of new associations, and the teacher should ensure that the several meanings of each word are understood.

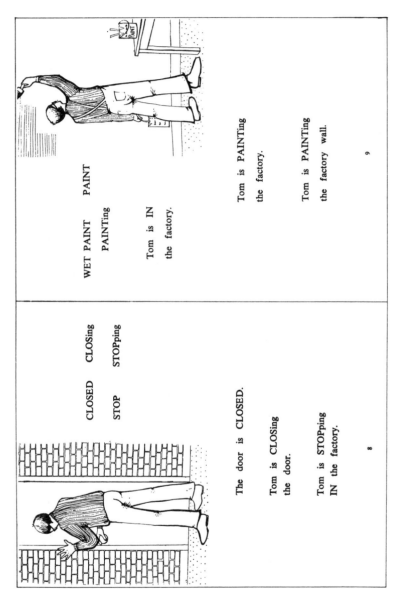

WET PAINT   PAINT

PAINTing

Tom is IN
the factory.

Tom is PAINTing
the factory.

Tom is PAINTing
the factory wall.

9

CLOSED   CLOSing

STOP   STOPping

The door is CLOSED.

Tom is CLOSing
the door.

Tom is STOPping
IN the factory.

8

Fig. 49. Sample pages of the OUT WITH TOM Reading Books
(Book 1: Out with Tom to Work).

of this deplorable habit. Hearing of the adventures of Clumsy
Charlie enables the mentally handicapped to appreciate the usefulness of reading the words. He may begin to understand the
relationship of 'reading' to often experienced situations, and this
in turn may help him to attach meaning to the mechanically learnt
words of the social sight vocabulary.

Learning to Read

An important advantage of the social sight vocabulary is the fact
that every word learned means one piece of socially useful knowledge acquired. The teacher of the mentally handicapped, unlike
other teachers, cannot rely on eight or more years in which to cover
her curriculum. Her pupils will start to learn to read when they are
12 or 13 and not at 5 or 6 as does a normal child. As the time for
teaching is considerably shorter and since the pupil is a slow
learner, his reading acquisitions will be very modest.

The reading requirements of the severely handicapped adult
should be met by a knowledge of the social sight vocabulary, but
the less handicapped should be taught to read. After the social sight
vocabulary which is of immediate practical usefulness, has been
thoroughly absorbed, a reading programme should be started which
is based on these words.

Whereas the Charlie books are designed for the lower level of
handicapped illiterates, another series OUT WITH TOM caters
specially for less retarded persons capable of advancing to a
higher level of both reading and understanding. The series OUT
WITH TOM (18 books) has been designed to help in teaching reading to the less retarded and to provide at the same time some
useful social knowledge (Fig. 49). The first set of three books
uses the words of the social sight vocabulary with various
suffixes and derivations, and adds a new vocabulary of 31 new
words. The contents are simple sentences on a more mature level
relating to factory work, football matches, and so on. From Book 4
onwards there is an average of 11 new words per book learnt by a
'look and say' method. The inclusion of simple phonetical exercises
permits an easy improvement of reading technique and gradually
more words are added to the vocabulary till eventually, short
stories can be read dealing with various situations.

The CLUMSY CHARLIE reading books were designed to avoid
giving offence to their prospective readers—they are not too
childish for the adolescent and adult because they deal, in a

'Nobody gets all of his wages.'

George looked at his wage packet. Then he said, 'But I don't understand. Why do they write down £7.0.0 if they only give me six pounds, two and three?'

For a time Mr Fox said nothing. Then he said to George, 'Now I am beginning to see why there has been all this trouble. Has nobody ever told you that money is stopped out of your wages? It is not just you. It is just the same for Mr Greensmith

16

Fig. 50. Sample page of the SPOTLIGHT ON TROUBLE Reading Books (Book 3: Trouble with the Wages).

humorous way, with minor incidents of real life, and the knock-
about comedy resulting from Charlie's clumsiness is within the
understanding of the younger reader. Tom, the main character in
the OUT WITH TOM series, is studious and successful on a simple
level, and it is probably easy for the mentally handicapped to
accept him as a friend. In this respect he differs considerably from
Charlie, whose attractiveness lies in his clumsiness which makes
the reader feel superior.

OUT WITH TOM is intended *only* for those who will benefit from
a more advanced knowledge of reading. The temptation to continue
teaching reading to the moderately mentally handicapped should be
avoided as time must be given to the more important skills that
will fit him for a place in the community.

Practising Reading for the Less Mentally Handicapped

A reading age of 8 is not very advanced, but to make best use of
the ability acquired, plenty of practice is necessary to advance
the skill to a higher level of efficiency. Unfortunately this is a
reading level which very often condemns young people to read
books and reading material which have been designed for the 6- and
7-year-olds. This is well below the interest level of even a mentally subnormal young man particulary if he has managed to stay in
the community for a while and feels that he is an adult. He does
not wish to read childish books, but there is little available which
is of immediate interest to him written in words simple enough to
be tackled with his limited skill of mechanical reading.

A series of eight reading books under the general title SPOTLIGHT
ON TROUBLE has been designed to meet the needs of the adolescent and adult mentally handicapped with poor reading ability. The
books provide easy reading material for the young adult with
limited reading skill, and they also deal with the social know-how
which is required once the shelter of home and school is no longer
available. Trying to follow directions in a bewildering maze of
streets, meeting the landlady for the first time, clashing with the
foreman at work, conforming to the demands of piecework and being
faced with the mysteries of deductions from a wage packet—these
are only some of the situations which confront the young people
who have left school.

The young adult reader who follows George's, the hero's, mishaps
may sometimes feel superior—he would not have done this, he
would have known better—but probably more often he will remember

wrong. Charlie opened his mouth to ask, but George guessed what was coming and nudged his brother's ribs to keep him quiet.

Just then the door opened and a man told George to go into court. A few minutes later George found himself standing before a long desk with three men looking at him. These must be the magistrates. He felt glad that Charlie was there sitting behind him. There were other people there too, but George did not notice them. All he could see were six cold eyes looking at him. They did not look angry, but neither did they look pleased. Another man asked his name and address, just as if they did not know, and George answered, "George Brown, 27 New Church Road." He wondered if all this would be put in the newspaper. Mrs. Smith would not like that. The man went on reading from a paper, "You are charged that on April the second last you did take and drive away a motor car without the owner's consent——"

Charlie had seen court cases on television. Someone always seemed to jump up and shout something. Then the case was dismissed and they all shook hands and went home. He jumped up!

"It wasn't like that at all. The Red Dragon hadn't got an owner. It had just been dumped there. My brother...." The words froze on his lips. One of the three magistrates was looking at him now and pointing a finger.

"Sit down. You must sit down and not interfere. Your brother will get an opportunity to speak for himself later." The voice was not unkind but it was very, very firm. Charlie sank back in his chair. He wanted to help George but what could he do? He just sat and listened while the clerk went through all the crimes which George was supposed to have committed. At the end of each charge he said, "How do you plead? Guilty? or Not guilty?" and George mumbled "Guilty".

At last the chief magistrate said to George, "Sit down and listen to the facts which will be outlined by the prosecution."

Charlie looked round eagerly. He knew the prosecution was the chap on the other side and wondered what he would look like. Perhaps he would be wearing a wig. He did not know quite what to expect, but he never thought the prosecution would turn out to be an ordinary police sergeant. He

One of the three magistrates was looking at him now and pointing a finger (p. 6)

Fig. 51. Sample pages of the SPOTLIGHT ON MYSTERY Reading Books (Book 4: The Mystery of the Bearded Man).

how he himself failed in similar situations. The events in the book link up with his own experiences—and since nothing is more interesting than reading and hearing about oneself—George and his troubles should have a ready reception from the socially and educationally retarded.

Easy vocabulary, short sentences, repetition of words, simple ideas, uncomplicated time sequence, few characters, absence of an intricate plot—all these factors bring the booklets within the comprehension of the backward reader. The same hero, the same people, the same places are found in each booklet, and each contains a story with a few telling incidents, humorous for the outsider who reads about them, exasperating for George, the victim Funny situations, expressions and idioms not generally found in educational readers but frequently heard in daily conversation make the reader feel 'at home'. They help to establish the adult nature of these easy books and they make George alive and familiar (Fig. 50). Obviously deficient reading skills, fluency, speed and comprehension will benefit greatly through practice with any suitable reading material, but these short 'Spotlight on Trouble' books link up with the reader's own world and help him to understand it better and therefore, perhaps to live more competently within it.

A new series of four books under the general title 'Spotlight on Mystery' continues the technique of presenting socially important situations in an easy, readable form, which makes not many demands of the poor reader. In order to make these books more attractive to the reluctant reader, they take the form of mystery stories (The Mystery of the Pop Singer, The Mystery of the Unfriendly Dog, The Mystery of the Red Dragon, The Mystery of the Bearded Man) giving thereby additional inducement to reading. In the interests of continuity, the same heroes already well known from the preceding stages experience a number of interesting adventures. There is Charlie the hero of the 'Clumsy Charlie' books, and by now possibly something of a mascot to the mentally handicapped reader, his brother George, who figures prominently in the 'Spotlight on Trouble' books, and also a new friend Sam. The books are intended to introduce everyday figures of speech to the reader. Like the preceding 'Spotlight on Trouble' books, they are concerned with social know how and talk about hire purchase, driving hazards, etc., though the mystery aspects dominate in these stories (Fig. 51).

Fig. 52. Sample page of CHARLIE WANTS TO HELP (Talking Points), see footnote, p. 131.

The Reading Interests of the Mentally Handicapped
(This section is based on a paper, 'The Subnormal Boy and his
Reading Interests', *Lib. Quart.*, (1948), XVIII, 4, 264-274.)

A considerable proportion of the mentally handicapped acquire
some mastery of the technical skills of reading. Many can read on
the level of an eight or nine year old child, and this suggests the
possibility of independent, purposeful and enjoyable reading
activities. This is, of course, one of the immediate aims of teaching children to read and it would be a pity if efforts to teach
reading to the mildly and borderline retarded were not utilized
later. Unfortunately, investigation of the reading habits of adult
readers at these intelligence levels shows that reading is not used
to any appreciable extent. Fluency and accuracy in reading does
not in itself indicate a corresponding understanding and a child
with a reading accuracy level of 14 may, when tested, have the
understanding of a child of only seven. Understanding of printed
matter depends primarily on intelligence, but also on an understanding of the vocabulary used and of the literary conventions employed
in story writing.

Limitation of comprehension means that much of the reading
material which is technically accessible is virtually beyond the
reach of understanding of the mentally retarded. It is, therefore,
useful to study his particular difficulties which are mostly due to
his comparatively limited mental outlook and limited experience in
order to select reading matter which can be understood and enjoyed
by him.

There has been little investigation into the reading habits and
attitudes of the mentally handicapped adult. The little that is known
is derived from studies of the educationally subnormal child (IQ
50 to 75) in his school years. There is, however, no reason to
suppose that the school child of fourteen and fifteen differs considerably from the young adult of sixteen or seventeen who is
admitted for further training and education to a hospital school or
a senior training centre. In the following section, the comments on
stories and books of the juvenile type are those of a number of
moderately and borderline retarded children who were asked to
write down their criticisms and general comments after they finished
their reading. But for correction of spelling mistakes and punct-
uation, the comments have been reprinted without alteration.

Generally speaking the educationally subnormal childrens' reading tastes and preferences are apparently very similar to those of their comrades with normal intelligence. They are attracted by descriptions of fighting, shooting and other dramatic events. 'I liked it because there were dead bodies in it' or 'it is a good fighting story' or 'I like to hear of daring deeds'.

Descriptions of escapes and last minute rescues are particulary liked, as are those of skilled practical ability, of invention, and the mastery of difficult situations. There is also interest in emotional events such as happy family re-unions and descriptions of family life. Stories of action, emotional impact, and those with heroes with whom the reader can identify are therefore of as great an interest to the mentally handicapped reader as to his normal contemporaries.

More important for an understanding of their attitude to reading are the difficulties which they encounter while trying to comprehend their reading matter. These difficulties are caused mostly by the complexity and unfamiliarity of vocabulary. Long words have to be spelt out laboriously and the exact meaning of many words is often unknown. References to well-known events and persons may not be understood and, once this sphere of abstract imagery is reached, the mentally handicapped reader is hopelessly lost. Nearly every book within the reading ability of a ten- to fourteen-year-old contains a certain amount of such matter and, though the story itself may be enjoyed, the impossibility of understanding certain points considerably mars the reader's satisfaction.

'Here are so many big words that I just could only understand some parts, but what I could understand was good'.

'I could not understand it because there were so many funny words in it, words which I have not heard'.

'It was quite interesting at the start and I could understand it too, but when I was half way through it I couldn't understand it at all, but near the end I could. Mind you I don't want very easy books, but ones that I can understand, I mean 'til I get better at dictionary words. Thank you'.

Such complaints are most frequent in relation to historical stories which use old-fashioned phraseology and vocabulary. Then the boys justifiably complain that:

'Some of the sentences were not understandable because it has been put down the way they used before in old days and there is a lot of dictionary words in it what I can't understand. Otherwise the book was all right'.

In consequence, a reader may approach stories of historical character already with some prejudice:

'When I first had this book I did think it was going to be hard because nearly every book I have read of olden days has always been hard. But this one was all right in understanding, and exciting'.

There is also a notable dislike for stories with many characters. It is difficult for the retarded to distinguish between a number of persons, and generally they cannot cope with a story containing more than five or six characters. Sometimes one person is referred to by two or three different names, surname, first name and nickname, and this proves to be highly perplexing:

'To my opinion I think this is one of the worst books I have read. My reason is I like a story book or adventure book with two or three names so that I can understand it'.

or

'I got mixed up with the names of the persons in it'.

There is pronounced agreement that books should not contain several stories because of the difficulty the readers have in separating the various persons and incidents of each story. The reader's unconscious assumption is that everything contained between the covers of a book pertains to the same story. If there are several stories within one book, the danger of overlooking the end of one and the beginning of the next is very real, and more misunderstandings occur than the normal reader is able to imagine. The resulting muddle of incidents and characters belonging to entirely different plots can be imagined!

'I do not like mixed-up stories and fresh people in them every time. I like one story. Then you know what you are doing and reading'.

'I do not like this book because there were two stories in it, and I do not like a book with so many stories in it'.

'I liked the book because it is all one story. That is how I like books'.

'Easy stories' are abhorred because they are associated with uninteresting reading matter of the fairy-tale type, written for much younger children. One can hear the undertone of disgust in the laconic comment 'all about a cat and a dog' or 'all about feather-bed land'.

Animal stories are generally disliked, but exceptions are made if the stories contain adventures. Stories of wild animals are preferable to those of tame and domesticated animals and there is also a preference for stories which include people.

'I can say this book wasn't so easy and would like to read it over and over again but I could understand it, and it always had some adventure in it. I mean, you don't usually get good animal stories like this. I can't say much more, but books like them are liked, thank you'.

'I don't mind having to put up with an animal in a story if it has someone who is a human being. But to have a book that is all about animals and nothing else is beyond me'.

There is also a tendency to withdraw from stories taking place in foreign countries.

'I do not like stories about foreign people', 'I do not like stories of other lands'.

These stories are considered 'funny', partly because of the difficult vocabulary and phraseology, partly because the whole background is unfamiliar and strange.

Since the mentally handicapped child grows up in a world of which he has only incomplete understanding, he feels especially lost and insecure if he wanders beyond his immediate sphere. His is no thirst for the unknown, no longing for a widening of knowledge, but rather a desire to find continuous reassurance in the world as he knows it. Terman (1926) states that the subnormal child 'derives pleasure from finding mention of himself and things that he has read of before. He may be contented through all his life with one simple 'literary' interest. Transferring him into far-away countries, with strange people, strange customs, and strange ideas deprives him of the possibility of drawing on his limited store of associations and experiences and makes him feel uncomfortable, insecure and resentful.' A similar observation was made by Huber (1928) who stated 'the preference of dull children (for stories) of family life and intimate social relationships—things that have happened to children—is so much greater than the preference of either average or bright children or all children combined as to make it a real and significant difference.'

It is rare for the mentally handicapped to comment on literary

mannerisms and style, and probably most of them overlook this
aspect. Still, here are some comments which show how irritation
with the subject matter of a book may fasten on an alleged defect
of style—the subnormal's critical attitude is not much different in
its outspokenness from that of many a 'normal' adult reader!

'The first two chapters were all right because they were about
Troy, but this about digging up libraries is, I think, boring. It tells
you what the man looked like and at least a page about his face
and how he dressed. I think that is too much about one thing in this
history book. It nearly always starts the story like this 'Once upon
a time, long ago' which I think is a baby's way. It always says that
girls have hair like the corn when it is ripe and their skin is like
milk. I think that is daft.'
'The one who wrote this book could not make up his mind what
to put.'
'I think it would be better without the first four pages in it, and
pages 14 and 15 would be better out of it because it's got nothing
to do with the story in one way.'
'I did not think much of it because of the last two or three
chapters and the part about the afternoon in the classroom where
the master told about the lost ship.'
'I could not understand it on two reasons. One was because there
was misunderstanding in the words and the second reason was there
was too much exclaiming when something had to be said, which was
not exciting at all.'

Here is another comment which is really aimed at the tedious
description of well-known scenes which take the interest out of
books while the reader is waiting for the 'real story' to begin.
'I have read books and they may start off like this: It was a nice
day and there were two little boys in the garden and their mother
told them to come in for breakfast and they have a wash and do
their beds and so on, the book gets boring when they put anything
like that.'
On the other hand, details and descriptions are appreciated if
they are really integrated into the interesting story.
'What I liked a lot in this, which is hardly in any other book I
have read, and that is, as the gang goes round, it does not only tell
you where the gang was and where they were going but it explains
exactly how the place is and that gives you a good idea of the

place itself. Of course, that's how you really want it, don't you? In conclusion, the subnormal boy's reading interests may be summarized as follows.

Although he is at a disadvantage on account of lower intelligence, narrower experience and limited vocabulary he could, if properly encouraged, be a keen reader with a critical attitude towards his books. He knows what he likes and what he does not like, and is not inclined to accept all that is offered to him without criticism. It is not correct to suppose that all mentally handicapped children need special urging and attention once they have acquired adequate reading skills (although there may be emotional blocking which interferes with the enjoyment of reading).

His reading interests are essentially the same as those of normal boys of his mental age although with some characteristic differences. Certain preferences in choice of subjects or incidents are directly attributable to his personality. There is not only the special interest in boy characters and their adventures that is to be found in every normal boy reader, but also a greater interest in familiar scenes and persons which is perhaps particularly characteristic of children with a mental handicap. This liking for homely and known settings is just as marked as the rejection of obtrusive historical or foreign settings beyond his comprehension. The natural urge for security and a tendency to identify the unknown with the fearsome are accentuated. Preference for familiar life does not mean dislike of an adventurous one but it is, so to speak, a 'geographical' liking which helps to keep the familiar landmarks in sight and gives the reader a better understanding of his surroundings.

The most important point however, is the need for a simplified vocabulary in his reading matter. It must be as simple and concrete as that of the everyday speech of the average boy, and all literary qualities have to be sacrificed to this necessity. The reading matter for the mentally handicapped who is able to read without much difficulty, should not be considered on the same level as reading matter for the normal child. No attempt should be made to extend his vision beyond his immediate needs or to widen his horizon; nor is reading for him a step up the ladder of literary values. On the other hand, if it is possible to collect a number of books which avoid the various pitfalls of complicated story construction and unaccustomed vocabulary, books can be used to augment the mentally handicapped child's and adolescent's social education.

The fact that the mentally handicapped adult who has a useful reading skill scarcely ever uses it to obtain pleasure or information from his reading is partly due to disillusionment with his reading matter. He is quite incapable of selecting reading matter which is within his grasp and which is not confusing. Not being of a very persistent nature, he will soon give up the struggle, and a reading skill which has taken years to acquire is left to deteriorate for lack of practice. On the other hand, the comments quoted show that there is understanding and enjoyment in reading, which could be utilized to strengthen the mentally handicapped child's social education.

C. Programmed Learning and a Teaching Machine for the Mentally Handicapped

It has been generally accepted that the educational needs of a severely mentally handicapped child are of such a nature that they require specialized assistance. This has led to the term 'Special Education'. Special education differs from normal education in many ways: smaller classes, different approaches, different subjects to be taught and a slower speed of teaching and learning than found in normal education. Yet in very few cases indeed has *special education* been achieved if this means a *tailor-made* education. Except for the private pupil, the teacher is faced with a group, even though a small group, which is heterogeneous in character. The majority are children who can only learn by doing things in an informal way. They have to be occupied and kept happy, they have to be supervised and their countless demands have to be satisfied. The two or three children in the group who could benefit by a specialized tailor-made education including some of the formal subjects have to be neglected to some extent because there is simply no time to attend to their needs.

This situation is very unsatisfactory, although it could be somewhat improved if the teacher were able to set aside one or two sessions a week to attend to the needs of these two or three exceptional children. The children are slow learners and the teaching of even very elementary knowledge takes up a disproportionately large amount of time. It will soon be felt that a few sessions are not sufficient to make any impact on the child since so much time must be spent on constant repetition and practice. In this situation the teacher may well think it would be useful if a great deal of the inevitable repetitive and mechanical teaching work could be taken over by an assistant, leaving her free to guide the pupil towards new knowledge. There is, after all, little doubt that a good deal of learning demands only simple practice which could be supervised by a person less qualified than the teacher.

A teaching machine could be useful, not to supplant the teacher, but to take off her shoulders some of the drudgery which most repetitive work produces. In this sense a machine can be regarded as an assistant who relieves the senior teacher of much of the mechanical work, which is nevertheless essential to make sure that knowledge is readily available.

The obvious difference between a machine and a teacher is that the teacher is adaptable for the changing needs of each pupil. A machine follows a rigid course of action for which it was constructed unless it is highly complex. Though this is an obvious disadvantage, there are certain advantages connected with this inflexibility of the machine.

A teacher, like any other human being, is very much subject to the influences of the moment. She may feel off colour, she may be disturbed, upset or particularly happy and may not be able to concentrate on her job. These and other factors may interfere and her performance may vary considerably from moment to moment. This is not necessarily a disadvantage, but there is little doubt that it leads to an unevenness in approach. At such times her efficiency may be impaired just when frequent systematic repetition may be most necessary in presenting the material in those very small steps which are required in work with the mentally handicapped. It is in this very area of systematic presentation of material in small steps, adjusted to the slow mental grasp of the mentally subnormal child, that the teaching machine can be of immense help. The machine is not subject to moods and will present the material in the same manner as often as required in an automatic and systematic way particularly suitable for practising repetitive operations, such as teaching the tables or the social sight vocabulary. A machine—if intelligently used—enables the teacher to devote her energy to teaching tasks which require a flexible approach.

If actual teaching rather than practising by repetition is the aim, the presentation of material must follow a certain programme and whatever is to be learned is taught in such small steps that even the slowest pupil will understand it. No essential step in the progress should be omitted, and each should follow logically from

the preceding one and lead logically to the next. This is good
teaching practice and there is no reason why the same method could
not be tried out in teaching the subnormal. This method is successfully used in programmed teaching machines and experiments have
shown that even the severely subnormal can acquire some knowledge
in this way.

Price (1963), using such machines with mentally retarded pupils
with an average age of 15 and an average IQ of 50, obtained
successes which compared well with classroom teaching. Setting
out to teach addition and subtraction he found that the teaching
machine achieved as much success in less time than the teacher
following conventional classroom methods. Malpass *et al.* (1964)
reported automated teaching of word recognition to be more effective
than conventional classroom instruction and pointed out that automated instruction was as effective in teaching word recognition
and spelling as individual tutoring. Stolurow (1963) reviews fourteen
studies of the effects of language and arithmetic programmes on
mentally subnormal children and Haskell (1966) summarizes this
literature relating to the mentally retarded. There is prejudice
against the use of teaching machines because they seem to threaten
the close personal link between teacher and pupil. But slide
projectors have been used for generations, and tape recorders and
television are becoming commonplace in the classroom. These are
aids to good teaching because they help to reinforce the spoken
word, and they leave the teacher free to devote more time to the
specialized tasks of individual teaching just as the housewife's
use of washing machine, vacuum cleaner and so forth help to free
her for other things. The teaching machine, too, should be con-
ceived as an aid that enables the teacher to devote more of her
time to those operations which need skilled attention.

As with many other aids which have been developed for normal
children, teaching machines now commercially available may
not be suitable for the social education of the mentally retarded.
In order to be useful in this context it should fulfil various conditions:

(a) The machine must permit the teacher to design programmes of
her own without difficulty. Very few published programmes will be
found generally satisfactory and the teacher will need to evolve
her own programmes which provide tailor-made education for each
individual.

(b) The teaching machine must be simple to operate.

(c) Because the mentally handicapped is not spurred on to increased endeavour simply by a desire to learn, the teaching machine must give its 'yes' or 'no' to each answer in a sufficiently interesting manner that this of itself provides some motivation to repeat the step or to proceed to the next question.

(d) In view of the child's small powers of application and sustained thought, the machine should incorporate a device which enables the teacher to see whether a child has proceeded by trial and error, or has learnt systematically.

The teaching machine discussed in the following paragraphs has been developed in accordance with the requirements.

The machine is housed in a box 16 inches × 18 inches (Fig. 53). In the lid are two Perspex windows through which the pupil can see the relevant parts of the programme card. The left-hand window shows the question and the right-hand window shows four possible answers. Next to the answer window are four buttons which operate a light signal (the dome light is seen protruding from the lid of the compartment at the right-hand top corner), a buzzer, and a magnetic counter situated in the front edge of the box. The material to be taught is written by the teacher onto cards which are provided with the machine (Fig. 54). The single frame on the left of the card displays either an item of information or a question to test the understanding of the information. On the right of the card are four frames, which permit the designer of the programme to draw or write three incorrect answers and one correct answer. The position of the correct answer is varied from card to card. The programmer cuts out the shaded piece on the right edge by the correct answer (Fig. 54), which allows the electro-mechanical mechanism of the machine to recognize the selected answer. If the pupils are illiterate the machine can be used in conjunction with a tape-recorder playing pre-recorded questions.

The procedure is simple. The teacher loads 30 to 40 programmed cards comprising the lesson to be taught into the left-hand compartment of the machine. The cards are stacked on a spring-loaded plate which presses the top card against the Perspex window. The lid is locked and the magnetic counter is set at nought. The machine is now ready for use by the pupil. The pupil reads the question and selects the answer which he thinks appropriate and depresses the button next to the answer frame of his choice. If he has selected

Fig. 53. PROLEMAC—4 teaching machine.

the correct answer the buzzer sounds and the dome lights up. The pupil moves now the sliding knob in the lid of the machine which removes the top card and brings the next into view. If the pupil has selected the wrong answer, the magnetic counter records his error and he should try again for the right answer.

At the end of the session the magnetic counter shows the number of incorrect responses made and the teacher will be able to judge from the score whether the pupil has understood the lesson or not. If the lesson has not been understood the teacher may choose to repeat the programme or design another one, or to give personal instruction.

For the mentally handicapped the machine should probably be used mostly in conjunction with other teaching aids and as a means to reinforce traditional methods. There is, however, no doubt that in some cases the subnormal pupil can learn from the teaching machine without the teacher having had an active part in the teaching process.

The following two cases illustrate the acquisition of words in the social sight vocabulary by using a tape-recorder and a Prolemac—4 teaching machine (Fig. 55).

The personal data of the two men were: F.W., age 23, WAIS FIQ 55, illiterate, B. H., age 17 WAIS FIQ 55, illiterate.

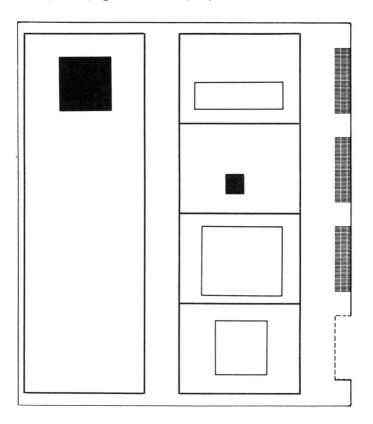

Fig. 54. A programme card used for perceptual training.

In this experiment, fifteen words of the social sight vocabulary were taught using the tape-recorder and appropriate cards in the teaching machine. Generally, only two new words were presented at each session. Words learnt in preceding sessions were tested by the teacher showing flash-cards, and if words were not remembered the unsuccessful lesson was repeated before proceeding to the next lesson.

The first session was taken up with an introduction to the teaching machine. Testing of actual learning could only start in the third lesson and be related to words learnt in the second session. There were fifteen sessions lasting half-an-hour each, during a period of 3 weeks. The maximum which could be learnt during that period was 26 words.

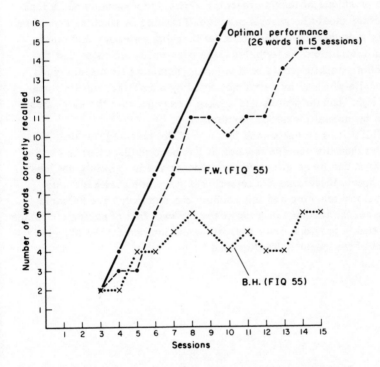

Fig. 55. Learning curves of two men with comparable intelligence.

The straight line in Fig. 55 extending from the bottom left-hand corner to the top right-hand corner shows the ideal progress there would have been if a pupil had remembered all the words learned at each session.

The graph of FW indicates good progress which, in the beginning, is pretty near to the optimal performance. At the end of the teaching period FW had acquired a knowledge of 15 words, which represented a teaching success of 58·7%. When he was re-assessed for retention, after an interruption of two weeks, he still remembered 11 words or 73% of the vocabulary he had learnt. BH, on the other hand, did not respond well to the teaching machine and learned only 6 words. For him the teaching machine is probably not an adequate method of learning.

This, of course, was an experiment to find out how far success could be attributed to the machine alone. It is not advocated that this technique of leaving teaching entirely to a machine and a tape-recorder should be general practice. Teaching by machine should be fully supported by the use of other teaching materials and classroom instruction. Nevertheless, the experiment indicates that the teaching machine could be a valuable assistant for certain types of pupils who may be better motivated by a machine with its flashing light, buzzer sounds and spoken messages over the earphones than by normal classroom instruction.

Whilst it is probably rash to say that the teaching machine is better than the average teacher, it has become clear that in certain tasks it can be as effective as a teacher and is certainly not less so. Speed of learning and retention is comparable with ordinary classroom teaching and the machine can certainly save valuable time for the teacher. In many cases the very fact of having a machine to operate provides extra motivation and interest for the sluggish mind of the mentally handicapped.

8

THE OUTLOOK

The Employability in the Open Community of Moderately Retarded People

A good part of the social incompetence of the mentally handicapped is due to his inadequate learning of social requirements during the formative years. Handicapped by his inferior intelligence, he is unable to develop on the impoverished 'general knowledge-nutrition' provided by a poor and adverse environment. The whole education and training process must therefore, at a later stage, attempt to provide those 'intellectual vitamins' that have been missing from the beginning. Although it would of course be preferable to train the handicapped person right from infancy, it is unlikely that the social, medical and community services will be improved so significantly in the near future that this will be possible. But it is essential that the available services are made sufficiently effective to ameliorate the worsening situation.

There is reason to believe that a good proportion of the mentally handicapped could make a reasonable adjustment to ordinary living and working conditions, provided they were given a good start and some assistance later. This is borne out by the discrepancies between the estimated numbers of mental defectives and those actually under care and supervision, and by a large number of studies which report the status of adults who had once been classified as mentally defective. This explains why statements of incidence of subnormality nowadays cautiously estimate the number of people who *will be retarded at some time in their lives.*

The available research, reporting on the subsequent social careers of people who came to the attention of the authorities on account of their mental subnormality, makes interesting reading, and has been ably summarized by Clarke and Clarke (1965). Most studies show a success rate of between 50% and 75% (if success is defined simply in terms of ability to hold down a job for a reasonable period of time and to keep out of trouble). Most reports however, deal mainly with the more intelligent subnormals and it

181

could be argued that their intellectual level is sufficient for social competence provided their personality make-up is adequate. As a group, they are undoubtedly more 'at risk' than normal people, but the fact that they can and do work and live satisfactorily outside institution walls is nowadays not wholly surprising.

The situation is rather different with the moderately retarded. These are people who have been considered unsuitable even for special school education, and they have received a mainly occupational training of doubtful value. The group consists largely of people whose mental subnormality is due to organic causes and, in their case, intellectual assessment offers little hope that an unrealized potential might lead to an improvement of performance at a later stage. Spectacular IQ score improvements are not found with the same frequency in their case as with the mildly and borderline retarded.

What about **their** chances to work and live in the community without constant **supervision**? Although much less research is available about this 'imbecile' group, enough is known to be able to form some impression of their capacity under optimal conditions.

The two principal questions to be asked are: Can the moderately retarded (high-grade imbecile) work sufficiently well to earn a wage which at least contributes substantially to his support? Can he live and work in the community with a modicum of support (from a home or hostel)?

The first question was investigated in the, by now, classic experiments associated with the names of O'Connor, Tizard, and Clarke & Clarke and their associates, carried out mostly at the Manor Hospital, Surrey. The results of these, admittedly laboratory experiments, and other relevant research can be studied in summarized form in the chapter on 'The Abilities and Trainability of Imbeciles' in Clarke and Clarke (1965). They suggested that the following points should be adhered to in training the moderately handicapped for industrial work, to reach a level of impressive competence.

a. There should be suitable incentives of a realistic type.

b. Work should be broken down into small constituent operations which have to be taught separately but in the right sequence.

c. Correct movements, which by definition are the easiest, should be taught from the very start.

d. Short teaching periods produce more learning than long sessions.

e. To make correct responses habitual, much 'over-learning' should take place.

f. It is important that the learning of skills is accompanied by the verbal reinforcement of a running commentary on the actions performed.

Highly interesting though these results are, they cannot provide evidence that the abilities which have been established under somewhat artificial conditions and in the shelter of an institution environment, would be adequate in the rough and tumble of life and over lengthy periods of employment. Whether there is sufficient 'transfer' from training to life to compensate for the considerable intellectual retardation is a question which must remain unanswered at present.

Other evidence, however, permits some judgment as to the employability of this group. Studies are not as plentiful as those dealing with the more intelligent mentally handicapped, and indeed it is only fairly recently that this group has been considered to have a chance at all in the labour market. The following paragraphs summarize some of the statistical results relating to the employment of the moderately handicapped. It bears out the impression among authorities that probably some 20% of the group could contribute substantially to their livelihood and do not require permanent custodial care or sheltered workshop arrangements.

In Tizard and Grad's investigation (1961), five out of 60 adult imbeciles were employed full-time for a regular wage, one worked full-time for meals and pocket-money and three others did casual work. Delp and Lorenz (1953) reported that of 66 adults whose IQ's were under 50 in their childhood 15% were gainfully employed and Saenger's (1967) investigation of 520 severely retarded adults showed that 27% were working for pay and an additional 9% had worked in the past.

The Annual Reports of the Special Services After-Care Sub-Committee of the City of Birmingham, for the years 1956 to 1960, show the type of work followed by those gainfully employed who had, as children, been excluded from school. In 1956, for example the report found no less than 20·3% (232 men and women) who lived at home and were gainfully employed. One third of these people were engaged in factory work, some 13% were employed as

porters, labourers and in odd jobs, and approximately 9% were **working** in bakeries, breweries and food manufacture. As subsequent **reports** show, these are the types of jobs which tend to absorb most of these people with low ability.

Craft (1962) investigated the careers of 53 patients discharged from hospital whose IQ's were between 35 and 49 when tested last within the hospital. The follow-up, carried out on an average of five years after discharge, established that 75% ($N = 40$) were working at the time of the follow-up. Further investigation showed that 49% of the group of 53 had been in continuous employment since their discharge, the women generally in domestic service and the men in unskilled labouring or semi-skilled gardening jobs. Craft was also able to compare these figures with 262 other patients discharged in the same period. He showed that 79% of those with IQ between 50 and 69, and 72% of those with IQ's over 70 were employed. These figures are comparable with the 75% of the low IQ group and this suggests that many mentally handicapped persons can hold down jobs in the open community, irrespective of their intelligence level, and that adequate placement would help considerably to overcome severe handicaps. Gunzburg (1963), investigating the records of a hospital for subnormals, found that 29% of the patients who, on a given day, were gainfully employed outside the hospital, had been classified as having an IQ below 50, and that their average earnings were £6 10s. 0d. with a range from £4 10s. 0d. to £9 0s. 0d.

Edgerton (1967) who made an extremely competent and detailed study of the mentally retarded outside institutions produced very relevant evidence regarding the social competence of people in the community. He stated that 'on the whole, the IQ of any given individual among these 48 former patients tells us little about what to expect from him following his return to the outside world. Even very low IQ is no sure indicator. For example, while it is true that the most dependent and incompetent person in the cohort had an IQ of 47, another person whose IQ was 48 was rated as the eleventh most independent and competent member of the cohort . . . it is clear that persons in this research cohort whose IQ's were over 70 possessed no obvious advantage over those whose IQ's were 70 or below. . . . many whose IQ's were over 70 were quite dependent, and hence not very competent persons. On the other hand, among the ten most independent and competent ex-patients we find persons with IQ's of 68, 56, 60, 57, and 52.'

If one considers that the few people studied in these surveys scarcely ever received an appropriate education and training for their jobs, it is surprising that so many succeeded despite their pronounced handicap, although it is probably correct to say that many were considerably helped by careful placement and by their own personalities. Nevertheless, these figures suggest that with adequate assistance which could influence their attitude to people around them, with careful placement and the belief that they could do better than they have done so far, moderately retarded people could well be placed in the open community for life and work, and the 20% mentioned by some authorities is not as unrealistic a target as might be thought.

Case studies illustrating the abilities of the severely retarded are not numerous yet, although they would help considerably to draw attention to successes which are possible despite very low abilities. Williams (1967) discusses in detail the training of a 17-year-old profoundly retarded mongol who had a non-verbal mental age of approximately 2 years and a verbal mental age of less than 18 months (the latter figure in an adult would correspond to an IQ of below 10!!!). This young man was able to take part in the industrial work of a sheltered workshop and earned consistently a small sum of money. Gunzburg (1960) gives the case history of one Freddie M. with a WAIS IQ 33 who was sent daily to work in a factory outside the institution where he held the job of a floor-sweeper 'and the manager could not find enough words of praise for his work.'

Even more intriguing is the following case of George P. This man was admitted to hospital at the age of 47 after his parents had died. He had held a labouring job in a laundry near his home for more than twenty years and the laundry was quite prepared to let him continue though his admission to hospital could have set a convenient end to his employment.

George had little communication and formal testing proved nearly impossible. He failed to answer the simplest verbal items on the WAIS test and was unable to understand performance tests. He was able to name all coins presented to him but was unable to do anything with this knowledge. He added two pennies together and counted serially up to four, but this was the limit of his mathematical knowledge and ability. When asked to draw a person he responded with a series of unclosed circles and continued until he was stopped. When asked to draw a house, he drew a number of horizontal lines.

There is no doubt about George's profound mental retardation and on formal testing his score was below Mental Age two. Yet this man had held a job satisfactorily for over 20 years earning now on the average £6 per week. It was decided that he should continue his employment from hospital despite the distance and travelling involved to get to work.

The nursing staff took on a patient daily training role, accompanying George to and from work, pointing out landmarks, demonstrating road crossings, showing how to get on buses, how to pay fares etc. —in fact a large number of social skills which were completely unknown to this man. His daily travel to and from work where each journey took over one hour, involved two different bus journeys, selecting the correct bus, and crossing the streets three times, (only once on a zebra-crossing, whilst the other two meant crossing extremely busy roads with heavy and dangerous traffic). The journeys also meant queuing up, having to pay two different bus fares and becoming part of the rush hour traffic.

The nursing staff managed to teach this man to do these journeys by himself in seven weeks' intensive training. Considering that this man had a Mental Age of less than two and was forty-seven years old when he had to learn a number of completely new and complex social skills which made him independent of further supervision, it appears that many of our traditional ideas of the imbecile's inability to adjust to life and work in the open community may have to be revised in the same way as we had to revise our ideas about his unemployability.

The Results of Directed Social Training in Adolescence

Having established that there is good reason to believe that the moderately and severely retarded are capable of living in the open community with some support and contributing to their livelihood, one inevitable question is whether the type of social education and training described in the preceding sections must always begin at a very early age, or whether it can also be effective later. This question is necessitated by the inadequacy of present provisions, which results in many moderately retarded people not receiving the right type of education and training at the right time.

The investigation described below[1] set out to explore the possibilities of a directed education and training programme begun after the age of 16 (Gunzburg, 1965). The setting in which the experiment took place was similar to that discussed on pp. 112–117. A training set-up was established in a small industrial town with the purpose of providing industrial occupational training for adult subnormals aged 16 to 25 with IQ's below 55. It was also decided that one group of approximately 30 young men and women should receive full residential social and educational training on the lines previously discussed, and that a second group consisting of a similar number of adolescent men and women should live locally and attend daily for industrial training only. (However, only 15 young people in the residential group and the people in the 'Workshop group' were still available for evaluation purposes two years later—see Table XXI).

Trainees were assessed by psychologists at admission and, on the basis of their results, individual training programmes were worked out. No further direct guidance and supervision was available from psychological staff. This made it possible to study the effects of training conditions which were not continually controlled by skilled and specialized staff. Trainees were regularly reassessed on their P-A-C forms and these served as guides to the social education provided throughout the trainees' stay. Reassessment on the intelligence test and on the Vineland scale took place approximately two years after admission to the project and was carried out by an independent psychologist.

Table XXI sets out the relevant data of the two groups before commencement of training. There were no significant differences in mental levels at the first assessment (mean 5y 11m and 5y 1m). There was also no significant difference between the levels of social competence (mean 7·62 and 7·49), and though the mean age of one group was two years more than that of the other (mean CA 19y 3m and 21y 3m), this was not statistically significant. Both groups were, therefore, comparable in intellectual attainments scores measured by the Terman-Merrill scale, in social ability as measured by the Vineland scale, and in chronological age. It is therefore reasonable to suggest that any differences between the

[1] This research was made possible by the National Society for Mentally Handicapped Children, which permitted the use of their National Hostels and Workshops, Elliman Avenue, Slough, for this purpose. The Society's support of this work is gratefully acknowledged.

TABLE XXI

Intellectual and social progress of two groups of severely mentally handicapped young adults

	Average MA ± S.D. 1st assessment	Average MA ± S.D. 2nd assessment	t Test	Average SA ± S.D. 1st assessment	Average SA ± S.D. 2nd assessment	t Test
Experimental group N = 15 Mean CA 19y 3m	5y 11m ± 1y 2m	6y 1m ± 1y 6m	0·5	7·62 ± 1·65	10·3 ± 2·35	6·3*
Control group N = 16 Mean CA 21y 3m at admission	5y 1m ± 1y	5y 3m ± 1y 4m	1·66	7·49 ± 1·75	7·91 ± 1·57	2·94*
t Test	1·78	1·65		0·18	3·28*	

*Significant at 1% level.

two groups, after completion of the training, would not be due to differences in age, intelligence or social ability, and that changes would be due to training or lack of it.

Trainees in the residential group lived at a hostel and received social training which particularly emphasized the skills needed for life outside the centre; this gave them experience in shopping, the use of public transport, delivering messages and running errands, etc. The day group attended only for work in the sheltered work-shop, and their social progress was due either to information picked up casually or to education and training given at home by their parents.

After two years, the re-assessment of intellectual and social functioning showed interesting differences (Table XXI). At that time the numbers had been reduced to 15 young people (10 men, 5 women) in the residential group and 16 young people (5 men, 11 women) in the day group. Though there was a slight increase of mean intelligence tests scores, the difference is statistically insignificant and the level of functioning intelligence, as measured by a traditional intelligence test, did not change in either group, despite the two-year interval, and the intensive educational train-ing of one group. This is in agreement with expectations and indirectly confirms the reliability of the first assessment of intel-ligence.

As far as social ability is concerned, both groups had improved significantly at the second testing. Figure 56 shows that some members of the control (non-resident) group had done comparatively well, even though others had added scarcely, if at all, to their measured social competence. The average gain of this group over two years was less than half-a-year. This advance is slight com-pared with the gains of each individual in the experimental group, and Figure 56 shows that each member of the residential group progressed well, and some of them extremely well; the average gain of the group measured on the Vineland scale was well over 2½ years. Although the difference in social functioning between the two groups was not statistically significant at the time of the first assessment, it had become so, at the 1% level of confidence, at the time of re-assessment two years later. The group living and working at the hostel and in the workshop had therefore advanced faster socially and developed a higher level of social competence than the group living at home and attending only for work.

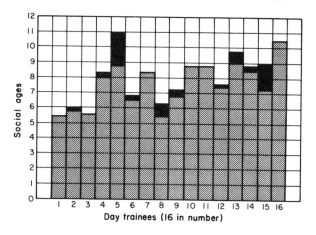

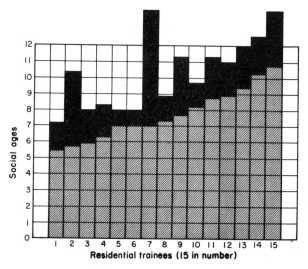

Fig. 56. Comparison between 'incidental' social learning and guided social education and training.

The fact that training does influence the social competence of moderately retarded people is not new; it has been shown to be the case with young children and it has also been shown that intellectual ability is unaffected by training and remains on the same level even though social competence increases (see for example the study by

R. E. Francey, 1960). The interesting feature of the present investigation is that these findings have also been shown to apply to young adults who are very often considered to be past the age when education might have any effect.

The progress of the group living at home and not receiving any particular training bears out the statement made by Doll (1953) that mental defectives show relatively little increase in social age after mental age reaches its final limit (p. 417). He suggests that there is only a slight tendency for social age to increase with chronological age during the period of 14 to 24 years (p. 120), and he provides a table (p. 164) indicating that social age increases in that period are zero. On the other hand, this investigation suggested that, if a determined effort is made to continue social education and training into adulthood, gains averaging 2½ years can be made by those given training *and* opportunities to practice new social skills.

Nonetheless, it would be a mistake to accept the figures of the Vineland scale at their face value. Some trainees improved quite considerably in terms of social age. One young man admitted with a social age of 7 had, on re-test, a social age of 14·4, and a young woman with the social age of 6·7 at the first assessment, had a social age of 10·3 on re-test. There are, as can be seen from Figure 56 several other examples of large increases, but it would be misleading to make a straight comparison and state that the young subnormal man's social ability was comparable with that of a young normal 14-year-old boy, and the woman's with that of a 10-year-old girl. The special atmosphere of the training situation has, without a doubt, produced considerable changes in *some* selected areas measured by the scale, but we cannot be sure that these changes are representative of the same all-round social development that would be found in normal children under normal conditions.

Several important points have been demonstrated by this investigation.

1 *The early stages of social competence consist of skills that can be mastered fairly easily because they require little intelligence as such.*

They represent attainments which generally can be acquired and practised with the help of intensive and directed training. Intelligence will determine the speed with which these skills are learned, but not necessarily whether they are learnt at all. It is legitimate to compare these primitive skills with the mechanical side of academic attainments such as reading ability. It is well-known that mentally handicapped people can acquire a fairly high level of reading attainment, despite a considerably lower mental level, for they recite the printed word without much understanding of what they are reading. Similarly, social skills acquired in a mechanical way may not always be fully applied by the mentally handicapped in unfamiliar situations or when adaptation to new circumstances is required, although they will be used adequately enough in ordinary daily routine.

2 Since social skills are, in the first stages, fairly independent of intelligence, *it is possible to raise the level of social efficiency well above the level indicated by mental age.* This has already been shown by surveys of the relationship between social attainment and mental age, and the present investigation has again demonstrated that a comparatively short time of training can result in an appreciable heightening of social competence. It also underlines the fact that a poor prognosis. based on the results of an intelligence test, will under-estimate potential social efficiency. If the mental age is taken as a guide and no special continued efforts are made to develop social skills, the mentally handicapped will under-function socially, and in consequence, a poor prognosis based on mental age will be borne out by the life performance.

3 The investigation also indicated *that social skills can be acquired in late adolescence.* It may well be that a mentally handicapped person needs much time before he is ready to learn on account of his slow grasp and slow maturation. On the other hand, there is no real evidence that the acquisition of many of those skills which were learnt during the 2 years of the experiment could not have been acquired at an earlier age: it could be argued that the results of the training were due to the omissions of the past and that the young people learnt these social skills simply because they had not been encouraged to acquire them when younger. Though this is probably true and underlines the fact that social education and training should be emphasized well before the age of 16, the important fact remains that there is a *capacity for social learning* which could be utilized for acquiring other social skills, if the more elementary skills have already been learned in the preceding stages.

4 *The learning of social skills requires opportunity.* The very name 'social' indicates that this type of skill has to be learnt, practised and used in the community and not only at home or in the classroom, workshop or institution ward. No special methods and techniques which could account for their significant improvement were used in the training of this group. Even though the type of classroom instruction they received was not available to the day trainees, it is reasonable to assume that competence in social skills would not result simply from being told what to do. The scoring method for social competence on the Vineland scale demands that a particular social skill should be used *habitually*, to receive credit and the mere knowledge of how it is done is not sufficient. After the men and women of the residential group had received instruction in the classroom and had been taught in real situations in shops, on public transport, and in the streets, they were encouraged to practice their skills on their own *outside* the hostel and workshops. Since they lived away from home, they were encouraged *to grow up socially* during the whole day and their classroom instruction was reinforced by daily practice. On the other hand, the day trainees received no social education in the classroom and were probably prevented from experiencing social activities by the protection and shelter afforded by their own homes.

5 *A major factor in achieving relative social competence was probably the 'living away from home' aspect of the training.* A closer analysis of the skills acquired during the two-year period, suggests that many successes were scored in areas which had probably not been encouraged at home or in training centres—going out, going shopping, running errands, etc. It is understandable that the mental handicap should induce an over-protective attitude in parents, but even the mentally handicapped child should learn to look after himself and to tackle a social situation. This encourages not only the technical competence with which he functions in society, but also helps him to develop self-reliance and confidence. The main reason for the high level of social competence achieved by the residential group on re-assessment, should probably be attributed to living away from home and to active encouragement to use their latent ability.

6 *It is essential that educational targets should be clearly defined.* A laissez-faire policy for mentally subnormal people will

achieve nothing. The provision of workshops, training centres and an increasing number of beds in hostels, will help only in ameliorating the problem of disposal, whilst the provision of more staff and the indroduction of some form of academic work will lead to expenditure of money, time and effort with poor and insignificant results, *unless* a determined attempt is made to define, at the outset, what it is hoped to achieve. One can expect very little if it is left to the imagination and goodwill of the individual teacher to interpret a vague aim which is often expressed as 'the full development of the mentally handicapped persons' potential'.

The social education scheme described produced these interesting and exciting results because it set limited, but very definite, targets which had been derived from an initial assessment of the social functioning of the child. The targets were realistic and usefully related to everyday life. The results could be attributed to either the training programme or the fact that the young people were living away from the over-protection of their own homes. It is probably true to say that it was the combination of both factors which was responsible for the achievement.

In conclusion, the results of this pilot project appear to point strongly to the need for augmenting the present arrangements for the education and training of the mentally handicapped. The facilities provided by training centres are inadequate because they are unable to give the prolonged twenty-four hour practical education in social functioning which is required to overcome the stifling climate of parental over-protection. The institutional or hospital facilities are also mostly inadequate, because they are too large and too typically institutional to permit the individualized and flexible training which would encourage a relative degree of independence and social competence. A third alternative should be provided which could act as a 'Finishing School' in social competence. In fact there should be provisions for training hostels (perhaps functioning only during a five-day week) where young severely handicapped adolescents can receive additional practical training in the skills of living and working in the community. By defining clearly and in practical terms the various targets of social education and training *throughout the whole career* of the young mentally handicapped person, and developing appropriate ways of teaching social skills, we shall probably achieve a better solution to the problem of the mentally handicapped than by shutting them away in institutions or sheltered workshops. Society has learnt to tolerate the subnormal—directed social education will help society to accept and integrate him.

The Impact of Present-Day Educational Programmes

It is probably not unfair to those who were concerned with the experiment discussed in the preceding section, to suggest that their results were due not so much to what was done whilst the pupils were in attendance as to what had *not* been done before they were admitted. It is quite possible that much less would have been achieved if training in the junior stages had been as effective as it should have been, for many of the successes were with comparatively minor skills which could have been learnt well before the age of 16. No doubt some measure of success would have been achieved simply by encouraging greater independence and responsibility, but progress would have been less marked because the additional skills to be learned at this late stage would have been more difficult to acquire.

This throws considerable doubt on the effectiveness of present training programmes. Some of the slow development of various skills, which has been shown in the Birmingham surveys (Figs. 18 to 29), is certainly due to the innate inferior capacity of the children, but much could also be due to the lack of directed education. Some corroboration of this comes from an important American study by Cain and Levine (1961).

They compared mentally retarded children in training centres, hospitals, and at home. It was assumed that 'the objective of the schools in educating trainable mentally retarded children, is the development of social competence.' It was also assumed that children who were not given training would show less gain in social competence than those attending schools.

The results of a very careful study over a two-year period showed that the children living in the community were socially more competent than those living in hospitals. In this respect the study confirmed the findings of many previous workers that hospital children generally have less opportunity to learn and to be independent than those living at home. The disturbing fact, however, was that those children who did *not* attend classes were not significantly less advanced than those receiving special education, and 'it was concluded that the public and institutional school programmes, as they are now conducted, do not foster the social competency development of trainable retarded children beyond that of children not attending such programmes'.

It would appear from this American study that at present it may make little difference whether a child attends a training centre or stays at home, although there are, no doubt, certain advantages in socialization and communication to be gained by children who work and live with others, and by parents who are relieved of the burden of having continually to look after their children. But whether the teaching programme exceeds a mere minding and occupying activity is perhaps doubtful. A further study of what was actually done in the training centres seems to bear this out.

The investigation (Cain and Levine, 1961) tried to determine the extent to which the school programmes were directed at the development of social competence. The school day was divided into instructional and non-instructional periods. Instructional periods, which were those in which an identifiable effort was made by the teacher to increase the children's social competence, self-sufficiency and social responsibility, were rated as high or low adequacy periods. Non-instructional periods were those in which there was no organized activity and in which little or no effect was made to increase the children's competence. In Cain and Levine's study approximately 44% of the community classroom time was categorized as instructional, and 56% as non-instructional; in the institutions instructional work accounted for 35% and non-instructional for 65% of the school day.

The American report suggests that much of the inadequacy of the programme 'appeared to be due to organizational difficulties in the use of classroom time and the teachers' assumptions regarding the abilities of these children. The amount of time devoted to recess, free activity and rest periods suggests that the school personnel may have devised their programmes on the assumption that trainable retarded children have a low energy level and diminished vitality. Although it is recognized that trainable retarded children differ from "normal" children in respect of these qualities, the general impression is that the school personnel treat these assumptions as expectations and, therefore, little or no demand is made of these children

This state of affairs is not limited to the American training centres as is shown by a smaller investigation made by Norris

(1961) in Britain. His analysis of the activities of 150 children, aged 5 to 9, attending training centres was as follows:

Time Allotted	Activity in Hand
14%	Sleeping and resting.
24%	Administrative business (assembly, register and dismissal).
40%	Lessons and play.
22%	Eating and going to the toilet.

The time available for lessons was divided into

17% free play.
33% group activity lessons.
50% sedentary group activities.

Norris commented that 'in view of the fact that the children being offered these time tables were young mentally handicapped children having a developmental level of their normal pre-school fellows, it is not encouraging to note that only 17% of the lesson time was given to independent activities, while the remaining 83% was devoted to group instruction'.

The main criticism made by Cain and Levine was that the teachers accepted 'deviating behaviour and performance below the level of the children's abilities. For example, when an activity was not proceeding satisfactorily, frequently the teacher would allow the activity to disintegrate into a free play period, rather than make an attempt to develop alternative means of successfully concluding the activity'. The rest periods were considered to be excessively long and often inappropriately placed in the sequence of school activities. There was a general assumption that there is little variability within the group, that the children are unable to sustain interest in an activity, to assume responsibilities, to respond to specific direction, and to function co-operatively within an organized programme.

It is interesting to note the reasons given by the teachers for not succeeding better than they did. Among those given for not planning an effective curriculum and instruction are inadequate training for the task and 'the lack of appropriate evaluational procedures and devices for assessing the children's progress'. This latter is probably a very important point, and it is hoped that the procedures outlined in the preceding pages will help to over-come this difficulty.

It is also noteworthy that according to Cain and Levine, much of the little time given to instructional work is of indifferent quality. These investigators found that of the approximately 44% community classroom time allocated to instructional periods, 25% was specifically devoted to increasing the children's self-sufficiency and social responsibility, half of which was judged to be low adequacy and half high adequacy time. In institutions the situation was even worse and all the time devoted to these activities was judged to be of low adequacy.

Whilst it was disheartening to see that training centre work in the community was not significantly more effective than the work carried out by the parents whose children were at home and not attending centres, the findings that children in institutional surroundings decreased in their social competence over two years is a warning that far more effective measures must be taken to overcome the lack of stimulation which seems to be invariably associated with institutional work.

Tizard (1962) stated that 'institutional children are particularly retarded in all aspects of language and speech and verbal intelligence, as compared with similar mentally handicapped children who live at home. The older the children, the greater becomes the discrepancy between their achievements and abilities and those of comparable children brought up in their own homes. The same is true of their personal independence—that is of their ability to dress themselves, manage their own meals and toilet, and generally help both themselves and the adults who are responsible for them. Observation shows them also be to extremely backward socially and emotionally, and it is clear that in these and in other ways institutional care today warps and stunts the development of already seriously handicapped children.'

Whilst it is probably true that no institutional set-up, however efficient and thoughtfully planned, could compensate for the stimulation provided by living in the community and at home, it is nevertheless true that institutional and hospital care is required because, in many cases, it cannot be completely replaced by community provisions. It is therefore important that a programme should be developed to counteract as much as possible the effects of living in an institutional atmosphere.

The criticism implied in the work of Cain and Levine, Norris, Tizard and many others, whilst raising doubts about the efficiency of present-day methods of educating the mentally handicapped child, must not be interpreted as casting doubt upon the possibility of educating the severely mentally handicapped child. There are many reasons to account for the little time devoted to furthering social competence and for the inadequacy of the approach adopted. Large classes of heterogeneous character and inadequate teaching facilities have certainly contributed to this situation, but even more to blame is lack of qualified teachers and of a clearly defined educational programme which would give meaning and direction to the teachers' undoubted enthusiasm and interest in their work.

The main reason for the inadequacy of educational work carried out in training centres and hospitals is probably the unjustifiably low expectations which would-be educators hold out for their pupils. Gunnar Dybwad in a paper pertinently titled 'Are we Retarding the Retarded?' (1964) quotes a Danish comment: 'A realistic adaptation of the mentally retarded to society can be achieved by not underestimating and by not overprotecting them' and he refers to the American worker Rick Heber who stated that a too gentle, too permissive, too undemanding regime which protects the retarded person from failure, works very much to his detriment and seriously interferes with future training.

Summary and Conclusion

The traditional division into educable and trainable children is no longer appropriate. Educable children were considered to be those with IQ over 55 and their education was more or less limited to academic subjects; trainable children had IQs below 55 and were those who could be expected to learn only simple occupations and handicrafts. This is an unfortunate division because it assumes the infallability of IQ, diagnostic testing and prognostic prediction, and fails to look at education as a preparation for life. In a sense, all activities designed to further competence in life situations are educational, and thus everything we do to develop and stimulate the child's competence is educative, even though the education given to the retarded may be very different from that given to normal children.

It is important that the education of the mentally retarded should be known as social education to emphasize that the traditional associations with books and paperwork must not intrude too far into a syllabus of work which is neither primarily academic nor primarily handiwork and manual occupation. The teachers are educationists and must apply the principles and techniques of sound teaching practice to the special requirements of the subnormal.

The word 'ineducable' should disappear from the official vocabulary of the educationists just as the word 'untestable' should be shunned in the psychologists' reports. These terms refer vaguely to a very severe handicap which causes very great difficulties in teaching and in obtaining meaningful responses, but even if only a little is learnt it means that the child is 'educable', and because it can be observed it means that it can be tested.

The social education of today should not be mistaken for the practical education of yesterday which was dominated by manual instruction. There is no question of training 'brawn-power' because 'brain-power' is so minimal. Social education represents a careful selection of academic knowledge and its amalgamation with social experience to give the mentally handicapped some familiarity with situations he is likely to encounter in work and life. It requires both the development of the mental processes of thinking and the practical application of thought to concrete situations.

Mentally handicapped people generally do considerably better in intelligence tests requiring non-verbal and performance abilities than they do in paper and pencil tests that require abstract thinking. Their ability to apply thought processes to situations which can be seen and manipulated far exceeds their ability to handle the symbols of language, number and time. Since the ultimate aim is to make the mentally handicapped function as effectively as possible in a community appropriate to his abilities, his education—learning to think in specific, concrete situations—must be aimed primarily at *social* attainments with only a modicum of academic and manual skills. Social education is suitable for all levels of mental handicap although, of course, the attainments and the speed with which they are acquired will vary and goals will be more ambitious the milder the handicap. Considering a programme of encouragement and furthering social skills as *education* towards certain well-defined targets of social competence will help to emphasize the teacher's role as an educationist rather than merely as a trainer of children who cannot be expected to achieve anything worthy of the name education.

The emphasis on norms, figures, graphs and tables in these pages may have given the impression that this is yet another attempt to measure and de-personalize mentally handicapped people. Far from it. It has probably been one of the greatest drawbacks in mental subnormality that the workers in the field had become so conscious of the intellectual deficit, which could be measured with such apparent ease, that it was invariably regarded as *the cause* of social incompetence. We now have reason to believe that, in many cases, social competence *and* low IQ scores are *the result* of a combination of factors—adverse environmental circumstances—and that the test score should often be regarded as a symptom rather than as an explanation of inadequacy. It is therefore not surprising that other approaches to the problems of subnormality are beginning to supersede reliance upon intelligence testing.

This book is an attempt to encourage systematic observation rather than laboratory-controlled measurements. It is unfortunate that the need for objectivity in laboratory studies has largely overshadowed the art and skill of systematic observation, because it is observation that enables us to see the subnormal as an individual with special needs rather than as a problem case to be measured.

Observation must be systematic and have a definite purpose, otherwise the collected data may become unmanageable. Using the P-A-C method helps the observer to see the problem in relation to certain clearly defined aspects. Results obtained by this method obviously do not give a complete picture and hundreds of other equally relevant observations could usefully be added. However, a start must be made and this is provided by a systematic technique. Since the standardization of a technique produces a mass of relevant observations relating to children of similar intellectual inferiority and similar age, a background is obtained against which to see any individual problem. The observer is therefore led to ask what can account for the difference between this child and others and what can or should be done about it?

In conclusion the argument for directed social education of the mentally handicapped can be summarized as follows:

1. The native endowment of the mentally handicapped person is insufficient to enable him to function on the same level of competence as a normal person, and there is no known treatment, education or training that will overcome completely the deficiency which affects his flexible and intelligent adaptation to the changing demands of life and work in the community.

2. There is reason to assume that many of the mentally handi-

capped people function on an even lower level of social efficiency than need be, and that this may be due to such environmental factors as lack of stimulation, cultural deprivation and inadequate teaching.

3. As many mentally handicapped people as possible should be educated and trained to enable them to meet the requirements of living and working in the open community. Preventive measures have so far failed to produce acceptable results and, although the increasing number of institutional facilities will be of some help they would have little effect upon the increasing burden on society.

4. To alleviate this burden society must find places in the open community for many of the mentally handicapped and must train and educate them to function as adequately as their handicap allows. Education must therefore deal with all requirements and not be limited to the work aspects alone.

5. Because of inferior intelligence, weak drive, disinclination to apply himself to a task, slow learning speed, limited time available for teaching, and, finally the fact that even in the best case the severely mentally handicapped will not succeed in more demanding work than unskilled or semi-skilled labouring, it is clear that an educational programme must be determined by these factors rather than by those which determine the education of normal children.

6. A consideration of what is possible and what it is desirable to achieve, leads to the conclusion that a form of social education is the only practical training that will enable the mentally handicapped to live in the open community even if marginally.

7. Education and training should be as direct and purposeful as we can possible make it. Keeping in mind the modest aims of a very low level social adequacy, the syllabus must help to make the child familiar with the surrounding world and less of 'a stranger in his own country,' when he is grown-up.

8. Only a comparatively small amount of academic knowledge essential to increase social competence should be taught and most of the contents of a normal education must be replaced by the essential skills necessary for social adequacy.

9. Since the mentally handicapped persons' weaknesses are pronounced and the social skills required for life are numerous, it will be important to select from a vast number of possible subjects only those which are relevant to social functioning and which can be taught in the time available.

10. It is essential for an adequate and purposeful teaching programme that a mentally handicapped child's social attainments should be carefully assessed and his weaknesses accurately pinpointed.

11. Careful assessment of social inadequacy, should be followed by purposeful education in underdeveloped areas. The aim of teaching should be not only to give knowledge and practice in those skills, but also thereby to increase confidence and self-assurance so that everyday situations can be tackled with greater ease.

12. Comparisons of the mental ages and intelligence quotients of mentally handicapped and normal children only indicate the degree of handicap compared with normal standards; they do not show how well a child performs *despite* his handicap.

13. An approximate idea of the efficiency with which a child uses his meagre mental equipment, can be obtained by comparing a mentally handicapped child with other children of the same intellectual level and age. In this way it is possible to obtain a fair idea whether a particular child is retarded, advanced, or normal in relation to other children of the same age and with a similar mental handicap.

14. This comparison enables an educational programme to be tailor-made for each individual and learning to be encouraged with due regard to the mental handicap.

15. Making available norms of social development for these handicapped children should ensure that neither too little nor too much will be demanded of them. It must however be left to the skill of the teacher to adjust her demands to the ability of each child and to solve, in each case, the problem of why one child will not do so well as other children of the same age and similar mental handicap.

16. Social skill and competence depend to a large extent on adequate social education *and experience*. If these are provided it is possible that slow but steady improvement may occur over the years, and that standards of social competence now accepted as norms for various groups may need to be raised in due course.

17. New teaching devices and new teaching approaches will have to be developed which take account of the specific aims of social education, the limited ability of the child and his low learning speed.

18. It has been said, and this is probably correct, that many mentally handicapped children do not learn as quickly as they might

because they do not understand what is required: the obstacle may be not so much the child's limited learning ability, but our own limited knowledge of how to teach him. It is therefore essential to develop new teaching programmes which take into consideration not only the different content of education but also the particular obstacles encountered in communication between teacher and mentally handicapped child. It may well be that a completely different way of teaching the mentally handicapped has to be developed—one which is not dominated by the misleading concept of mental age.

Despite a long tradition of training the mentally handicapped child, it is only now that we see the beginning of a systematic and more promising approach to a partial solution of the problem. We cannot reasonably expect spectacular advances in the near future which will enable the individual mentally defective to become completely independent as an adult. The mentally handicapped is more vulnerable than normal persons to emotional difficulties, social requirements and economic conditions. Although breakdowns will affect them more frequently than normal people, to speak of failure and wasted effort shows a complete misunderstanding of the real issues: there is no failure because no permanent success has ever been envisaged. To contribute to the ability of a mentally handicapped person to fend for himself even for a limited period under favourable circumstances, is a substantial achievement, especially when the alternative is a life of custodial care and supervision. He will require help and assistance from time to time, and it is as well to remember that a great many people of normal intelligence also require help during periods of nervous stress, insecurity at work or difficulty in getting on with other people. The mentally handicapped especially needs a firm and helping hand at such times, but failure, even frequent failure, should not discourage us from helping to equip him with the 'social know-how' which would enable him to make a success of his life for varying periods.

The problem of the social adequacy of the subnormal is inextricably linked with the well-being of society. As a weak, vulnerable and less capable member of society, he will be tolerated and accepted as long as there is room for him in a community which can afford his modest, and often rather inefficient contribution. In times of affluence the mentally handicapped can generally be accommodated in large numbers, but in times of economic depression and poverty he is unable to compete with the normal individual who has more to offer and requires more from life.

This is a point that needs emphasis. The rehabilitation of the mentally handicapped can only be seen against the background of the society into which he is to be adjusted. As long as society can afford to tolerate his existence, education and training efforts will have to be directed towards this adjustment. There may well be times when this tolerance can no longer be afforded by society and a form of custodial care and institutionalization may be the only way of protecting the weakest member of society against that same society. But even then, social education and training will still be of importance as it will decrease the burden of complete dependence on those who have to care for them. Whilst particular goals within the social education programme might have to be altered to suit the new demands, the general aim of making the mentally handicapped relatively efficient and *at home in his own country,* will still be valid.

APPENDIX A

Standard Deviation and Correlation Coefficient

The term standard deviation (SD) has been used in this book and
it is important to know what exactly is meant by it. Figure 57 shows
the frequency distribution of scores obtained in a test. High scores
are placed at the right-hand side of the curve, low scores on the
left-hand side; most scores are around the average and they are
placed in the middle. The frequency distribution curve is therefore
higher in the middle and lower on the extreme right and left sides
because comparatively few people score very high and very low
marks. Whilst it is easy to calculate a mathematical average, it is
a matter of convenience to decide how far a given score may deviate

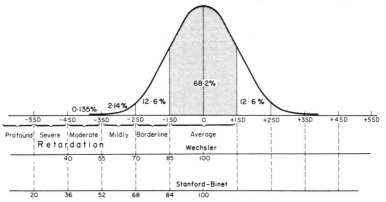

Fig. 57. Classification ranges based on standard deviations

from the mathematical mean and still be called average. Let us
assume the mathematical average on a particular test is 117, should
a score of 116 or 118 still be regarded as average because the slight
difference may in fact be due to chance? A decision has to be
made; it can be done quite arbitrarily or it can be done by using
the standard deviation. This is a mathematical computation which
sets acceptable numerical limits to the mean.

The first SD indicates that 68·26% of a given population obtain scores *within the average range*. Such a score may therefore be close to the mathematical mean or separated from it by 10 or more points, but as long as it is within the limits indicated by the Standard Deviation, it will be considered an average score.

A score outside the limits of the first SD will be below or above average depending on whether the score is below or above the limit indicated by the first Standard Deviation. The next Standard Deviation comprises the same range of scores but includes far fewer people (Fig. 57). In fact only 12·6% on either side of the frequency curve of a given population, or 25% of the total population, will be contained by the second SD.

In the classification discussed on pp. 25 to 28, adoption of this method means that the borderline retardation of measured intelligence (Wechsler IQ 70 to 84), reaches from below one SD to two SD from the mean, and we can estimate that no more than 12·6% of the population will show this degree of retardation. The third SD to the left of the mean (the mildly retarded—Wechsler IQ 55 to 69), will contain even fewer people (2·14% of the general population).

The next group, the third to the fourth SD, comprises very few people indeed, only 0·13% of the population (moderate retardation of measured intelligence, Wechsler IQ 40 to 54). People below the fourth SD (Wechsler IQ 25 to 39—severe retardation of measured intelligence) and those below the fifth SD comprise only a fraction of the general population.

The same principles apply to the upper deviations: scores above the first SD are obviously of above average, those in the third SD are superior and those past the third SD are very superior indeed. Although the examples given refer to intelligence test scores, the same principles apply to any other measurable quantity.

For convenience the mathematical average in an intelligence test is taken to be 100, so that the hypothetical score of 117 mentioned above, could be referred to as 100 IQ (which means simply the mathematical mean of scores obtained on a particular test). The size of the standard deviation is settled arbitrarily, say as a range of 90 to 110 points; the SD would then be 10 points on either side of the mean. As far as the standardized intelligence test scales are concerned, it has been found convenient to mark the Standard Deviation as 15 to 16 points from the mean.

On the WAIS scale, the SD is regarded as 15 IQ points, and so anyone with an IQ score of 85 to 115 on this test has, in fact, obtained a score which puts him among the 68·26% average of the population. The next SD also comprises 15 points and so anyone with an IQ between 70 and 84 will be regarded as having borderline retardation of measured intelligence and belonging to the 12·6% of the general population.

Unfortunately the various tests use different Standard Deviations. The SD for the Stanford-Binet is 16 points which means that the average is between 84 and 116 IQ. In consequence IQ scores between 83 and 68 on the Stanford-Binet are equivalent to those between 84 to 70 on the WAIS. It is therefore important to state in reports which intelligence test scale has been used, particularly in the case of less well-known tests.

A correlation coefficient (r) expresses the degree of relationship between two variables, for example, height and weight. It indicates whether increase in one dimension is generally, but not invariably, accompanied by a corresponding increase in the other.

A perfect correlation expressed as $r = +1·00$ indicates that both variables are so closely related that additions of equal units in one dimension are accompanied by additions of constant units in the other, and predictions from one dimension to the other can be accurately made. Such perfect correlations are few in psychological testing although thermometers, clocks and other apparatus must correlate perfectly. Generally correlation coefficients indicate imperfect relationships. A coefficient of 0 indicates an absence of relationship, one near to $+1$, for example $r = 0·85$ or $0·92$, indicates a high degree of relationship between the two measures. In intelligence test scores a correlation coefficient of $r = 0·52$ would indicate that just over half of the reasons for differences of scores on the tests influence the results in the same way and may be identical, but there are many other causes which account for the differences.

A high test-retest correlation coefficient is important to gauge the reliability of a test used on two different occasions within reasonable time limits. The test should give the same or similar results on the two occasions. Differences of up to 5 points between two results from the same intelligence test are, however, so common that no significance can be attached to such an occurrence. Even larger discrepancies can be entirely due to inherent weaknesses in test construction and need not indicate significant changes. It has been demonstrated by Shapiro (quoted by Clarke and Clarke, 1965) that even in a test with a high test-retest correlation of 0·9, one child out of three assessed as having an average score of 100 would score above 107 or below 93 on retest, and one out of 10 would score above 112 or below 88 on retest. It is clear that very careful investigation is necessary in every case to establish whether changes in test scores reflect genuine changes in ability, and there is certainly no reason to believe that an intelligence test score is by itself as reliable a measure as a thermometer or a pair of scales are in the physical field.

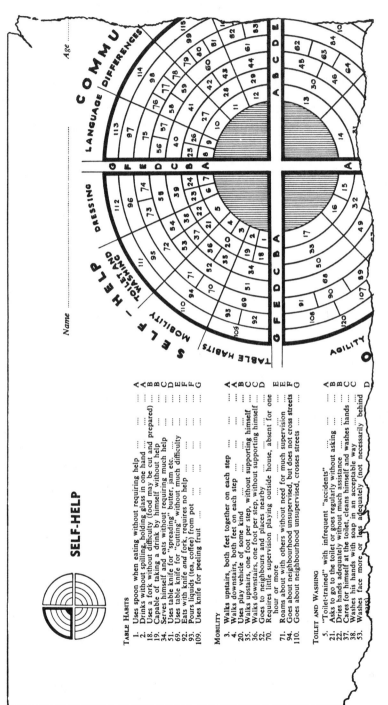

Fig. 58. Facsimile reproduction of the inside lay-out of the P-A-C 1

APPENDIX B

The Use of the P-A-C and P-E-I

There are, at present, five versions of the Progress Assessment Chart (P-A-C):
A. The *Primary Progress Assessment Chart* (P-P-A-C) deals with very young children and is also suitable for the severely and profoundly mentally handicapped.
B. The *Progress Assessment Chart 1* (P-A-C 1) deals mainly with the school child and is the form which is generally used in work with the young mentally handicapped child.
C. The *Mongol Progress Assessment Chart 1* (MP-A-C 1) is based on the P-A-C 1 and contains the same social skills but in a different order. It has been designed for use with mongol children and reflects the typical development of mongol children.
D. The *Progress Assessment Chart 1A* (P-A-C 1A) is a supplementary form which extends the range of social skills measured on the P-A-C 1. It provides additional teaching aims for children who have pretty well reached the ceiling level of the P-A-C 1, but who are not ready yet for assessment on the P-A-C 2.
E. The *Progress Assessment Chart 2* (P-A-C 2) has been designed for adolescents and adults, and, unlike the preceding P-A-C's, deals with 'parcels of behaviour' rather than single skills.

Although the charts are by and large related to definite age groups it is quite appropriate to use the P-P-A-C and P-A-C 1 for adults and on occasions the P-A-C 2 for children.

The skills on the P-P-A-C, P-A-C 1, MP-A-C 1 have been arranged in order of difficulty on the basis of published research. The sequence in the P-P-A-C and P-A-C 1 follows normal childhood development and indeed the P-A-C's of normal children will tend to show systematic growth from the centre according to the developmental level reached with few or no gaps in the diagrams. On the other hand subnormal children will show quite a few gaps in their social competence (Fig. 4, p. 19).

The skills of the MP-A-C 1 have been re-arranged in order of difficulty as experienced by mongol children. Thus the sequence of skills shown on the diagram corresponds to the progress in learning these skills, as found in research with Down's syndrome (see, Gunzburg, 1974b).

The skills of the P-A-C 1A and P-A-C 2 have been arranged according to difficulty and their importance for living. This had of necessity to be based on empirical knowledge and a personal decision as to which skills are important. An attempt has been made to place the most important and most useful skills near the centre to indicate that these should be acquired first of all. The order of skills in the P-A-C 2 has been slightly revised from the 10th edition onwards, in the light of recent research (Jackson and Struthers, 1974).

There are five *Progress Evaluation Indexes* (P-E-I).

The *Primary Progress Evaluation Index* (P-P-E-I) is based on the P-P-A-C assessments of 156 children, aged 2 years to 7 years.

The *Progress Evaluation Index 1* (P-E-I 1) is based on the P-A-C 1 assessments of 337 children, aged 6 years to 18 years. The P-E-I 1 presents the results of the surveys summarized in Figs. 18 to 29, on pages 84 to 86 in diagrammatic form. (See Fig. 42 p. 94.)

The *Mongol Progress Evaluation Index 1* (MP-E-I 1) is based on the P-A-C 1 assessments of 200 children with Down's syndrome, aged 6 years to 15 years. The survey of 100 boys and 100 girls indicated the existence of considerable sex differences, and as a result, the MP-E-I 1 is available in a male version (m) and a female version (f).

The *Progress Evaluation Index 2* (P-E-I 2) is based on the P-A-C 2 assessments of 144 mentally handicapped young people, aged mostly 17 to 23 years.

There is no Progress Evaluation Index available for the P-A-C 1A, which is still in its experimental form.

All children included in the P-P-E-I and P-E-I 1 surveys had been addressed as being severely mentally subnormal, that is to say, having IQs below the 50 mark. As far as the P-E-I 2 is concerned, the results refer to three different groups. Moderately mentally handicapped with IQs between 40 and 54 on the Wechsler Adult Intelligence Scale, the mildly mentally handicapped with IQs between 55 to 69 on the WAIS and the borderline metally handicapped with IQs between 70 and 84 on the WAIS.

The five Progress Evaluation Indexes indicate the average achievement levels in social competence of mentally handicapped children and adults as assessed on the corresponding P-A-C's.

Figure 58 shows the inside layout of the P-A-C 1, the diagram and some of the 120 social skills listed in that form. The P-P-A-C and P-A-C 2 follow the same pattern (see Fig. 8, page 74). On page 95, Fig. 43 shows in the upper half the filled in P-A-C 1 and in the lower half the P-E-I 1 of an individual child. The crosshatched sections of the P-E-I 1 indicate in this case the average performance of 15 year old mentally subnormal children. The P-A-C 1 record of an individual child, shown in the upper half of Fig. 43, can be summarized by shading in the total number of skills in each subsection of the diagram of the P-E-I 1. As can be seen, the first subsection corresponding to 'table habits' shows only 6 successes and these are, therefore, shaded over the crosshatching of the P-E-I 1. This leaves 2 crosshatched spaces still visible, indicating that this child is underfunctioning in this area compared with the average performance of this age group. In the 'mobility' subsection 5 skills have been credited to the child in the P-A-C 1 and thus 5 skills are shaded in in the corresponding subsection of the P-E-I 1. In this case the shaded part covers completely the printed crosshatching, indicating that as far as mobility is concerned the performance of this child corresponds to the average performance of the age group. This procedure is continued in the other subsections of the P-E-I 1.and, as a result, it can be seen that this particular child is under achieving in most areas, except in 'mobility' and 'paper pencil work', whilst in 'number work' he is functioning on a higher level than would be expected considering the average performance of his age group.

This procedure is the standard approach to evaluation of the P-A-C record and should be repeated every half year.

In the P-E-I 1 folder provision has been made for two assessments each year. The first assessment is entered on the left inside cover, the second on the right inside cover. Thus, the succession of diagrams on each side shows a child's development at yearly intervals comparing it, at the same time, with his age group. By shading in the summary of the P-A-C results, it is easy not only to see the progress of the child over six-monthly periods during a number of years, but also to compare each assessment with the standard set by the average achievement of each age group.

Group Comparisons

Just as important as keeping track of the progress of individual trainees is the analysis of the progress of a whole training scheme. Since so much of a trainee's progress depends on providing adequate learning opportunities and emphasizing those aspects of social learning which he finds difficult, it will be necessary to evaluate a teaching programme by reference to the lack of progress which has been shown by a group of trainees over a certain period. It is only too easy to assume that everything is well, because remarkable successes are achieved in various subsections of the P-A-C by most pupils. Encouraging as these successes are, it is more instructive to have a good look at those areas where little or no progress is made and to ask whether this is due to a trainee's innate inability to learn or to weakness in the training scheme.

In this section two examples will be given to indicate what sort of analysis can be carried out using the P-A-C and P-E.I.

Table XXII presents in numerical form the findings of the P-A-C survey shown graphically in Figs. 18 to 29 and in the Progress Evaluation Index (see Fig. 42).

Since each subsection of the P-A-C 1 contains 10 skills Table XXII indicates how many skills out of ten the average moderately and severely retarded child has acquired at a particular age. To assess whether such a child is backward or average for his age in any aspects of social functioning, first find out his age. In the column corresponding to each age are shown the mean number of skills mastered in each subsection by children of that age. For example, the average 10-year-old has acquired 6 table habit skills, 3 mobility skills and 6 toilet and washing skills. The adjustments to be made in individual cases have been discussed on pp. 78 to 97. Generally speaking the figures in Table XXII refer to the skills in the order in which they are listed in the P-A-C 1 which reflects the normal emergence of ability in course of growing up.

TABLE XXII
Social attainments of children with IQs below 55

					How many skills?						
Age:	6	7	8	9	10	11	12	13	14	15	16
SELF-HELP											
Table Habits	4	4	5	6	6	6	6	7	7	8	8
Mobility	3	3	3	3	3	3	4	4	4	5	5
Toilet and Washing	4	5	5	5	6	6	6	7	7	8	8
Dressing	4	4	4	5	5	5	5	6	7	7	8
COMMUNICATION											
Language	3	3	3	3	3	4	4	4	5	6	6
Differences	1	2	2	2	3	3	3	4	4	5	6
Number Work	1	2	2	2	2	2	3	3	4	4	4
Paper and Pencil Work	2	2	3	3	3	3	3	3	3	4	4
SOCIALIZATION											
Play Activities	3	4	4	5	5	5	5	6	6	7	7
Home Activities	2	3	3	3	3	3	3	4	5	5	5
OCCUPATION											
Dexterity	2	2	2	3	4	4	5	5	6	6	7
Agility	2	2	2	3	4	4	5	5	6	6	6

Thus we would expect the 6 self-help skills of the average 10-year-old mentally handicapped child to be the first 6 skills listed in the P-A-C 1 (Nos. 1, 2, 18, 19, 34, 51) but omitting the more complicated skills of pouring liquids or using a knife for peeling. Although the skills are arranged in hierarchical order, the older mentally handicapped child shows a typical scatter: competence on more advanced levels and some ignorance of the easier stages.

It will be observed that generally even the 16-year-old never manages to obtain the 100% score of ten rather simple skills in any subsection, although such proficiency is within the capability of particular children. Table XXII should therefore be considered as representing a reasonable minimum of efficiency within the grasp of most moderately subnormal children who have no additional handicap.

The information contained in numerical form in Table XXII and in graphical form in the P-E-I Folders (Fig. 42) can be used to tabulate the achievements of a group of children and assessing their progress. The data justify now the use of descriptive 'labels' such as 'average', 'superior' or 'backward' by referring to objective measurement rather than relying on subjective impressions. Using a simple convention whereby deviations of one skill above or below the figure indicated in the P-E-I or Table XXII are still regarded as being within the 'average range', the familiar terms can be applied though they are now closely defined. 'Better than average' or 'superior' would be achievement exceeding the average rating on the P-E-I or Table XXII by two or more skills, whilst 'backward' can be defined as being a performance falling below the average by two or more skills.

Table XXIII shows the application of this convention to a group of children at the first and second assessment. The analysis of the first assessment indicated the particular areas of backwardness of the whole group and individual children. The reassessment showed various improvements and many children who had been backward in specific areas at first, were subsequently rated as 'average' justifiably and objectively.

In accordance with the philosophy underlying all our work, the P-A-C record indicates in effect the size of each individual trainee's handicap and a reassessment can, therefore, indicate how far this handicap has been reduced due to directed teaching. If, for example, a trainee could not succeed on any item of the self help section in the P-A-C 1 (40 skills) then his handicap in P-A-C terms would be

100%. Most trainees, however, have acquired competence in some skills and thus a few of the spaces in the self help area of the P-A-C would be filled in. For example, in Fig. 43, nineteen skills of the self help area have been credited, which represents 47.5% of this particular area. Thus the remaining 21 skills, which have not

TABLE XXIII

P-A-C analysis of gains in social competence in a directed training scheme
(time interval—9 months, IQs below 50)
A = Average, S = Superior, B = Backward

Name	CA	TH	Mo	T&W	D	L	D	NW	P&P	PA	HA	D	A¹
		Self-help				Communication				Social		Occupation	
PG	11	A⁺	S	A⁺	A⁺	A	(B)	B/(A)	A	A	(A)	S	A⁺
	12	A⁺	S	A⁺	A⁺	A	(A)↓B	(A⁺)	A	A	(A⁺)	S	A⁺
PH	11	A⁺	S	(A)	A	B✓	(A)	A	(A)	(B) A	A	A	(A)
	12	A⁺	S	(A⁺)	A	B	(A⁺)	A	(A⁺)	(A)↓A	A	A	(A⁺)
DD	12	A	A	S	A	(A)	(B) B/(B)	B ✓(B)	A	A	(A)		
	13	A	A	S	A	(A⁺)	(A)↓B	(A)↓	B	(A)↓	A	(A⁺)	
SW	12	(A)	A	(B) A	A	(B)	B /A	A	A	B✓	A	(A)	
	13	(A⁺)	A	(A)↓A	A	(A)↓	B✓	A	A	A	B✓	A	(A⁺)
ES	13	S	S	S	S	(B) (B) A	A	A	A	A	(A)		
	14	S	S	S	S	(A)↓(A)↓A	A	A	A	A	(A⁺)		
KB	13	A	A	A	A	B/	A/	A	A	B/	B/	B/	(A)
	14	A	A	A	A	B✓	B✓	A	A	B✓	B✓	B✓	(A⁺)
EG	13	B/	A	A	A↓(B)	B/	B/B/	A	A	A	A		
	14	B✓	A	A	A↓(A)	B✓	B✓ B✓	A	A	A	A		
EF	13	S	S	S	S	S	S	S	S	A	S	A	A
	14	S	S	S	S	S	S	A	S	A	S	A	A

¹ These abbreviations refer to the subsections of the P-A-C 1, e.g. TH —Table Habits, Mo — Mobility, etc.

In this example reassessment showed that there were no changes in 72 aspects of which 14 had been found 'backward' on the first assessment. These aspects (and the numberwork of KB) will require particular attention and have been marked thus: ✓. On the other hand, children had improved from 'backward' to average standing in 10 aspects (shown (B/A)↓) and had improved their 'average' status in 12 aspects, meriting now an A+ rating and shown as (A/A⁺) Thus improvement had been objectively scored in 22 aspects or in 23 per cent of the areas assessed.

been mastered, make up 52.5% and represent this particular child's handicap.

Appropriate training should show in the reassessment. If by that time the child has acquired more skills, say for example 28 skills (70%), then this child's handicap would have been reduced from 52.5% to 30%, that is to say the training period would have improved his performance by 22.5%. In this particular case, a reference to the P-E-I 1 would also show that by achieving this level of 28 skills at the age of 15, he might have achieved the average functioning of 15 year old subnormal children in terms of the P-E-I, provided the distribution of achievements in the various subsections corresponds to the pattern of the P-E-I 1.

When dealing with a larger group, it is at times useful to add the successes and failures of the individual members of the group and to compare the results with the reference points provided by the P-E-I.

Table XXIV gives the results of a training programme for adolescent mentally subnormal people. In this example a group of 45 trainees was subdivided according to intelligence scores and each group was compared with the 'average achievement levels' of the groups on the P-E-I 2.

In each subsection of the P-A-C 2 the average score of the members of each intelligence group was computed by simply adding the number of successes and dividing the results by the number of trainees in the group. An average score in one particular area, tabulated in the second column (let us say 'health'), was then compared with the average performance level of the P-E-I 2, indicated in the first column. In this particular case it was seen that the moderately retarded was underfunctioning compared with the reference points and the score was, therefore, marked minus, indicating this fact. If, on the other hand, the average score was above that of the first column (showing the P-E-I 2 average performance) then the space was marked +, indicating an above average performance (as, for example, in the case of subsection 'Money' of the borderline retarded group). If the average score of the group was equal to that of the P-E-I 2 average performance level, then it was shown by an = sign. Carrying this procedure through for each of the 3 intelligence groups, the results indicated that members of the moderately retarded group were underfunctioning in 10 aspects, that in 5 aspects average functioning had been achieved, but that this group did not function above average in even one of the aspects of the P-E-I 2. The same procedure was applied to the other two intelligence groups and the results are summarized at the bottom of Table XXIV.

TABLE XXIV

Comparisons with Expectancy Levels of the P-E-1 2 (Gunzburg, 1973).

	Moderate N=15			Mild N=20			Borderline N=10		
	Expec. Levels	1st Assess.	2nd Assess.	Expec. Levels	1st Assess.	2nd Assess.	Expec. Levels	1st Assess.	2nd Assess.
SELF-HELP									
Table Habits	5	−	=	5	=	+	5	=	=
Cleanliness	4	−	=	4	=	=	5	−	−
Care of Clothes	4	=	+	4	=	=	5	−	=
Mobility	3	−	=	4	−	=	5	−	−
Health	3	−	+	4	=	=	5	−	−
COMMUNICATION									
Language	2	=	+	3	=	=	4	−	=
Money	2	−	−	3	=	=	4	+	+
Time and Measure	1	=	+	2	=	+	4	−	=
Writing	2	−	−	3	−	=	5	−	−
Reading	1	=	=	2	−	=	3	=	+
SOCIALISATION									
Shopping	3	−	=	3	=	+	5	−	=
Social Graces	4	=	+	4	=	=	4	=	+
Home Assistance	3	−	=	3	=	+	4	−	+
Financial Dealings	2	−	=	2	=	+	3	=	+
Social Initiative	3	−	=	3	=	+	4	=	+

Total Group (N=45)

	−	=	+
1st Assessment	22	22	1
2nd Assessment	6	22	17

This tabulation of successes and failures in the second column of each group indicated quite clearly that on the whole the group of 45 adolescents was underfunctioning in many aspects, but that the underfunctioning was more pronounced in the case of the moderately and borderline retarded groups than in the mildly retarded group. Whatever the reasons for this situation, it was a clear indication that much emphasis should be paid to the needs of these two groups.

The reassessment, shown in the third column of each intelligence group, showed that training had succeeded very substantially in

TABLE XXV
*Identification of skills[1] requiring 'more' attention in the training scheme
(Gunzburg, 1973)*

	Failures	
	1st	2nd
SELF-HELP	Assessments	
10 Knows how to deal with simple injuries	13	14
44 Shaves himself regularly (men), looks after personal hygiene adequately (women)	15	16
46 Can be relied on to change underclothes regularly	21	19
47 Uses public transport for journeys requiring at least one change of transport	29	27
89 Knows how and where to obtain a general practitioner's help	30	30
90 Knows that simple remedies should be at hand and where to obtain them	11	10
COMMUNICATION		
13 Gives change out of ten new pennies or (in the USA) makes change for a quarter	17	18
14 Adds coins of various denominations up to 10 new pennies or (in the USA) adds coins of various denominations up to one quarter	17	17
15 Tells the time and associates times on clock with various actions and events	10	8
18 Addresses an envelope in an adequate manner	29	30
53 Gives change out of 50 new pennies or (in the USA) gives change out of a half dollar	25	25
56 Understands time intervals, e.g. between 3.30 and 4.30	34	32
91 Uses public telephones	34	30
92 Makes enquiries from operator for telephone numbers	38	36
99 Reads books requiring advanced reading skill, i.e. novels	45	43
SOCIALIZATION		
68 Can state several items required in weekly expenditure	26	25
110 Can obtain forms and licences when required, e.g. application forms	38	38

[1] Numbers refer to identification number on P-A-C 2.

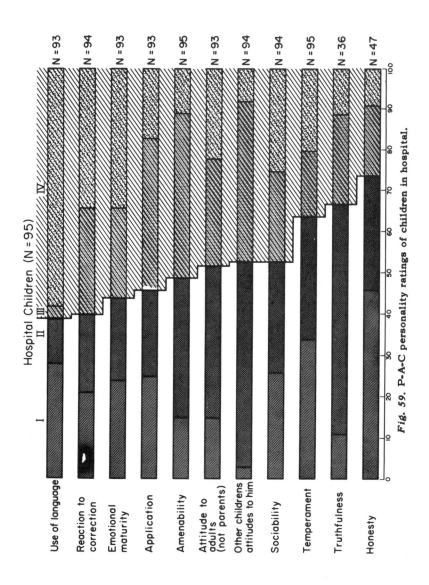

Fig. 59. P-A-C personality ratings of children in hospital.

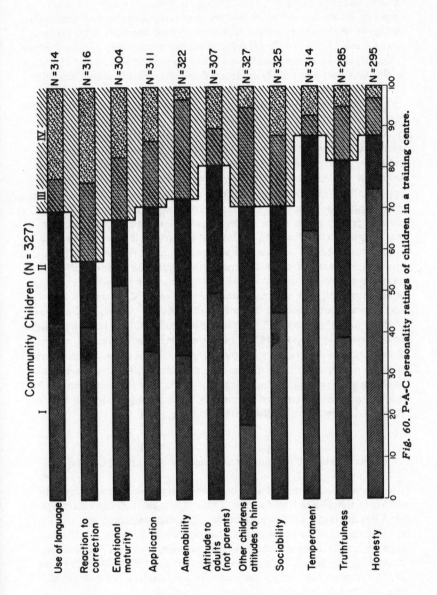

Fig. 60. P-A-C personality ratings of children in a training centre.

certain aspects of social functioning, but not so much in others. Areas of under achievement had been greatly reduced and generally the level of the three groups had been raised but with less success in the case of the mildly retarded than the moderately and borderline.

Gratifying as these results are, they, nevertheless, draw attention to the fact that the mildly retarded does not seem to have benefited as much as the other two groups and also that in some areas the trainees were still underfunctioning. Whilst it is obvious that under-functioning could be due to intellectual shortcomings, it is well worthwhile to make a further analysis of the skills in which there was comparatively little success. Table XXV (Gunzburg, 1973) indicates how carefully the areas of comparative failure should be analysed. In this particular case it was shown that several training opportunities had been overlooked or not been arranged for and that the training programme should correspondingly be adjusted to provide in future for these experiences. For example, because of the geographical situation of the particular institution where this survey was carried out, there had been no need to use more than one bus to arrive at most destinations. Thus, the trainees did not have opportunities for using public transport for journeys requiring at least one change of transport (P-A-C 2: item 47), though they had become quite competent in P-A-C 2: item 7: 'uses public transport for short journeys'. There is little doubt that no training scheme can adequately respond to the needs of individual trainees, unless it adjusts constantly its syllabus by providing a tailor-made education for people who have different needs and different experiences. Methods as outlined in the preceding pages are extremely useful to draw attention not only to failures in the trainees' progress but to failures in the teaching system (Gunzburg, 1974).

The Mentally Handicapped at Home and in Institutional Care

The average achievement levels of mentally handicapped children shown in the P-E-I 1 and in the Table XXII, reflect the attainments of children living in the community. Children in hospitals and institutions tend to achieve less, as shown in Figures 34-37 on page 89, partly because they have fewer opportunities (as demonstrated by the Brooklands experiment—Tizard 1962 and 1963) and partly because they often have severe personality difficulties which may have made institutionalization advisable.

The more troublesome personality make-up of children in hospital compared with the personalities of children living at home and attending training centres, is reflected in the two diagrams of

Figs. 59 and 60. They are based on the personality ratings by teachers on the P-A-C 1 forms. Ratings I and II (heavily shaded) refer in each respect to statements indicating degrees of socially acceptable behaviour. Ratings III and IV (lightly shaded) refer to socially unacceptable behaviour (IV indicating very negative behaviour—irregular dots). As can be clearly seen 'acceptable behaviour' is far more dominant in the children living in the community (Fig. 60) than in children in hospital (Fig. 59).

It is, of course, quite possible that many of the unfavourable personality aspects have been caused or at least been increased because the children have been institutionalized. Yet, irrespective of the cause, difficult behaviour will affect social functioning and lead to lower social achievements.

Figs. 34 to 37 show the rate of acquisition of social competence in a child population resident in hospital compared with a similar population at training centres. Although the children were comparable as far as their intelligence levels were concerned, the hospital children were often less competent socially than children living outside. Similarly, Elliott and MacKay (1971) who compared the social competence of subnormal children living in a hostel and in the community with those who had been in hospital for longer or shorter periods, came to the conclusion that 'the subnormal living in the community have more social skills and higher verbal ability than their counterparts living under different types of residential care', and they also point out that 'the difference in social competence between the two groups of hospitalized subnormals suggests that length of hospitalization is important, at least in the young patients of the kind involved in this study'. Since the level of competence and social skills is relatively low in the subnormal, the difference over one year in social age (as demonstrated in that article) is great enough to show that, with increasing length of stay, the development of social abilities is stunted. Mitchell (1955) also found a relationship between length of stay and social competence in her institutionalized feebleminded girls who lived in small cottage groups.

It could easily be concluded from these researches that institutional care would always be less successful in teaching social competence than community residence. This would in fact suggest that all subnormal children would do better in community placements than when living in hospitals or institutions. On the other hand, it is quite conceivable that a new type of institutional environment with training programmes which aim at helping the subnormal to help himself rather than to protect him, would be more effective than mere residence in the community provided institution life becomes outward orientated rather than inward looking, as is so often the case at the present time. The marked gap between the performance of children in the community and that of institutionalized children could be narrowed considerably by providing more individual attention, increased opportunities and more purposeful training.

The Social Competence Index (SCI)

The Social Competence Index relating to the four sections of the P-A-C, has been introduced to enable the researcher to summarize the social attainments of a mentally handicapped person and to relate them to a well-defined standard. It also makes it possible to report in quantitative terms the position of a particular person in relation to his peers.

This quantitative summarizing must in no way be interpreted as taking the place of the qualitative assessment of the deficits and assets in the P-A-C or the setting of definite objectives in the various subsections of the P-E-I. The detailed analyses of the P-A-C and P-E-I are essential for the educationalist who is concerned with the management of individual teaching and training schemes. However, the SCI will be helpful when demonstrating to people less intimately involved with the day-to-day work, how particular children or adults function, in relation to their peers and whether education and training are effective in changing their relative position to 'average attainment levels'. The P-A-C and P-E-I diagnoses are for the expert worker, the SCI for people outside these circles, and it would be quite indefensible if the easier and more obvious method of the SCI were used by the teacher and tutor in preference to the more informative but also more demanding interpretations of the P-A-C and P-E-I diagrams.

The SCI are based on the P-E-I. The P-A-C Manual, 3rd edition (Gunzburg, 1974b) provides 'skill values' derived from the average attainment levels contained in the P-E-I. The number of skills contained in each shaded sector of the P-E-I has been equated with 100%. Each component skill will, therefore, derive a different 'skill value' in percentage terms depending on age and intellectual standing. The SCI is, therefore, simply expressing in percentage terms the degree of achievement in relation to the average attainment level of the reference group. An SCI 100 indicates average functioning in relation to a group similar in age and intelligence group, SCI below a hundred would suggest under functioning, whilst SCIs above one hundred indicate superior functioning.

To avoid as much as possible the disadvantage of turning a qualitative assessment, as given by the P-A-C, into a quantitative score, the SCI's relate to the four areas of the P-A-C only. The following example will clarify the situation.

A mildly retarded woman aged 55 had been in institutional care for 45 years. When assessed first she obtained these scores: SCI (SH) in self-help 71, SCI (C) communication 23, SCI (S) socialization 87, SCI (O) occupation 100. When re-assessed after two years training, the SCI (SH) self-help was 105, SCI (C) communication 85, SCI (S) socialization 153, and SCI (O) occupation 117. There had obviously been considerable improvement (Gunzburg, 1975).

The Personal Assessment

The purpose of the 'Personal Assessment' (introduced in the P-A-C 2, 10th edition and P-A-C 1, 12th edition) is to bring into juxtaposition the social and personal assets and deficits required for a fuller appraisal of a mentally handicapped person's resources for social adjustment. Impressive attainments in social skills—as observed on the P-A-C diagram—can only become effective in a life situation if backed by an adequate personality constellation. The shading of the personal diagram and social diagram provides visual impressions whether the degree of competence in the social skills is matched by an acceptable personality make-up, which does not require much tolerance and understanding from other people, though help is, and always will be needed. It is often possible to observe a lack of balance between the two assessments which should be taken into account when making decisions. A poor social assessment may be compensated for by a full personal assessment which indicates a stability and social acceptability of a higher degree than usually found. On the other hand, a full P-A-C diagram indicating competence in the social skills may not be regarded such an asset if the corresponding personal assessment is 'meagre' because various personal attributes have been rated on a very low level.

Figure 61 indicates clearly such a case. The poor ratings in the sphere of sexual attitudes and dominance suggest that this trainee's adjustment to the demands of the community is rather precarious despite his knowledge of social know-how.

SOCIAL ASSESSMENT

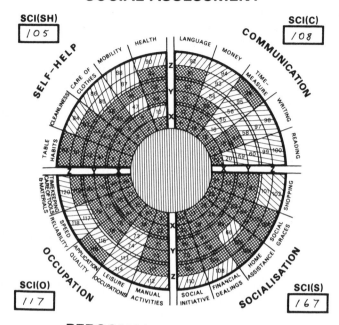

SCI(SH) 105

SCI(C) 108

SCI(O) 117

SCI(S) 167

PERSONAL ASSESSMENT

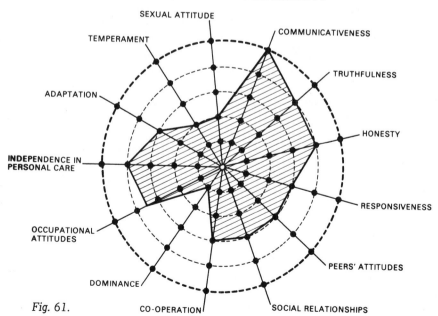

Fig. 61.

REFERENCES

Bernstein, B. (1960). 'Language and social class.' *Brit. J. Sociol.*, **11**, 271-6.
———— (1962). 'Linguistic codes, hesitation phenomena and intelligence.' *Language and Speech*, **5**, 31-46.
Cain, L, F. & Levine, S. (1961). *A Study of the Effects of Community and Institutional School Classes for Trainable Mentally Retarded Children.* San Francisco State College.
Charles, D. C. (1953). 'Ability and accomplishment of persons earlier judged mentally deficient.' *Genet. Psychol. Monogr.*, **47**, 3-71.
City of Birmingham Education Committee (1956-1960). *Reports of the Special Services After-Care Sub-Committee.*
Claridge, G. S. (1959). 'A re-analysis of 'excitability' and its relationship with improvement in performance of imbeciles.' *J. ment. Def. Res.*, **3**, 116-127.
———— (1962). 'The Senior Occupation Centre and the practical application of research to the training of the severely subnormal.' *J. ment. Subnorm.*, **8**, 11-16.
———— & O'Connor, N. (1957). 'The relationship between incentive, personality type and improvement in performance of imbeciles.' *J. ment. Def. Res.*, **1**, 16-25.
Clarke, A, D. B. & Clarke, A. M. (1954). 'Cognitive changes in the feeble-minded.' *Brit. J. Psychol.*, **45**, 173-9.
————, ———— & Reiman, S. (1958). 'Cognitive and social changes in the feeble-minded—three further studies.' *Brit. J. Psychol.*, **49**, 144-57.
———— & ———— (1965). *Mental Deficiency, the Changing Outlook.* (2nd ed.) London: Methuen.
Craft, M. J. (1962). 'The rehabilitation of the imbecile: a follow-up report.' *J. ment. Subnorm.*, **8**, 26-37.
Delp, H. A. & Lorenz, M. (1953). 'Follow-up of 84 public school special class pupils with IQ's below 50.' *Am. J. ment. Defic.*, **58**, 175-182.
Department of Health and Social Security (1971). *Better Services for the Mentally Handicapped*, London: H.M.S.O.
Doll, E. A. (1953). *The Measurement of Social Competence.* Washington: Ed. Test Bureau.
Dybwad, G. (1964). *Challenges in Mental Retardation.* New York: Columbia University Press.
Earl, C. J. C. (1961). *Subnormal Personalities; their Clinical Investigation and Assessment.* London: Baillière, Tindall & Cox.
Edgerton, R. B. (1967). *The Cloak of Competence*—Berkeley and Los Angeles: University of California Press.

227

Elliott, R. & MacKay, D. N. (1971). 'Social competence of subnormal and normal children living under different types of residential care'. *Brit. J. Ment. Subn.* XVII, 32, 48-53.

Francey, R. E. (1960). 'Psychological test changes in mentally retarded children during training.' *Canad. J. Publ. Hlth.*, 51, 69-74.

Gunzburg, H. C. (1948a). 'Experimental approach to the improvement of reading of educationally subnormal boys.' *Spec. Schools Journal*, 37, 77-86.

———————— (1948b). 'The subnormal boy and his reading interests.' *Library Quarterly*, 18, 264-274.

———————— (1959). 'A survey of reading deficiency in Monyhull Hall Hospital.' *J. Midl. ment. defic. Soc.*, 5, 36-42.

———————— (1960). *The Social Rehabilitation of the Subnormal.* London: Baillière, Tindall & Cox.

———————— (1962a). 'The school and social failure.' *Assoc. for Spec. Education, 26th Biennial Conference.* pp. 21-27.

———————— (1962b). 'Training for employment' in *Training and Employment of the Mentally Handicapped.* London: N.S.M.H.C.

———————— (1963). 'Employment of the mentally subnormal.' *Trans Ass. Indust. Med. Officers*, 13, 57-61.

———————— (1964a). 'Social competence of the imbecile child.' *Proc. int. Congr. sci. Study ment. retard.* Copenhagen, 2, 693-706.

———————— (1964b). 'The reliability of a test of psycholinguistic abilities (I T P A) in a population of young male subnormals.' *J. ment. Subnorm.*, 10, 101-12.

———————— (1965). 'A finishing school for the mentally subnormal.' *Med. Officer*, 114, 99-102.

———————— (1974) . 'The Monitoring of Rehabilitation Programmes.' in Gunzburg, H. C. (Ed.). *Experiments in the Rehabilitation of the Mentally Handicapped.* London: Butterworth.

Haskell, S. H. (1966). Programmed instruction and the mentally retarded in *The Application of Research to the Education and Training of the Severely Subnormal Child.* Monograph. J. Ment. Subnorm., pp. 15-24.

Heber, R. (1959). 'A manual on terminology and classification in mental retardation.' *Am. J. ment. Def.* 64, Monograph.

Huber, M. B. (1928). *The Influence of Intelligence upon Children's Reading Interests.* New York Teachers College, Columbia University.

Isaacs, N. (1960). *New Light on Children's Ideas of Number.* London: ESA.

———————— et al. (1959). *Some Aspects of Piaget's Work.* London: National Froebel Foundation.

Jastak, J. E. (1949). 'A rigorous criterion of feeble-mindedness.' *J. abnorm. Soc. Psychol.*, 44, 367-78.

———————— (1952). 'Psychological tests, intelligence and feeble-mindedness.' *J. Clin. Psychol.*, 8, 107-12.

Kellmer Pringle, M. L. (1965). *Deprivation and Education.* London: Longmans.

———————— (1966). *Social Learning and Its Measurement.* London: Longmans.

Kirk, S. A. (1958). *Early Education of the Mentally Retarded.* Urbana, Illinois, Univ. Illinois Press.

———————— & McCarthy, J. J. (1961). 'The Illinois test of psycholinguistic abilities—an approach to differential diagnosis.' *Amer. J. ment. Def.*, 66, 399-412.

Kirk, S. A. (1962). 'The effects of educational procedures on the development of retarded children.' *Proc. Lond. Conf. Scient. Stud. Ment. Def.*, 1960. 2, 419-28.

Locking, J. R. (1966). 'An arithmetic programme for the subnormal pupil' in *The Application of Research to the Education and Training of the Severely Subnormal Child.* Monograph J. ment. Subnorm., p. 33-42.

Lovell, K. (1961). *The Growth of Basic Mathematical and Scientific Concepts in Children.* London: University of London Press.

Luria, A. R. (1963). *The Mentally Retarded Child.* London: Pergamon.

Lyle, J. G. (1959). 'The effect of institution environment upon verbal development of imbecile children. 1. Verbal intelligence.' *J. ment. Def. Res.*, 3, 122-28.

———— (1960). '2. Speech and Language.' *Ibid.*, 4, 1-13; '3. The Brooklands Residential Unit.' *Ibid.*, 4, 14-22.

Malpass, et al. (1964). 'Automated Instruction for retarded children.' *Am. J. ment. Def.*, 69, 405-412.

Marshall, A. (1967). *The Abilities and Attainments of Children Leaving Junior Training Centres.* London: NAMH.

Masland, R. L., Sarason, S. B. & Gladwin, T. (1958). *Mental Subnormality.* New York: Basic Books.

Matthew, G. C. (1964). 'The social competence of the subnormal schoolleaver.' *J. ment. Subnorm.*, 10, 83-88.

Mein, R. & O'Connor, N. (1960). 'A study of the oral vocabularies of severely subnormal patients.' *J. ment. def. Res.*, 4, 130-43.

Mein, R. (1961). 'A study of the oral vocabularies of severely subnormal children. *J. ment. def. Res.*, 5, 52-9.

Ministry of Health (1962). *A Hospital Plan for England and Wales.* London: H. M. S. O.

Mitchell, A. C. (1955). 'A study of the social competence of a group of institutionalized retarded children.' *Am. J. Ment. Def.* 60, 354-361.

Moorman, C. (1967). A Social Education Centre. *J. ment. Subnorm.*, 13, 88-92.

Neale, M. D. (1966). 'Perceptual development of severely retarded children through motor experience.' in *The Application of Research to the Education and Training of the Severely Subnormal Child.* Monograph. J. Ment. Subnorm., pp. 49-60.

———— & Campbell, W. J. (1963). *Education for the Intellectually Limited Child and Adolescent.* Sydney: Ian Novak.

Norris, D. (1961). 'Education in the Training Centre.' *J. ment. Subnorm.*, 7, 62-66.

O'Connor, N. & Hermelin, B. (1963). *Speech and Thought in Severe Subnormality.* London: Pergamon.

———— & Tizard, J. (1956). *The Social Problem of Mental Deficiency.* London: Pergamon.

Piaget, J. (1952). *The Child's Conception of Number.* London: Routledge & Kegan Paul.

President's Panel on Mental Retardation (1962). *A Proposed Program for National Action to combat Mental Retardation.* Government Printing Office, USA.

Price, J. E. (1963). 'Automated teaching programs with mentally retarded students.' *Am. J. ment. Def.*, 68, 69-72.

Ryan, W. F. (1963). *Rehabilitation of the Mentally Handicapped.* (Thesis) Cork: University College.

Saenger, J. E. (1957). *The Adjustment of Severely Retarded Adults in the Community.* Albany. New York State Interdepartmental Health Resources Board.

Sampson, O. C. (1962). Speech Development and Improvement in the Severely Subnormal Child. *J. ment. Subnorm.*, **8**, 70-77.

Sampson, O. C. (1964). 'The conversational style of a group of severly subnormal children.' *J. ment. Subnorm.*, **10**, 89-100.

———— (1966). 'Helping the severely subnormal child to develop language' in *The Application of Research and Training of the Severely Subnormal Child.* Mongr. J. ment. Subnorm., pp. 25-32.

Schiphorst, B. (1968). 'Social education of the Subnormal' *Special Education*, **57**, 26-29.

'Scott Report' (1962). *The Training of Staff of Training Centres for the Mentally Subnormal.* London: H.M.S.O.

Sellin, D. F. (1967). The usefulness of the IQ in predicting the performance of moderately retarded children. *Am. J. ment. Def.*, **71**, 4, 561-562.

Spradlin, J. E. (1963). 'Language and communication of mental defectives' in N. R. Ellis (Ed.) *Handbook of Mental Deficiency.* New York, McGraw-Hill Book Comp.

Stolurow, K. M. (1963). 'Programmed instruction for the mentally retarded.' *Rev. ed. Res.*, **33**, 126-236.

Terman, L. M. & Lima, M. (1926). *Children's Reading: A Guide for Parents and Teachers.* New York: Appleton.

Tizard, J. (1962). 'The residential care of mentally handicapped children.' *Proc. Lond. Conf. Scient. Stud. Ment. Def.* 1960, **2**, 659—66.

———— (1964). *Community Services for the Mentally Handicapped.* London: Oxford Univ. Press.

———— & Grad, J. C. (1961). *The Mentally Handicapped and their Families.* Maudsley Monographs 7. London: Oxford Univ. Press.

Training Council for Teachers of the Mentally Handicapped (1972). *Guide to Diploma Course in the Training and Further Education of Mentally Handicapped Adults.* London (Alexander Fleminyhouse, SE1).

Wall, W. D., Schonell, F. J. & Olson, W. C. (1962). *Failure in School.* Hamburg: Unesco Institute for Education.

Williams, P. (1967). Industrial Training and Remunerative Employment of the Profoundly Retarded. *J. ment. Subnorm.*, **XIII**, 24, 14-23.

Woodward, M. (1961). 'Concepts of number in the mentally subnormal studied by Piaget's method.' *J. Child Psychol. Psychiat.*, **2**, 249-59.

———— (1962). 'The application of Piaget's theory to the training of the subnormal.' *J. ment. Subnorm.*, **8**, 17-25.

———— (1962). 'Concepts of space in the mentally subnormal studied by Piaget's method.' *Brit. J. Soc. clin. Psychol.*, **1**, 25-37.

ADDITIONAL REFERENCES (1975 reprint)

Bland, G. A. (1974). 'Encouraging Communication skills in the Institutionalized Adolescent Mentally Handicapped' in H. C. Gunzburg (Ed.) *Experiments in the Rehabilitation of the Mentally Handicapped.* London: Butterworths.

Browne, R. A, Gunzburg, H. C., Johnston Hannah, L. G. W., MacColl, K., Oliver, B. & Thomas, A. (1971). The Needs of Patients in Subnormality Hospitals if discharged to community care. *Brit. J. Ment. Subn. Vol. XVII.*, 32 7-24.

Gemmel, E. (1974). 'Progress in the Rehabilitation of the Mentally Handicapped in Sheffield' in
   H. C. Gunzburg (Ed.) *Experiments in the Rehabilitation of the Mentally Handicapped.*
   London: Butterworths.

Gunzburg, A. L. (1974). 'The Physical Environment as a Supportive Factor in Rehabilitation' in
   H. C. Gunzburg, (Ed.) *Experiments in the Rehabilitation of the Mentally Handicapped.*
   London: Butterworths.

Gunzburg, H. C. & Gunzburg, A. L. (1973). *Mental Handicap and Physical Environment.* London:
   Baillière Tindall.

Gunzburg, H. C. (1974). *The P-A-C Manual (3rd Edition).* London: NSMHC.

Gunzburg, H. C. (1975). Institutionalized People in the Community—a critical analysis of a
   rehabilitation scheme. *REAP*, Vol. I, No. 1.

Jackson, S. & Struthers, M. (1974). *A Survey of Scottish Adult Training Centres.* Unpublished
   Report, Jordanhill College of Education, Scotland.

Leck, I., Gordon, W. L. & McKeown, T. (1967). Medical and Social Needs of Patients in Hospitals
   for the Mentally Subnormal. *Brit. J. prev. soc. Med.* 21, 115-121.

McKeown, T. & Teruel, J. R. (1970). An Assessment of the Feasibility of Discharge of Patients in
   Hospitals for the Subnormal. *Brit. J. prev. soc. Med.* 24, 116-119.

Morley, K. G. & Appell, J. (1974). 'An Appraisal of the Social Progress of 59 Mentally Handicapped
   Persons in Community Centres' in H. C. Gunzburg, (Ed.) *Experiments in the Rehabilitation
   of the Mentally Handicapped.* London: Butterworths.

Whelan, E. (1974). 'The 'Scientific Approach' in the Practical Workshop Situation' in H. C. Gunzburg,
   (Ed.) *Experiments in the Rehabilitation of the Mentally Handicapped.* London: Butterworths.

ASSESSMENT AND TEACHING MATERIALS

P-P-A-C	Primary Progress Assessment Chart
P-A-C 1	Progress Assessment Chart 1
M/P-A-C 1	Mongol Progress Assessment Chart 1
P-A-C 1A	Supplementary Progress Assessment Chart 1 (A)
P-A-C 2	Progress Assessment Chart 2
P-P-E-I	Primary Progress Evaluation Index
P-E-I 1	Progress Evaluation Index 1
M/P-E-I 1	Mongol Progress Evaluation Index 1, in two versions: male, female
P-E-I 2	Progress Evaluation Index 2

The P-A-C forms are also available in Dutch, French, German, Norwegian, Portuguese, Spanish and Swedish.

The P-A-C Manual (3rd Edition) contains full scoring instructions for the P-A-C and P-E-I. Available also in translation: Dutch, French, Spanish.

Clumsy Charlie Flashcards
Clumsy Charlie Reading Books (4 books)
Out with Tom Reading Books (18 books) – 2nd Edition (13 books)
Spotlight on Trouble Reading Books (8 books)
Spotlight on Mystery Reading Books (4 books)

Charlie Wants to Help - (Talking Points)

PRINCIPAL DISTRIBUTORS

Australia: Australian Council for Educational Research, Frederick St., Hawthorn E2, Victoria 3122.

Belgium: Association Nationale d'Aide aux Handicapés Mentaux, Rue Forestière 12, 1050 Bruxelles.

Brazil: Sociedade Pestalozzi do Brasil, Rua Gustavo,Sampalo, 29-(Leme) Rio de Janeiro-Gb.

Germany & Holland: N.V. Swets & Zeitlinger, Keizersgracht 471-487, Amsterdam.

Norway: Spesialpedagogisk Laeremiddelutvalg, Birkelid Off. Skole, 4647 Brennåsen.

Spain: Fundacion Centro de Enseñanza Especial, Pozuelo De Alarcón, Madrid-23.

United
Kingdom: **National Association for Mental Health, 39, Queen Anne St.,
             London.W.1.**

             National Society Mentally Handicapped Children-Books,
             Pembridge Hall,
             17, Pembridge Square,
             London W2 4EP.

U.S.A.   Aux Chandelles, P-A-C Dept.,
             P.O. Box 398-Bristol,
             Indiana 46507.

INDEX

Numerals in italic type indicate references to illustrations